APOSTOLIC AGENDA

Translation of the original cover page above:
Top frame: "Saul, Saul, why are you persecuting me?" (written upside down)
Center: Of Dr. Friedrich Balduin, general superintendent and P.P. [Professor Primarius, "First Professor"] at Wittenberg. Commentary on All the Epistles of Paul with prior indices and the addition of a new general [index]. Frankfurt, by means of the typesetting and expenses of Balthasar Christopher Wustius, in the year 1692.
Bottom right: A. Fröhlich engraved [this].

Apostolic Agenda

With Intercessions for Securing Grace for a Converted Servant from His Lord, 1630

That Is:
The Epistles of the Holy Apostle Paul to Titus and Philemon

Explained with clear commentary

Translated by
Eric G. Phillips and James L. Langebartels
Historical Introduction by Benjamin T. G. Mayes

Emmanuel Press ✠ Fort Wayne, IN

Published by Emmanuel Press
Fort Wayne, Indiana
www.emmanuelpress.us
emmanuelpress@gmail.com

Translation copyright © 2020 Concordia Theological Seminary, Fort Wayne, IN, www.ctsfw.edu.

All rights reserved. No part of this publication may be reproduced, stored in a retrieval system, or transmitted, in any form or by any means, electronic, mechanical, photocopying, recording, or otherwise, without the prior written permission of Emmanuel Press.

Translated from Friedrich Balduin, *Commentarius In Omnes Epistolas Beati Apostoli Pauli*, vol. 2 (reprint, Francofurti ad Moenum: Balthasar Christophorus Wustius, 1664), pp. 1462–1538.

Cover design by Meghan Schultz. Portrait of Balduin enlarged from the original title page, photographed by Mark J. Kranz and Roger Peters. Layout and production by Emmanuel Press.

ISBN 978-1-934328-20-0

Manufactured in the United States of America

Contents

Patrons of this Translation vii
Historical Introduction ix

The Epistle of St. Paul to Titus

Introduction 1
The First Part of the Text [Titus 1:1–4] 5
The Second Part of the Text [Titus 1:5–16] 28
The First Part of the Text [Titus 2:1–10] 77
The Second Part of the Text [Titus 2:11–15] 106
The First Part of the Text [Titus 3:1–8] 145
The Second Part of the Text [Titus 3:9–15] 183

The Epistle of St. Paul to Philemon

Introduction 208
The First Part of the Text [Philemon 1–7] 210
The Second Part of the Text [Philemon 8–26] 223

Works Cited 252
Index of Persons 256

Patrons of this Translation

This translation of Friedrich Balduin's *Apostolic Agenda: Commentaries on Titus and Philemon* was commissioned by pastoral and diaconal students of Concordia Theological Seminary—Fort Wayne, Indiana, meeting in 2017, as their class gift. It is our prayer that this, the first full length work of Balduin available in English, would edify the hearts and minds of Christ's Church from now until His glorious return.

Jakob Andrzejewski	Hanna Kern
Christopher Antonetti	Mark J. Kranz
Tyler Arends	Kurt Laskowsky
Albert Bader	Timothy Magill
Patrick Baldwin	Gino R. Marchetti, II
Michael Bekx	Blake Martzowka
Steve C. Berndt	Sawyer Meyers
Alexander Blanken	David Miller
Wendy Boehm	Jonathan Olson
Jon Carpenter	Joshua Reber
Simeon Cornwell	David Rosenkoetter
Jonah Domenichelli	Brock Schmeling
Keith Emshoff	Christian Schultz
Robert Etheridge	Timothy Sheridan
Carolyn Ferguson	Kaitlin Sheridan
Daniel Fickenscher	Grant Sorenson
Taylor Fickenscher	Berett Steffen
Trae Fistler	Alan Thoe
James Grady	James A. Tuell
Daniel Harrison	Thomas C. Van Hemert
Scott Hedtke	John Widmer
Edward Holschuh	Nathan J. Wille
Donald P. Henry	Isaac Wirtz
Nathaniel Jensen	Brett Witmer
Jason M. Kaspar	Daniel A. Wojtowicz
Jeffrey Kazmierski	Justin Woodside
David Keating	Terry J. Worst
Timothy Kern	William Zwick

Historical Introduction

Friedrich Balduin (1575–1627)

Friedrich Balduin was a significant Lutheran theologian of the early 17th century, a well-respected exegete and churchman in his day, who deserves to be rediscovered in our day. Balduin was born in Dresden on Nov. 11, 1575, to Paul and Magdalena Balduin, and the next day he was baptized and given the name "Friedrich."[1] His parents were working people in the fur business. Early in life, his parents and teachers noticed his strong mind and hoped he would become a useful instrument for God's Church. From his earliest childhood his parents spared no expense to give him a good education, both in the pursuit of piety and in good literature. In Dresden he attended school until age 14. Thereafter he was educated in Meissen, and then soon enrolled at the University of Wittenberg in September 1593. Here he was first in his class, obtaining his master's degree in philosophy on May 15, 1597. At the time, theologians usually studied "philosophy" before proceeding to theology. "Philosophy" was quite broad, including nearly everything that we now call "liberal arts."[2]

The course of study at a German university at that time included not just hearing lectures but also hearing and sometimes participating in disputations. These were debates on predetermined topics that gave students the opportunity to research a topic in advance and then use

---

[1] The biography of Balduin is drawn from Erasmus Schmidt, *Oratio Funebris, Viri Reverendi & Optimi Friderici Balduini, SS. Theol. D. Et In Academia Wittebergensi Professoris Solertissimi. Eiusdemque Ecclesiae Pastoris, Et Vicinarum Superintendentis Supremi, Longe Dignissimi, Τοῦ Ἐν Ἁγίοις Memoriae* (Wittebergae: Sumptibus & Typis Iohannis Gormani, 1627). A recent full-length study of Balduin is Daniel Wolfgang Bohnert, *Wittenberger Universitätstheologie im frühen 17. Jahrhundert: Eine Fallstudie zu Friedrich Balduin (1575–1627)* (Tübingen: Mohr Siebeck, 2019).

[2] Johann Gerhard, "Method of Theological Study," in *On Interpreting Sacred Scripture and Method of Theological Study*, ed. Benjamin T. G. Mayes, trans. Joshua J. Hayes, Theological Commonplaces, I–II (St. Louis: Concordia, 2017), 164–69.

their research in carefully-reasoned argument.³ Balduin's disputations as a student at Wittenberg showed his mastery of logic and metaphysics. In 1599 he was crowned as a "poet laureate" by Nicholas Reusner—a significant honor.⁴ In the meantime Balduin studied theology and prepared himself for the ministry. In 1602 he was called to the office of "deacon" in Freiberg, an office equivalent to what we call an "assistant pastor," with preaching and sacramental duties, working under the supervision of a senior pastor.

As so often happened in those times, Balduin waited to marry until he had finished his studies and had been established in an ecclesiastical position. So on Oct. 9, 1602, he married Dorothea Meisner, sister of Balthasar Meisner, a Wittenberg theology professor. He was 26 years old. The next year he was called to a different parish—Oelsnitz in the Vogtland, south of Leipzig. That same year his first theological book was published, a defense of Luther against a Jesuit at Mainz who had claimed Luther was a disciple of the devil.⁵ His time in Oelsnitz did not last long. In 1604 he was called by Elector Christian II of Saxony to be a professor of theology at Wittenberg, replacing David Runge (d. 1604). This required that he earn his doctorate, which he accomplished on June, 28, 1605, with a disputation on the will of God in the doctrine of predestination.

In 1607, Balduin was called to be pastor in Wittenberg and general-superintendent of the Electorate of Saxony,⁶ in addition to his duties as

---

3 See Kenneth G. Appold, *Orthodoxie als Konsensbildung* (Tübingen: Mohr Siebeck, 2004).

4 John Flood, *Poets Laureate in the Holy Roman Empire: A Bio-Bibliographical Handbook* (Berlin: Walter de Gruyter, 2011), 113–17.

5 Friedrich Balduin, *Hyperaspistes Lutheri, adversus maledicam orationem Nic. Serarii, Esauiticae factionis monachi* (Lipsiae: Rhodius, 1603).

6 The old sources do not agree on the extent of Balduin's diocese. Schmidt calls him the superintendent of the "electoral diocese," which means all of electoral Saxony. Schmidt, *Oratio Funebris . . . Friderici Balduini*, 23. Zedler, however, makes him the superintendent only of Wittenberg. Johann Heinrich Zedler and Carl Günther Ludovici, eds., *Grosses vollständiges Universal-Lexikon* (Graz: Akademische Druck- u. Verlagsanstalt, 1961), s.v. "Balduinus (Fridericus)." Bohnert explains that the office of Wittenberg senior pastor was combined with the general superintendency for Electoral Saxony. Bohnert, *Wittenberger Uni-*

a professor. His duties expanded yet again in 1617, when Elector John George put him in charge of visitations of all the provincial schools. In 1622, his wife Dorothea died from complications in childbirth. They had been married for twenty years. Two years later Balduin married a young woman, Sophia Barwasser of Torgau. His biographers say the 48-year-old widower especially needed help with housework and raising his children. In later years, Balduin suffered from gout in the feet and kidney stones, brought on by his hard work. In 1625 Balduin was unable to carry out his annual visitation of schools due to poor health. The next year there was a plague in Saxony, so he was unable to carry out his visitation that year, also. Finally on May 1, 1627, he was called home to his Lord. Before his death, he requested the body and blood of Christ, and was communed by the Rev. Michael Blum, who at the time was deacon (assistant pastor) of the Wittenberg church. On May 4, he was buried in the parish church (St. Mary's) in Wittenberg.

In the time immediately after his death Balduin was remembered as the great churchman and pastor of Wittenberg. In the centuries since then, however, he has been remembered for his other accomplishments.

Balduin's Writings

Today, Balduin is mainly remembered for his casuistry—the study of cases of conscience, in which a person is uncertain on the right thing to believe or do in various difficult situations. The year after his death, his *Cases of Conscience* (1628) were published, based on lectures he gave from 1622 to 1626.[7] Due to his position as general-superintendent of churches, as well as his position on the Wittenberg faculty, Balduin had much experience with casuistry. As general-superintendent of electoral Saxony,[8] he had the highest seat in the ecclesiastical

---

versitätstheologie im frühen 17. Jahrhundert, 124.

7 Balduin, *Tractatus Luculentus, Posthumus . . . De materia rarissime ante hac enucleata, Casibus nimirum Conscientiae* (Wittenberg: Helwig, 1628); see Roderick Henry Martin, "The Reformation of Conscience: Rhetoric in the Lutheran Casuistry of Friedrich Balduin (1575–1627)" (Ph.D. dissertation, University of Virginia, 2008); Wilhelm Loehe, *The Pastor* (St. Louis: Concordia, 2015), 304.

8 Schmidt, *Oratio funebris*, 23.

consistory and judged marriage cases. He was dean of the university eleven times, and his role here required him to issue official opinions and to prepare responses to requests for counsel in difficult situations. Likewise, his commentaries on Scripture are full of tough questions of right doctrine and practice. His Wittenberg colleagues considered his *Cases of Conscience* to be the first Lutheran work of casuistry. That is not completely true; books answering cases of conscience were published by Lutherans ever since the end of Martin Luther's life, and especially five years previously, in the monumental *Treasury of Counsels and Decisions* published by the Hamburg pastor and editor Georg Dedekenn (1564–1628). But Balduin's posthumous work was the first Lutheran book to be called "On Cases of Conscience," and was seen as more systematic than collections of official opinions. Balduin's casuistry and the entire Lutheran casuistry literature is not just the resolution of moral problems. Rather it is primarily an attempt to remove doubt and establish certainty of one's conscience. This doubt and certainty deals not just with questions of right behavior, but also with questions of right faith. Balduin's work was recognized as an aid to pastoral care and the advising of consciences in difficult situations.[9]

Most of Balduin's publications were exegetical, written either in Latin as the result of university lectures and disputations, or written in German as the result of sermons in the Wittenberg parish church. His exegetical method will be discussed below.

Besides his casuistry and his exegesis, Balduin should also be remembered for his teaching on the Christian's union with Christ through faith. Balduin has been called the "inaugurator" of this doctrine within Lutheran Orthodoxy, a doctrine that was later called the "mystical union."[10] Balduin's teaching on the mystical union could

---

9   See Mayes, *Counsel and Conscience*, pp. 28–39; Hans Leube, *Die Reformideen in der deutschen lutherischen Kirche zur Zeit der Orthodoxie* (Leipzig: Dörfling & Franke, 1924), 46–47.

10 Theodor Mahlmann, "Die Stellung der unio cum Christo in der lutherischen Theologie des 17. Jahrhunderts," in Matti Repo and Rainer Vinke, eds., *Unio: Gott und Mensch in der nachreformatorischen Theologie* (Helsinki: Suomalainen Teologinen Kirjallisuusseura, Luther-Agricola-Gesellschaft, 1996), 128.

be seen as a response to the false mysticism of the time. Valentin Weigel's writings began to be printed in 1609, 21 years after Weigel's death. Likewise, at the beginning of the 17th century writings of Paracelsus were being printed, along with the fictitious Rosicrucian writings. Other Lutherans saw this "mystical theology" as being directed against the Orthodox Lutheran churches and universities. Proponents of the heterodox mystical theology saw themselves as being essentially united to Christ and thereby as having the Holy Spirit indwelling them substantially. What Balduin rejected in these writings was not the spiritual indwelling of Christ in believers, but the manner of this indwelling and union, which Valentin Weigel called "essential." This cannot take place, according to Balduin, since the substances are diverse and distinct. The fruit of Weigel's enthusiastic "essential union" is the despising of Scripture and the ecclesiastical ministry.[11] Therefore Balduin, basing his teaching especially on the epistles of the New Testament, sought to teach clearly the substantial *nearness* of believers not just with the gifts of Christ and with the Holy Spirit, but with Christ Himself, the God-Man, mediated through the church's ministry as it distributes Christ's means of grace.[12]

Balduin's main Latin writings include: doctrinal disputations, especially on the Trinity; commentaries on the Smalcald Articles (1606)[13]; on the Saxon Visitation Articles of 1592[14]; on the Pauline epistles (of which the present commentary on Titus and Philemon is a part)

---

[11] Mahlmann, "Die Stellung," 78–82.

[12] Balduin, *Disputatio ordinaria De Communione Nostri Cum Christo. Opposita tum Calvinianorum, tum Fanaticorum quorundam erroribus, qui ex Theophrasti Paracelsi Philosophia novam plane de Christo & Christianis Theologiam comminiscuntur* (Wittenberg: Johann Matthäus, 1618).

[13] Friedrich Balduin, *De Articulis Smalcaldicis: Quos ut commune Ecclesiarum orthodoxarum Symbolum Concilio exhibendos, Beatus Lutherus Anno Christiano 1537. conscripsit, Disputationes XXII. Habitae in Illustri Academia Wittebergensi. & nunc denuo in nonnullis locis correctiores editae* (Wittebergae: Gormanus, 1609).

[14] Friedrich Balduin, *Disputationes tredecim pro aureolo Visitationis Misnicae libello . . . Habitae Witebergae: In quo articuli 4, cardinam salutis nostrae concernentes: de coena domini, de persona Christi, de baptismo, de praedestinatione ad vitam, praeside Friderico Balduino* (Witebergae: Schürer, 1607).

(1611–1630)[15]; sermon studies for the church year (one-year series); his *Idea of Biblical Dispositions* (1622, on hermeneutics and preaching)[16]; polemical works against Roman Catholics, Reformed, and Unitarians (Socinians); *The Passion of Christ in Types* (1614)[17]; and his *Cases of Conscience* (1628).[18] His main German writings include: sermons on the Gradual Psalms (1608)[19]; and his postil (1624–1625, sermons for the whole church year).[20] Besides his exegesis and casuistry, his opposition to early 17th-century Socinianism deserves to be rediscovered and would be most useful to faithful Christians of our day.[21]

The Exegetical Literature of Lutheran Orthodoxy

Lutheran exegesis in the Orthodox period (1580–1750)[22] took place in a

---

15 Friedrich Balduin, *Commentarius In Omnes Epistolas Beati Apostoli Pauli* (Francofurti: Mevius, 1654).

16 Friedrich Balduin, *Idea Dispositionum Biblicarum* (Wittebergae: Helwigius, 1622).

17 Friedrich Balduin, *Passio Typica Seu Liber* (Wittebergae: Selfisch, 1614).

18 Friedrich Balduin, *Tractatus Luculentus, Posthumus, Toti Reipublicae Christianae Utilissimus, De Materiâ rarissimè antehac enucleatâ, Casibus nimirum Conscientiae* (Wittenberg: Paulus Helwigius, 1628).

19 Friedrich Balduin, *Psalmi graduum: Das ist, Die Schönen Lieder im Höhern Chor, des heiligen Königs und Propheten Davids, welche in seinem Psalmenbüchlein zu finden, von dem 120. Psalm biß auff den 135. / In besondern Predigten einfeltig erkleret in der Schloßkirchen zu Wittenberg* (Wittenberg: Paul Helwig, 1608).

20 Friedrich Balduin, *Postilla oder Außlegung der sontäglichen und vornembsten Fest Evangelien uber das gantze Jahr*, 3 vols. (Wittenbergk: Samuel Selfisch Erben, 1624); Friedrich Balduin, *Postilla/ Oder Außlegung der Sonntäglichen und fürnehmsten Fest-Evangelien über das gantze Jahr: Auß unterschiedlichen Predigten vieler Jahren also zusammen getragen/ daß deß Texts rechter Verstand/ und heilsamer Gebrauch von Anfang biß zum Ende deß Evangelii ordentlich gezeiget wird* (Franckfurt am Mäyn: Wust, 1671).

21 For fuller bibliographies of his works, see Bohnert, *Wittenberger Universitätstheologie im frühen 17. Jahrhundert*, 289–308.; Flood, *Poets Laureate in the Holy Roman Empire*, 114–17; Schmidt, *Oratio Funebris . . . Friderici Balduini*, 28–31.

22 Robert Kolb, "Lutheran Theology in Seventeenth-Century Germany," *Lutheran Quarterly* 20, no. 4 (2006): 429–56; Ernst Koch, *Das konfessionelle Zeitalter: Katholizismus, Luthertum, Calvinismus (1563–1675)* (Leipzig: Evangelische Verlagsanstalt, 2000), 211–59; Markus Matthias, "Orthodoxie: I. Lutherische Orthodoxie," in *Theologische Realenzyklopädie* (Berlin: de Gruyter, 1995); Johannes Wallmann, "Lutherische Konfessionalisierung—Ein Überblick," in *Die*

wide variety of contexts and forms. Much has been explored regarding Orthodox Lutheran dogmatics, and more has been done recently to study their piety and meditation.[23] But the history of scriptural exegesis is still mostly untouched.[24] In textbooks of church history, the military history of the Thirty Years' War takes far more space than the theology and religious life of Lutherans in the seventeenth century. The theology of the period is remembered as scholastic. The work of hymn writers is remembered, but nothing more.[25] The theology of the period was supposedly based on Scripture, but due to "rigid, exact, and demanding intellectual conformity,"[26] faith had become impersonal, consisting of assent to dogma. This Protestant Scholasticism, so it is often thought, was influenced by the rationalism against which it struggled.[27]

This view of the era, however, is quite narrow. It knows the theology of the era only via the dogmatics texts, superficially considered. Not surprisingly, scholars who only know of dogmatics texts think that Lutheran exegesis in the seventeenth century declined sharply. Humanism was set aside, they think, and the scholasticism that Luther had condemned marched victoriously into Lutheran theology. Even though Johann Gerhard, as a prominent example, used Scripture copiously in his *Theological Commonplaces* and other works, many still think that, as a whole, Scriptural exegesis retreated. The Bible was

---

Lutherische Konfessionalisierung in Deutschland (Gütersloh: Gerd Mohn, 1992), 33–53.

23 This section draws from Benjamin T. G. Mayes, "Not Just Proof-Texting: Friedrich Balduin's Orthodox Lutheran Use of Exegesis for Doctrine," *Concordia Theological Quarterly* 79, no. 1–2 (2015): 103–6.

24 Johann Anselm Steiger, "The Development of the Reformation Legacy: Hermeneutics and Interpretation of the Sacred Scripture in the Age of Orthodoxy," in *Hebrew Bible / Old Testament: The History of Its Interpretation*, ed. Magne Sæbø, vol. 2 (Göttingen: Vandenhoeck & Ruprecht, 2008), 699; Kolb, "Lutheran Theology in Seventeenth-Century Germany," 444.

25 Williston Walker, *A History of the Christian Church*, 4th ed (New York: Scribner, 1985), 526–34.

26 Walker, A History of the Christian Church, 587.

27 Walker, *A History of the Christian Church*, 587; Jürgen Quack, *Evangelische Bibelvorreden von der Reformation bis zur Aufklärung* (Gütersloh: Gütersloher Verlagshaus G. Mohn, 1975), 176.

used, they think, merely as proof-texts for preconceived dogmatic theses. While it may have been pious, the Lutheran Orthodox system was supposedly only the production of an uncreative age, deficient of authority; dogmatics and polemics choked all other theological disciplines, including exegesis; the Bible became nothing more than a collection of proof texts; the results of this "phony philology" were grotesque, according to this view, such as the attempt to find all of Lutheran dogma in the book of Genesis.[28]

Thankfully, a number of recent studies have called into question this view of the Orthodox Lutherans only as defenders of rigid dogma to the neglect of exegesis. These recent studies have noticed the central role that exegesis played for the Orthodox Lutherans in general.[29] Richard A. Muller's words are fitting: "Since it has so often been implied that the Reformation was a time of exegesis, virtually without dogma, and the era of orthodoxy was a time of dogmatic system without exegesis, it must be added that at no time before or since the era of orthodoxy was systematic theology so closely wedded to the textual and linguistic work of the exegete."[30] In both Latin and German,

---

28 Friedrich Uhlhorn, *Geschichte der deutsch-lutherischen Kirche* (Leipzig: Dörffling & Franke, 1911), 135; Karl Heussi, *Kompendium Der Kirchengeschichte*, 11. Aufl. (Tübingen: J.C.B. Mohr, 1956), 356–66.

29 Kenneth G. Appold, "Abraham Calov on the 'Usefulness' of Doctrine," in *Hermeneutica Sacra: Studies of the Interpretation of Holy Scripture in the Sixteenth and Seventeeth Centuries*, ed. Torbjörn Johansson, Robert Kolb, and Johann Anselm Steiger (Berlin: De Gruyter, 2010), 312; Kenneth G. Appold, "Scriptural Authority in the Age of Lutheran Orthodoxy," in *The Bible in the History of the Lutheran Church*, ed. John A. Maxfield (St. Louis: Concordia Historical Institute, 2005), 26; Michael Coors, *Scriptura efficax: Die biblisch-dogmatische Grundlegung des theologischen Systems bei Johann Andreas Quenstedt* (Göttingen: Vandenhoeck & Ruprecht, 2009), 23–25; Steiger, "The Development of the Reformation Legacy: Hermeneutics and Interpretation of the Sacred Scripture in the Age of Orthodoxy," 723; Volker Jung, *Das Ganze der Heiligen Schrift: Hermeneutik und Schriftauslegung bei Abraham Calov* (Stuttgart: Calwer Verlag, 1999), 222–23; Robert D. Preus, *The Inspiration of Scripture: A Study of the Theology of the Seventeenth-Century Lutheran Dogmaticians*, 2nd ed. (St. Louis: Concordia, 2003), 193–94; Bengt Hägglund, *History of Theology*, trans. Gene J. Lund, 4th English ed. (St. Louis: Concordia, 2007), 299–303.

30 Richard A. Muller, "Biblical Interpretation in the 16th & 17th Centuries," in *Historical Handbook of Major Biblical Interpreters*, ed. Donald K. McKim (Downers Grove, Ill.: InterVarsity Press, 1998), 135–36.

Lutherans in Germany wrote cursory explanations of biblical books; preached through books of the Bible and the Apocrypha at midweek services; published postils and sermon studies for the liturgical year; published polyglot Bibles and study Bibles; wrote rhymed paraphrases of biblical books; and published pedagogical, philological, and exegetical Bible commentaries. Indeed, the center of theological study was the philological study of the Bible.[31]

Much Orthodox Lutheran exegesis, but by no means all of it, was dogmatic and polemical. In this Lutheran dogmatic exegesis, exegetes were interested in presenting the doctrines of the Christian faith as resting on certain, clear passages of Scripture (*loci classici* or *sedes doctrinae*).[32] This approach to exegesis, which gathered dogmatic points of teaching as a result of exegetical work, can be seen first of all in Johann Gerhard's locus *On Christ* (1625), in which his entire chapter on the two states of Christ is an extended commentary on Philippians 2.[33] The same approach can be seen, secondly, in Gerhard's *Method of Theological Study*. From the very beginning of theological study, Gerhard leads his students to read Scripture in two ways: cursorily

---

31 Benjamin T. G. Mayes, "Scripture and Exegesis in Early Modern Lutheranism," in *The Oxford Handbook of Early Modern Theology, 1600–1800*, ed. Ulrich L. Lehner, Richard A. Muller, and A. G. Roeber (New York: Oxford University Press, 2016), 283–97; Ernst Koch, "Die 'Himlische Philosophia des heiligen Geistes'. Zur Bedeutung alttestamentlicher Spruchweisheit im Luthertum des 16. und 17. Jahrhunderts," *Theologische Literaturzeitung* 115 (1990): 706–20; Koch, *Das konfessionelle Zeitalter*, 227; Stephen G. Burnett, *Christian Hebraism in the Reformation Era (1500–1660)* (Leiden: Brill, 2012), 93–137; Johann Georg Walch, *Bibliotheca Theologica Selecta Litterariis Adnotationibus Instructa*, vol. 4 (Jenae: sumtu viduae Croeckeriane, 1765), 400–1050; Muller, "Biblical Interpretation in the 16th & 17th Centuries," 146.

32 Jung, *Das Ganze der Heiligen Schrift*; Hägglund, *History of Theology*; Steiger, "The Development of the Reformation Legacy: Hermeneutics and Interpretation of the Sacred Scripture in the Age of Orthodoxy"; Appold, "Abraham Calov on the 'Usefulness' of Doctrine"; Preus, *The Inspiration of Scripture*; Muller, "Biblical Interpretation in the 16th & 17th Centuries"; Koch, "Die 'Himlische Philosophia des heiligen Geistes'. Zur Bedeutung alttestamentlicher Spruchweisheit im Luthertum des 16. und 17. Jahrhunderts"; for bibliography, see Walch, *Bibliotheca Theologica Selecta Litterariis Adnotationibus Instructa*, 4:147–48, 845–49.

33 Johann Gerhard, *On the Person and Office of Christ*, ed. Benjamin T. G. Mayes, trans. Richard J. Dinda, Theological Commonplaces, Exegesis IV (1625) (St. Louis: Concordia Publishing House, 2009), 298–317.

and painstakingly. In the cursory reading, the student reads through the Bible every year in the vernacular or Latin, reading didactic books of Scripture in the morning and historical books in the evening. The painstaking reading of Scripture requires students to study the Bible in Greek and Hebrew every day, reading a trusted commentary alongside, and writing observations and excerpts in large blank books that would serve future ministers as a portable library. In disputations, students were instructed to take the foundations of their position first from Scripture, including necessary conclusions drawn from Scripture, and only thereafter to bring forth testimonies of the early church fathers and decrees of councils as witnesses, followed by an argumentative use of the adversaries' assent and philosophy. Doctrinal and exegetical tradition was cultivated and revered, but not seen as above criticism.[34]

Balduin's Commentary on Titus and Philemon

At some point in his career Balduin wrote his commentary on Titus and Philemon, most likely as a result of academic disputations. The book was not published until 1630, three years after Balduin's death, under the title: *Apostolic Agenda with Intercessions for Securing Grace for a Converted Servant from His Lord, That is: The Epistles of the Holy Apostle Paul to Titus and Philemon.*[35] Each chapter of this commentary begins with a simple two-part outline. Then the Greek text of the Epistle is printed with a translation alongside. Following this is Balduin's "analysis and explanation." In this section he explains

---

34 Johann Gerhard, *Methodus Studii Theologici* (Jenae: Tobiae Steinmanni, 1620); Johann Gerhard, *On Interpreting Sacred Scripture and Method of Theological Study*, ed. Benjamin T. G. Mayes, trans. Joshua J. Hayes, Theological Commonplaces, I–II (St. Louis: Concordia, 2017); Benjamin T. G. Mayes, "Lumina, Non Numina: Patristic Authority According to Lutheran Arch-Theologian Johann Gerhard," in *Church and School in Early Modern Protestantism: Studies in Honor of Richard A. Muller on the Maturation of a Theological Tradition*, ed. Jordan Ballor, David Sytsma, and Jason Zuidema (Leiden: Brill, 2013), 457–70.

35 Friedrich Balduin, *Agenda Apostolica cum intercessoriis pro impetranda servo converso, Domini sui, gratia. Hoc est, S. Apostoli Pauli Epistolae Ad Titum Et Philemonem. Commentario perspicuo illustratae: In quo praeter Analysin & Explicationem textus, multiplices commonefactiones ex textu eruunter* (Wittebergae: Helwigius, 1630).

the context of each verse, indicates parallels to other biblical passages, discusses geography and history, gives the contents of each verse (often in numbered lists), and defines words (often with rich references to classical and patristic literature). When there are different possible meanings of words or phrases, he lists and discusses the possibilities. Next come "questions" with their answers. These are often apparent contradictions between the text and other passages of Scripture or the received Evangelical-Lutheran doctrine. The questions are often taken from the Bible commentaries of opponents, who used the biblical text to try to prove false doctrine. This is where Balduin shines as a casuist. In America, William Arndt's *Bible Difficulties and Seeming Contradictions* did the same thing and has been popular for generations.[36] What Balduin offered, however, is much more extensive.[37] Finally there are the "theological aphorisms." Here the biblical text provides a harvest of *credenda et agenda*, the things that God gives us to believe and the things that He calls us to do. These doctrines are drawn from the text, just as he taught his students to do.[38]

The 1630 edition of the commentary includes a dedication letter, written by "the sons of Dr. Friedrich Balduin, left behind to God and pious people." It is dedicated to Rev. Sigismund Scherertz (1584–1639), superintendent of Lüneburg and inspector of the upper school (*gymnasium*) there. Scherertz had been a friend of Balduin. Unfortunately, the dedication says nothing about the commentary and how it came into being.[39]

---

36   William F. Arndt, *Bible Difficulties and Seeming Contradictions* (St. Louis: Concordia Publishing House, 1945).

37   Many works harmonizing apparent contradictions were written by the Orthodox Lutherans. See Walch, *Bibliotheca Theologica Selecta Litterariis Adnotationibus Instructa*, 4:854–57, 862–83, 901–4, 907–12, 914–18; cf. Robert D. Preus, *The Theology of Post-Reformation Lutheranism*, vol. 1, A Study of Theological Prolegomena (St. Louis: Concordia, 1970), 358–61.

38   Mayes, "Not Just Proof-Texting: Friedrich Balduin's Orthodox Lutheran Use of Exegesis for Doctrine."

39   Balduin, *Agenda Apostolica*, fols. I2r[– I3]r.

Balduin's Exegetical Method

The few who have studied Balduin's exegesis have found it excessively full of dogmatic polemics.[40] Indeed, to modern readers some of his views may seem strange. But this is an advantage. Balduin can challenge modern assumptions and help readers to view the biblical text with new eyes. Instead of simply agreeing with him or rejecting his statements, the most fruitful reading will be the one that asks instead about why he says what he does and why the feeling of strangeness arises in the reader's heart and mind.

Balduin's contemporaries valued his use of the original languages. Erasmus Schmidt noted how Balduin used the languages to investigate the emphasis of the text in its original wording, and to find the genuine sense of Scripture.[41]

The method that Balduin followed in his commentaries was set forth explicitly in his *Way of Biblical Dispositions* (1622).[42] Here Balduin teaches that the reader of Scripture should first pray. After the text has been explained and analyzed regarding its structure and philology, Balduin instructs his students to take another step, and collect doctrines from the text. After that, the text along with the doctrines derived from it are to be applied to the spiritually "well" and "sick." Part two of the book introduces the various books of Scripture. Part three deals with how to interpret kinds of biblical genres. This is also where allegories and types are discussed, along with how to preach.

Balduin does not do exegesis starting from a blank slate. He knows the Creed and Reformation doctrine, and he does not pretend to be unbiased as he does exegesis. At the same time, he is very clear that the literal sense of Scripture in its original context must be understood; only after that may doctrines be discovered from the text for the purpose of teaching and preaching.

Balduin practiced his exegesis in a way that was very common

---

40 Preus, *The Theology of Post-Reformation Lutheranism*, 1:337; Walch, *Bibliotheca Theologica Selecta*, 4:669–70.

41 Schmidt, *Oratio Funebris . . . Friderici Balduini*, 11.

42 Balduin, *Idea Dispositionum Biblicarum* (Wittebergae: Helwigius, 1622).

among the Lutheran Orthodox. Not only did he aim to find out what the biblical text had to say, he also was looking for how it should be used and applied to the lives of Christians. In biblical exegesis, this meant that doctrines must be gathered from the biblical text after its literary structure had been recognized and it had been explained (1 Cor. 8:1; Isa. 48:17; Rom. 15:4; 2 Tim. 3:16).[43] From this book, it is clear that "doctrines" are not primarily words written in catechisms and textbooks, but "teachings" that a preacher communicates to his hearers. Doctrines are for preaching and for the *use* of Christians. The search for doctrines from the biblical text was motivated by 2 Tim. 3:16: "All Scripture is given by inspiration of God, and is profitable for doctrine, for reproof, for correction, for instruction in righteousness."[44] That is, Christians need to make *use* of Scripture for teaching, admonition, warning, and consolation. For Balduin, doctrinal, dogmatic exegesis served practical purposes. Dogma was set forth both because preachers loved the truth and also because they loved their people. Balduin's dogmatic exegesis shows that the search for doctrines in the text of Scripture did not occur in just a polemical context. More than anything it was the desire to make salutary application [*usus*] of the text to the lives of Christians that directed Orthodox Lutheran exegesis. Since Scripture is God's Word in written form and was "written for our learning" (Rom. 15:4), the old Lutherans sought doctrines and applied them.

An example of this doctrinal exegesis can be seen in Balduin's Old Testament commentaries. In his commentary on the Gradual Psalms, Balduin says that Ps. 120 contains the "commonplace" [*locus communis*] on slanderers. Therefore his first sermon on this text deals, first, with various reasons why a Christian should guard himself from the vice of slander (a warning). Second, Balduin explains how we should act when we are slandered (admonition and consolation).[45]

---

43 Balduin, *Idea Dispositionum Biblicarum*, 31. See Benjamin T. G. Mayes, "The Useful Applications of Scripture in Lutheran Orthodoxy: An Aid to Contemporary Preaching and Exegesis," *Concordia Theological Quarterly* 83, no. 1–2 (2019): 111–35.

44 *The New King James Version* (Nashville: Thomas Nelson, 1982).

45 Balduin, *Psalmi graduum*, 3.

Balduin himself practiced this kind of "dogmatic exegesis" throughout his lengthy commentary on the Epistles of St. Paul.[46] Thus this whole commentary on Titus and Philemon should prove conclusively that Lutheran Orthodox theologians successfully joined exegesis and dogmatic theology, and that the latter was derived from the former. Exegesis was not made to conform to preconceived dogmatics. Rather, the Lutheran Orthodox theology truly is biblical theology, and is based on the close, attentive, pious interaction with the Bible, which is confessed and revered as the Word of God.

Acknowledgments

The Master of Divinity class of 2020 at Concordia Theological Seminary, Fort Wayne, Indiana, was motivated to commission a translation of a significant Lutheran book as their class gift, and they were soon joined by the Alternate Route class of 2019 and by deaconess students in various degree tracks. The individuals listed as patrons of this translation contributed their funds so that this work could be translated.

Early in their course of study here, these students appointed Mark Kranz to be the project manager. He and I have guided this project from beginning to end. In his first year at our seminary, Mr. Kranz approached me for suggestions on what to translate. Since Johann Gerhard's commentary on 1 and 2 Timothy was in the process of being published by Concordia Publishing House,[47] I was eager to have an Orthodox Lutheran commentary on the last of the pastoral epistles translated, too. The students agreed, and the project began.

The translator of the Titus commentary is Rev. Dr. Eric G. Phillips, pastor of Concordia Lutheran Church, Nashville, TN. With a doctorate in patristics and experience translating for the new volumes of *Luther's Works: American Edition*, Dr. Phillips was well suited to translate Balduin, who cites the early church fathers and classical Latin and

---

46 Mayes, "Not Just Proof-Texting."

47 Johann Gerhard, *Commentary on 1 Timothy and Commentary on 2 Timothy*, trans. Joshua J. Hayes (St. Louis: Concordia Publishing House, 2017).

Greek literature so often. The translator of the Philemon commentary is Rev. James L. Langebartels, emeritus, who likewise has much experience translating for *Luther's Works*. Not only did the translators translate the text, they also provided the vast majority of the footnotes.

The editing of the text was undertaken by me along with students Nathaniel Jensen and Berett Steffen. Students Trae Fistler and Blake Martzowka reviewed the Greek text. Thanks are due to Mark Kranz and librarian Rev. Roger Peters for the photo of the woodcut from Balduin's commentary. Dean of Students Gary Zieroth gave advice and approval for the project. Finally, Rev. Michael Frese of Emmanuel Press undertook the layout, publication, and distribution of the book.

May this commentary guide its readers to discover the depths of God's holy Word, and to make salutary use of it for the glory of God and the edification of His people!

Benjamin T. G. Mayes
August 15, 2019 A+D
Festival of St. Mary, the Mother of God

The Epistle of St. Paul to Titus
(Παύλου τοῦ Ἀποστόλου πρὸς Τίτον Ἐπιστολή)

Introduction
Of the Occasion, Argument, and Division of this Epistle

A summary of both Epistles to Timothy is this one, which the Apostle Paul wrote to Titus a little while after the first to the Corinthians, about the year of Christ 57, the twenty-second year of his conversion. For when he had left Ephesus, he traveled to Macedonia and Greece, during which journey he passed through Crete, that most celebrated island, situated in the midst of the sea, which Homer called ἑκατόμπολιν, *Iliad* book 2, famous for its hundred cities. He was first to preach the Gospel there, for he wanted to preach in those places where Christ had not yet been named, "lest he should build upon another's foundation" (Rom. 15:20). But because he was in a hurry to get to other places, he could not complete the task of his preaching that had been begun: so he left his faithful disciple Titus there, that he might continue that excellent work, and lest anything should be lacking to the churches of that place, he appointed presbyters throughout all the towns. Therefore, in the same way as he instructs Timothy, Bishop of the Ephesian church, with two Epistles, with this Epistle he instructs Titus, the Cretan Archbishop, how he ought to carry out the office [*officium*] of a faithful teacher of the church, reviewing his teaching that he had transmitted to the Cretans by word of mouth [lit: *viva voce*], and confirming Titus in his office [*munus*], that he might be certain that he was declaring divine words, and that the church might not be in doubt concerning the truth of Titus's teaching. For there were many there, as is reported in the first chapter, who were attempting to seduce the believing people with a pretense of law. It is against these that [Paul] furnishes Titus with public authority.

Now, Titus was from both his parents a Gentile and a Greek, and as it seems to Chrysostom, born in Corinth (*Homil. per hanc Epistolam 2 Cor. 7:7*), an opinion that we finally leave in doubt, but this is certain, that he was familiar with the Corinthians, and was for some time a teacher in its church. For as is established from 2 Cor. 7:15, he had been "received" by the Corinthians "with fear and trembling," and when Paul, seeking Titus, had come into Macedonia on his account, Titus came to him from Corinth, reporting with great joy how great a desire gripped the Corinthians for their Apostle. In the same church, he collected alms, by Paul's command, for the needy brothers at Jerusalem (2 Cor. 8:23). Paul converted this Titus to the faith of Christ, and joined him to himself in his travels, together with others of his allies. On the Jerusalem trip, he was unwilling to circumcise him for the false brothers who had come in, who were insisting that circumcision was something necessary, although he had circumcised Timothy, Gal. 2:3. Indeed, he held him to be in all things a compliant disciple, and in the end a faithful παραστάτην [companion] in spreading the Apostolic teaching, whence he also calls him his "beloved son" (Tit. 1:4, *Vulgate*), and his "brother" (2 Cor. 2:13), his associate and helper (2 Cor. 8:23), with whom he walked in one Spirit, in the same footprints (2 Cor. 12:18). And since he had judged his faith and aptitude sufficient, at length he established him as Pastor and Archbishop of Crete and the adjacent islands, for which reason he is called the first Bishop of the Cretans by Eusebius (*histor. Eccl.*, Book 3, Chapter 4), having been set in place by Paul. When he visited Paul near the end of his imprisonment, he was sent by him into Dalmatia, that he might take care of the church there, too (2 Tim. 4:10). It is thought that he returned thence to the island of Crete, where he also died, Sophronius writes,[1] and that in the 94th year of his life,

---

[1] Possibly: Sophronius of Jerusalem, *Epistola ad Arcadium Cyprianum*.

The Epistle of St. Paul to Titus—Introduction

as Baronius has noted in his *Martyrology*.[2] In this Epistle, the Apostle Paul writes to this Titus about the correct arrangement of the church, that in this way you might have here an idea of how the church ought to be arranged. He commands him to ordain presbyters throughout all the towns; he teaches what sort of men those presbyters ought to be; he commands that useful teachings be set forth, and that it might be possible to do this, that false teachers be restrained; he prescribes rules for hearers of all stations; he commends sound teaching about the Savior; and finally he ends the whole Epistle with certain private matters. The Epistle was written at the city of Nicopolis in Epirus, situated on the coast near Actium,[3] into which Paul had decided to turn after he had traveled through Macedonia, and to winter there (Tit. 3:12). And that this is an Epistle of St. Paul, which Marcion and Basilides[4] once doubted, is shown by (1) the similarity of style with the rest of Paul's writings, (2) the grandeur of the matters being clearly Apostolic, (3) the harmony with either letter to Timothy, (4) the universal consensus of the early church, in which there was no doubt on this matter, (5) the customary salutation at the end, with which Paul signed all his Epistles (2 Thess. 3:17). We make two parts of the Epistle. The first deals, in the first chapter, with the duties [*officium*] of the Teachers. The second, in

---

2 The Roman Martyrology of Cardinal Cesare Baronius (1538–1607), published 1586. Interestingly, Baronius also wrote the 12-volume *Annales Ecclesiastici a Christo nato ad annum 1198* (Ecclesiastical Annals from Christ's birth to 1198), published from 1588 to 1607, as a rebuttal to the *Magdeburg Centuries*, a Lutheran church history published at Magdeburg (1559 to 1574).

3 Literally, "on the Actian coast" (in Actiaco littore). Nicopolis is (and was) about 13 km northwest of Actium, and is not on the same coast. Probably the only reason Balduin mentions Actium is that he is thinking of the Battle of Actium (31 B.C.), in which Octavian (later Caesar Augustus) made his camp just north of Nicopolis, or of the Actian Games (Actia or Ludi Actiaci), which Octavian instituted (or revived) at Nicopolis to celebrate his victory. These games were held every four years in honor of Apollo, until the mid-3rd century A.D.

4 Second century heretics: Marcion (c. 85–c. 160), Basilides (fl. 117–138). Basilides was an early gnostic teacher in Alexandria, Egypt. Marcion came from Pontus in Asia Minor, and is known for developing his own canon of the New Testament, excluding many books and extensively editing the ones he kept (those being the Gospel of Luke and most of the Pauline corpus). What led him to do this was the gnostic (or at least gnostic-compatible) belief that Yahweh and the Father of Jesus Christ were different deities.

the two latter chapters, deals with the duties [*officium*] of hearers in any station of life. The principle Loci are: On the Requirements of the True Church, On the Incarnation of the Son of God, On the Corruption of the Human Nature after the Fall, On the Justification of Man before God, On Heretics and Their Punishment. May the Father of Men bring it to pass that we might produce sound and useful comments concerning all these things, through Jesus Christ our Lord, Amen.

Chapter 1

Argument and Division of the Chapter

The salutation having been communicated first, he commits the examination of the whole church of Crete to his faithful disciple and assistant [Titus], and places the pastors of all the towns under him, and teaches at length what sort of men they ought to be. There are two parts to the chapter: the former, up to verse 5, has a brilliant introduction in which Paul gives an account of his vocation with the most exquisite words.

The latter part, from verse 4 to the end of the chapter, deals with the organization of the church and the duty [*officio*] of the teachers.

The First Part of the Text [Titus 1:1–4]

Παῦλος δοῦλος θεοῦ, Ἀπόστολος δὲ Ἰησοῦ Χριστοῦ κατὰ πίστιν ἐκλεκτῶν θεοῦ, καὶ ἐπίγνωσιν ἀληθείας τῆς κατ' εὐσέβειαν.

1. Paul, the servant of God, and also an Apostle of Jesus Christ, according to the faith of God's elect, and the knowledge of the truth that is according to piety.

Ἐπ' ἐλπίδι ζωῆς αἰωνίου ἣν ἐπηγγείλατο, ὁ ἀψευδὴς θεὸς, πρὸ χρόνων αἰωνίων.

2. In the hope of eternal life, which He has promised, God who knows not how to lie, before eternal times.[5]

Ἐφανέρωσε δὲ καιροῖς ἰδίοις τὸν λόγον αὐτοῦ,[2] ἐν κηρύγματι ὃ ἐπιστεύθην ἐγὼ κατ' ἐπιταγὴν τοῦ σωτῆρος ἡμῶν θεοῦ.

3. And in His own times He has manifested His word through the preaching that was committed to me according to the assignment of God our Savior.

Τίτῳ γνησίῳ τέκνῳ κατὰ κοινὴν πίστιν χάρις, ἔλεος, εἰρήνη³ ἀπὸ θεοῦ πατρὸς, καὶ Κυρίου Ἰησοῦ Χριστοῦ, τοῦ σωτῆρος ἡμῶν.
Notes in text.⁵

4. To Titus, my true son according to a common faith, grace, mercy, peace from God the Father and our Lord Jesus Christ, our Savior.

Analysis and Explanation of the First Part

Here again the three customary parts of Introductions, conspicuous in the Pauline Epistles, come together, namely: (1) the Subscription, (2) the Inscription, (3) the Salutation. The Subscription consists of fine words, by which Paul wished both to obtain good will and to establish his authority, because this Epistle, which we ought to esteem highly on account of an author of so great a name, was written not only for the sake of Titus, who already both knew and honored the Apostle as his teacher, but also for our sake. These words of the Apostle are: *"Paul, the servant of God, and also an Apostle of Jesus Christ, according to the faith of God's elect, and the knowledge of the truth that is according to piety"* (v. 1).

These, Paul's epithets, are his badges of honor. He calls himself a servant lest he should seem to have pursued either this writing, or his whole office [*munus*] of teaching, on his own impulse; but it should be

---

5   Verse 2 (English): varies a little from the Vulgate, and also from the version quoted below: "In the hope" (in spe) instead of "Unto the hope" (in spem), "who knows not how to lie" (qui mentiri nescit) instead of "who does not lie" (qui non mentitur), and "before eternal times" (ante tempora aeterna) instead of "before the times of the world" (ante tempora saecularia) are the significant differences.
    Verse 3 (Greek): the preceding half-sentence shows a few differences between Balduin's Greek text and modern critical texts [WH and NA28 consulted], which have the separable nu at the end of Ἐφανέρωσε, an acute accent instead of a grave in ἰδίοις, and a smooth breathing mark instead of a rough on αὐτοῦ.
    Verse 4 (Greek): Modern critical texts read χάρις καὶ εἰρήνη instead of χάρις, ἔλεος, εἰρήνη. In the Latin column, Balduin translates the Greek text rather than just quoting the Vulgate, which also has only "grace and peace" (gratia et pax). Balduin addresses this difference below.

believed that he did this by the command and instigation of his Lord, to whom should redound everything that ought to be expected from this work, whether glory or ignominy. He calls himself a servant of God, at which point it must be understood that one can be a servant of God in three ways: (1) through creation, in which way every creature is servile to God, because it serves to the glory of God, and has been created by God for the use of others. In this way God is said to produce the green plant for the service of men (Ps. 104:14), and Paul teaches that the whole creation has been subjected to the servitude of vanity (Rom. 8:20). (2) Through regeneration, which is a servitude only of the faithful, who serve God in holiness and righteousness all the days of their life (Luke 1[:75]). Thus Jerome writes on this text, "He is a servant of God, who is not a servant of sin. 'For everyone who commits sin is a servant of sin'" (John 8:34). (3) Through deputation or administration [*ministerium*], in which way Moses is called the servant of God (Deut. 34:5, Josh. 1:2), and Christ Himself (Isa. 42:1, 44:21, 53:11). Our Paul calls himself a servant of God in this third sense, that is, one sent as His minister in order to teach the Gospel and plant churches.

Now, this is a general term that belongs also to the Prophets, and whomever has been sent as an ambassador of God, so he adds something more specific when he calls himself an Apostle of Jesus Christ, that is, a man sent directly by Christ to teach the Gospel among Jews and Gentiles. He accordingly limits that service of God to a particular aspect, namely that of the Apostolic function, which was the service of a very small number of people. Thus he says, "Paul, the servant of God, and also an Apostle of Jesus Christ," where the particle δὲ, "and also,"[6] is διορθωτικὴ [that is, corrective], for it corrects what seemed to be said in a meaner sense, in order that the meaning might be, "Indeed, I am a servant of God, but also[7] an Apostle of Jesus Christ, so that no one might understand my service to be something lowly and mean, but might hold it to be such a service as is shared by only a few." Phil. 2:8 is

---

6   The equivalent Latin term he cites is *autem*.

7   The primary meaning of δὲ (and the Vulgate *autem*) is adversative, and Balduin is referring to that here.

said of Christ in almost the same sense: "He humbled Himself, having become obedient to death"; then lest this should seem too servile, it adds, "and also the death of the cross," which is indeed an ignominious death, but is nevertheless esteemed as salutary and divine, because of the redemption of the human race. These words were chosen in order that the world's judges might seem to be more noble than Him (something Jerome writes on this text) on account of the kings whom they serve, and the dignity with which they are puffed up. So also the Apostle, claiming for himself a dignity that is great among Christians, marked himself from the beginning with the title "Apostle of Christ," that by it he might cow readers with the authority of the name, indicating that all who believe in Christ should be subject to him.

And now Paul's Apostleship is described according to all four kinds of causes. The Efficient Cause is Jesus Christ, whose Apostle he calls himself. The Material Cause is noted by the added clause, "according to the faith of God's elect," *etc.*, where the "according to" (*secundum*) is the same as "with respect to" (*circa*), as in Rom. 8:5: "Those who walk according to (*secundum*) the flesh, do the things that are of the flesh." That is, those who have been occupied with respect to (*circa*) fleshly things, or with respect to (*circa*) the desires of the flesh. Chrysostom understood "faith" to mean "committal,"[8] as did Theophylact, as if the meaning were, "God's elect have been entrusted or committed to me; 'I have received this dignity not because of deeds done righteously, nor from labors and sweat, but it is entirely of His favor, who entrusted them to me.'"[9] But we take "faith" here to mean "saving faith," by which we believe in Christ, which he calls "the faith of the elect," which is the principal requirement of election,[10] for "he elected us… in belief (*fide*) of the truth" (2 Thess. 2:13), and is the universal mark of the elect, who are not found outside the assembly of the faithful. The Apostle

---

8   The Greek πίστις can also mean "that which is entrusted, a trust."

9   "I have received… entrusted them to me" is a direct quotation of the Chrysostom excerpt featured in the *Glossa Ordinaria* for Titus 1:1.

10 The Latin is, *praecipuum requisitum electionis*. This wording hints at the *intuitu fidei* view of election that he articulates in Question 4 on this portion of the text.

wants to teach, therefore, that he is not the same kind of minister of God as Moses was, who was occupied with respect to (*circa*) the law and the ceremonies, for he has been occupied with respect to (*circa*) faith and the promises of grace. And he also adds, "according to the knowledge (*agnitio*) of the truth that is according to piety." This knowledge is elsewhere called *notitia* ("knowledge"), and is the explanation of "faith," a part of which is knowledge of the truth. When Paul teaches faith, therefore, he leads men at the same time to the knowledge of the truth, for which reason "knowledge of the truth" is put for faith itself in 1 Timothy 2:4. And the truth is understood not as just any kind of truth, but that which is according to piety. For both arts and sciences have their own truth, but one that does nothing with respect to piety. Heavenly truth, on the other hand, includes the piety in which the practice of faith consists, for which reason it was once the case that εὐσέβεια (piety) was called "practical theology" or "religion," but in actuality it is contemplative theology *par excellence*, or "wisdom," as it is in Augustine, book 10, *De civitate Dei*, chapter 1, and in the *Enchiridion ad Laurentium*, chapter 2. Theophylact sets the truth here in opposition to the legal shadows: the latter are found in the teaching of Moses, the former is found in the teaching of the Apostle.

The Final Cause of the Apostolic office (*munus*) is expressed in these words: "*Unto the hope of eternal life, which God has promised, who does not lie, before eternal times*" (v. 2).[11] For on this account is the heavenly truth taught and believed, that by it we might obtain eternal life; which although it is not yet clearly possessed, still the hope of it has been accomplished for all the faithful, who on this account are said to be "saved by hope" (Rom. 8:24). "And this hope does not confound" [Rom. 15:5], for we rely on the promise of God, who does not lie, nor can He lie (Heb. 6:18). Now the promise is said to be before temporal or eternal times, for in Greek it is τῶν αἰωνίων, the eternity that precedes, in a manner of speaking, the creation of the world and of

---

11 As noted above under the text of verses 1–4, Balduin here quotes a different variant of this verse, one that is closer to the Greek for the omission of "who knows not how to."

all ages. The promise of eternal life was made then, when God decreed that He was going to give it to the faithful. For "promise" is put here in place of "decree," in the same way as the giving of life is put in place of "predestination" in 2 Timothy 1:9. For God is said both to promise and to give because the outcome of the matter was most certain, because [Paul] concluded that he was going to give, although the ones to whom He was giving did not exist yet.

Finally, the Formal Cause of the Apostolic office (*munus*) is the preaching of the Word, by which the hope of eternal life in Christ, promised before the ages, is announced in time. Of this Paul speaks thus: *"And in His own times He has manifested His word through the preaching that was committed to me according to the assignment of God our Savior"* (v. 3). He calls the times of the New Testament "His times," καιροὺς ἰδίους, because in Gal. 4:4 he calls them πλήρομα τοῦ χρόνου, "the fullness of time." Clearly when the Word was made flesh, it was then the proper time to reveal to men the things that God had determined from eternity to do through His Word, since without that manifestation, neither the counsel of God nor that Word would have become known to men. Hence it happens that Jerome takes τὸν λόγον (the Word) in this passage to mean the Son of God, and it is well established by John that He is called λόγον (John 1:1,14; 1 John 1:1, 5, 7; and Rev. 19:13). In part this is because of the eternal and immutable generation of the Son of God from the Father, and in part because of His office (*officium*), because He is the interpreter of the Father's will among men. This consubstantial[12] Word of God had been hidden from eternity in the Father's bosom (John 1:14), but was manifested through the preaching of the Apostles (1 John 1:2), who for this reason are called ministers τοῦ λόγου (of the Word; Luke 1:2). But because that Word is not to be viewed by us absolutely, in Himself, but in that the Father's decree concerning our salvation has been accomplished in Him, therefore in this passage we do not take it to mean, in an absolute sense,

---

12   The Latin is *substantiale*, not *consubstantiale*, but what Balduin means is that this Word is a Substance at the same level as the Father, and not just one of His powers, thoughts, or declarations. And this can only mean that He is the *same* Substance, since there is only one God.

that consubstantial Word, but rather the word of promise and of the decree concerning the salvation of men, which Word has indeed been prepared from eternity in the counsel of God, but manifested in time through preaching, by which it has been published in the whole world, as if by the voice of a herald (for the Greek word κήρυγμα [proclamation, preaching] has that in the background). It pleased God to use the Apostle Paul's works in this way. Therefore he says that this preaching has been entrusted to him according to the command of God our Savior, that is, of Jesus Christ, who is True God (John 1:1) and the Savior of the world (John 4:42). Christ is adorned with this title fairly often in this Epistle, as in the second chapter, vv. 10 and 11, and 3:4, because it was a trait of the Apostolic office (*munus*) to announce that He is such a Savior who is God, and of Paul in particular to show that he had received the command to preach from that same Savior who had called the rest of the Apostles. And this happened at his conversion (Acts 9:15, 22:14). This is the first part of the Introduction.

The second runs thus: "*To Titus, my true son according to a common faith*" (v. 3). This is the Inscription, which regards Titus as the Archbishop of the Cretan Church. He calls him his γνήσιον (true) son, his own son, as he also does Timothy (1 Tim 1:2); that is, the son of a sincere faith, who both affirms it with his character and declares with his entire life that those do not, are not γνήσιοι (true), but νόθοι (illegitimate). Now he calls him his son because when he converted him to the faith of Christ, he begot him in God, through his Gospel. Therefore he calls him his "son according to a common faith," which faith Paul, to be sure, shared not only with Titus, but which also all the saints hold in common among themselves. For there is one faith of all those who believe, at whatever time, just as there is one God of all (Eph. 4:5). So he takes as his son, by reason of his instruction, the one who acknowledges him as his father by way[13] of his confession: this is the great humility of the Apostle.

The third part of the Introduction adds the customary Salutation, "*grace and peace from God the Father and Jesus Christ, our Savior*" (v. 4).

---

13 "By reason of" and "by way of" are the same word in the Latin (*ratione*).

In the Greek text ἔλεος, mercy, is inserted between "grace" and "peace," as in the other Epistles to Timothy, for since Paul takes both men as his own sons, he also shows his greater affection to both. Now the augmentation of the language in this Salutation should be noted, for "grace" signifies the benevolent love of God toward us, and the mercy that is bestowed upon our miseries flows from this, and mercy eventually produces peace of conscience; and these three have their origin from God the Father, but their foundation is in Christ the Savior, who brought it about by His merit and obedience that God might be benevolent to us, might be moved by our distresses, and might still our conscience.

Questions from this Part of the Chapter

Question 1

Why does St. Paul call himself the servant of God in v. 1, when elsewhere (Gal. 4:7) he treats "servant of God" and "son of God" as opposites?

Answer: Servitude, as it is generally understood, is opposed to liberty, for it is an institution of the law of the pagans, by which one is subjected, against nature, to the lordship of another. But when it is attributed to a man with respect to God, it rarely differs from liberty. For the servitude of God is either common or particular. The common kind is either lawful or unlawful. Lawful servitude is the condition of all men, for all owe obedience and subjection to God. "For you are slaves of the one whom you obey" (Rom. 6:16). We are all such servants of God in four ways: (1) by the law of birth, inasmuch as those who are born from slaves and servants are called slaves (Ex. 21:4). And thus from our birth we have all been subjected to God, from whom, through our parents, we have received our life and fortunes. This is the way some understand what Paul writes in 2 Timothy 1:3, that he "serves God from his ancestors." (2) By the law of captivity or war, just as Daniel and his associates were made slaves of Nebuchadnezzar, by whom they were led away into captivity, and were handed over to the instruction of the

Chaldaeans (Dan. 1:4). In the same way, all of us have been freed from Satan's captivity and redeemed by the precious blood of the spotless Lamb, and by this name have all become slaves of Christ (1 Pet. 1:19), of whose servitude Paul admonishes us in 1 Cor. 6:20. (3) By the law of poverty, doubtless, in the same way as the Egyptians, pressed hard by famine, were offering their servitude to Pharaoh in order that they might have necessary provisions (Gen. 47:19). So also we have brought nothing into the world. Whatever we possess, we have received from God, whom therefore we serve not undeservedly. (4) By the law of weakness, because we are certainly not able to govern ourselves. Thus we serve God as our superior, on whose will and counsels we depend. Accordingly, all men are God's slaves, whether they are pious or impious; and this is a lawful servitude that, because it is done willingly and from the mind, is liberty: for to serve God in this fashion is to rule.

The unlawful servitude of God is when someone does indeed obey the Lord's commands, but not out of the mind's inclination, nor with a free spirit, but as coerced; or even from fear of punishment or hope of rewards, which is mercenary behavior. Servitude of this kind is opposed to τῇ υἱοθεσίᾳ (adoption) as a slave and a son (Gal. 4:7), a slave and a friend (John 15:15), and the spirit of servitude and of [adoption][14] (Rom. 8:15) are opposed, for it is not in men who are reborn, but who are carnal, who hate and flee God. Paul in this passage calls himself the servant of God according to neither kind of servitude. His own servitude of God is that of certain persons who act in the place of God on earth, and through whom God deals with men, as through His vicars and legates. In this sense the very Son of God was a servant of God (Isa. 41:9, 43:10, 49:6, 53:11), Moses the leader of the people is called a servant of God (Deut. 34:5, Jos. 1:2), and Obadiah the prophet of the Lord received a name from servitude,[15] for a servant is obedient. Our Paul too is a servant of God in this way, by reason of his ministry and Apostleship, in which embassy he is engaged for the sake of Christ (2 Cor. 5:20).

---

14 Read *adoptionis* instead of *timoris* (fear).

15 In *Hebrew* the name Obadiah means "servant of the Lord."

Question 2

Why does St. Paul call himself the servant of God in this passage, but elsewhere (Rom. 1:1) the servant of Christ?

Answer: Theophylact replies, "He used these titles indiscriminately; sometimes, for instance, 'servant of Christ,' but 'Apostle of God'; and vice-versa; for he knows no difference between the Father and the Son." And Theodoret: "He calls himself without discrimination the servant, sometimes indeed of Christ, but sometimes of God; for he knows that the name is shared." And Jerome: "If the Father and the Son are one, and he who believes in the Son believes also in the Father, then the servitude of the Apostle Paul also should be referred indifferently either to the Father or to the Son." Hence it has happened that some refer the word "God" in this passage to the whole Trinity, because Paul's Apostleship is a work of the whole Trinity in common, although he is called an Apostle of Jesus most especially, because he was called immediately by Christ (Acts 9:3ff.); because the will of Christ and of God is still the same in calling Paul, which is why it is written that he was called through Jesus Christ and through God the Father (Gal. 1:1), and "an Apostle of Jesus Christ according to the will of God" (2 Cor. 1:1, Eph. 1:1), and "according to the command of God" (1 Tim. 1:1), all of which things indicate the identity of the Father with the Son in this shared work. For whatever Christ teaches the Apostle, and commands him to do, that also is pleasing to the Father, as He Himself says: "The speech that you have heard is not mine but the Father's who sent Me," (John 14:24), and "All that the Father has is mine" (John 16:15).

Question 3

Does no one have faith except for the elect, because faith is said (v. 1) to be of God's elect?

Answer: Indeed the Calvinists want it to be thus. They say that faith is an exclusive trait of the Elect, nor do they think it can be lost. On this, see Beza, Answer 2 to the Colloquy of Mömpelgard,[16] p. 75. For this reason, Piscator[17] in his analysis of this chapter explains those words ("according to the faith of the elect") this way: "in order that He might lead the elect to faith." Also, in his observations from this chapter, he writes (Observation 2), "The faith by which we believe in Christ, and through which we are eternally saved, is an exclusive trait of God's elect. That is, it is given by God only to the elect, namely those whom He has elected to eternal life." However, although it is certain that faith is not a trait of all men, which Paul teaches in 2 Thess. 3:2, nevertheless it is not the case that only the elect have faith, and that Paul's function (*officium*) was to lead only the elect to faith. For faith is indeed a requisite property of the elect; therefore those who do not believe are not of Christ's sheep (John 10:26). Still, it does not belong only to the elect, for many others are found who believe, and yet are not properly elect, that in this way faith might be more broadly accessible. For faith is also a trait of the called, who are not all elect. Hence some who believe are said to be πρόσκαιροι (temporary), those who believe only for a time, but in time of persecution fall away (Luke 8:13). But the elect, properly so-called, do not fall away, but persevere in the faith all the way to the end, for election properly so-called always attains to salvation (Rom. 11:7).

Some believers are said to have been vacated by Christ and to have fallen from grace (Gal. 5:4, Vulgate), which cannot be said of the elect. But every error of the adversaries stems from this, that they think faith, having once been received, cannot be lost—which is quite false. For to this end appear, in other passages, the most severe threats, punishments, and warnings of God, by which the Holy Spirit strives to keep the reborn within the limits of piety (Gal. 5:21, Eph. 5:5, Rom. 8:13, Col.

---

16 Also called the Colloquy of Montbéliard. It was held in 1586 to discuss differences between Lutheran and Calvinist doctrines. The principals were Jakob Andreae for the Lutherans and Theodore Beza for the Calvinists. See Jakob Andreae and Theodore Beza, *Lutheranism vs. Calvinism: The Classic Debate at the Colloquy of Montbéliard 1586*, trans. C. J. Armstrong (St. Louis: Concordia Publishing House, 2017).

17 Johann Piscator (1546–1625), Reformed theologian and writer of Bible commentaries.

3:5). Surely Aaron by his idolatry and David by adultery lost faith, which cannot remain with such sins done against the conscience, and if they had not repented, they would not have been in the number of the elect. Therefore David, as soon as he was restored to repentance, prayed that the Lord would not take the Holy Spirit from him [cf. Psalm 51:11], which he surely would not have done if he had not thought that he could lose faith and the Holy Spirit. Also, Ezekiel affirms that the righteous man is able to turn thus away from all his righteousness, with the result that the Lord no longer remembers all his preceding righteousness (Ezek. 18:24). Therefore, because it is quite false that faith, once received, cannot be lost, it is also false that faith is a trait only of the elect. It should be understood, then, that God grants many a faith that they nevertheless do not retain, but they fall away from it through sins against the conscience, and that happens either: totally but not finally, as happens sometimes among the elect, who nevertheless receive faith through repentance, as the example of Aaron shows, and of David and of others; or totally and also finally, as happens among the reborn who fall into sins against the conscience and do not repent, as the example of Saul teaches, from whom it is written that the Spirit of the Lord departed (1 Sam. 16:14), and of Judas, into whom one reads that Satan entered (John 13:27).

So when faith is said to be of the elect, it should be understood in the highest degree, because the faith of the elect is without a doubt before other faiths, not as if those who are not of the number of the elect have never had faith, but because the elect are never found to be without faith, insofar as they are elect, and they persevere in that faith all the way to the end. For this reason also, the title of "elect," used properly, does not fit all believers indiscriminately, but those who persist in the faith; because election in its proper and specific signification is concerned not only with the beginning, but also the end of faith, which is the salvation of souls. Hence we are said to have been made partakers of Christ, if we hold fast the beginning of His substance all the way to the end (Heb. 3:14, Vulgate). In the same way, then, as baptism is said to be a possession of the faithful and the saints, even though the baptism of hypocrites is also a true baptism, so also faith is said to be a trait of the elect, although for a time it is also in those who do not properly belong to the number of the elect on account of the failure of perseverance. But Paul has used this phrase for this reason: because he wants to show that he teaches such a faith, not that anyone invents for himself, but such as is a trait of the elect, which constantly takes hold of Christ, and cannot be utterly driven out by any devices of errors or temptations.

Question 4

If faith is a trait of God's elect, does it enter into the decree of our election?

Answer: The Calvinists, Hofmann, and Huber,[18] who all construct some kind of disordered election, deny this, judging (if it may be said) that to suggest that faith enters into the decree of election is Pelagianism, and establishes faith as the cause of election, when it is actually a special effect of the same. See Paraeus[19] on chapter 9 of Romans, article 6, and Hoffman on the question, "Is faith foreseen the cause of election?" argument 3. Pererius[20] also argues in disputation 22 on Romans chapter 8, that faith is not a reason and cause of predestination (argument 3), because it is one of its special effects. But the text of our Apostle is clear enough, and he says that faith is a trait of God's elect. Therefore it cannot be separated from the decree of election, for however the elect are constituted in time, is how they were constituted also in the foresight of God before the foundation of the world, because the reason is the same for a decree and its execution. That is why God is said to have elected us in Christ (Eph. 1). Now, no one is in Christ without faith, and He is distinctly said to have elected in faith in the truth (2 Thess. 2:13). For He did not elect us as men, else all were elected—the kind

---

18 Samuel Huber, professor at Wittenberg who was dismissed from the faculty in 1594 for teaching that God elects all men, but this election saves only those who believe.

19 David Pareus (1548–1622), Reformed theologian and writer of Bible commentaries.

20 Isaac de la Peyrère (1594–1676), Reformed theologian who speculated that the ancestors of the Gentiles lived before the creation of Adam. Later in life he renounced this theory and joined the Roman Catholic Church.

of indiscriminate election that Scripture, which declares the elect to be few, knows nothing of. He elected us as sinners, and not absolutely or without any order, but in such a way that all who believe in the Son might have eternal life. Therefore, although neither the men nor their faith was from eternity, yet the condition of all men was not unknown to God. Therefore, whomsoever He saw was going to believe in the Son, and persevere in that faith, those He also decreed to save, that is, elected. Hence the faith of the elect is said to be *par excellence.*

This consideration from this doctrine excludes all Pelagianism, for by faith we are doing nothing deserving of election, as the Pelagians claim, but a middle thing, or a part of the order,[21] something that God has considered in election because it takes hold of and gives attention to Him in whom election has been done. Hence we are said to be elect not on account of faith, but through it. It follows from this that faith may indeed depend on election, not as an effect depending on its cause, but as a limit depends on what has been limited, because election does not bring about faith, but finds it, and includes it as part of the order. For God sees from all eternity those who are going to believe in time, but on the other hand, election does not depend on faith as an effect depends on its impelling and Meritorious Cause, but is only by reason of looking (*intuitus*) to Christ, the true cause of election, which cause, nevertheless, is never considered apart from faith in the decree of election, for we are not elected simply in Christ, but in Christ taken hold of by faith. Fulgentius[22] writes concerning this verdict in *ad Monimum* book 1: "He predestined to the kingdom those whom He foreknew were going to return to Him by the help of prevenient mercy, and were going to remain in Him by the help of subsequent mercy."

---

21 Meaning the *ordo salutis*, the Order of Salvation.
22 St. Fulgentius of Ruspe (c. 465–533), a North African theologian who championed Augustine's teachings on grace against the Semi-Pelagians, and Nicene Christology against the Arians (Vandals) who ruled North Africa in his day.

Question 5

Is there any truth without piety? Because Paul here names "the knowledge of the truth that is according to piety" (v. 1).

Answer: Jerome raises this question in this passage, and replies, "There clearly is truth that has no piety, if anyone knows the Grammatical Art, or the Dialectical, so that he has the art of speaking properly, and distinguishes between true and false. Geometry also, and Arithmetic, and Music have truth in their knowledge, but that is not the knowledge of piety. The knowledge of piety is to know the Law, to understand the Prophets, to believe the Gospel, not to ignore the Apostles.[23] And on the other hand, there are many who have true knowledge of piety, but no firm handle on the truth either of those arts which we have mentioned above, or the other arts." In this passage, therefore, St. Paul understands "truth" to mean "the Christian religion," which alone teaches piety, and is elsewhere called ἀλήθεια, "truth," *par excellence*, as in John 8:32 and 17:17, Gal. 3:1, Col. 1:5, 1 Tim. 2:4 and 3:15, or with the label "the truth of the Gospel" (Gal. 2:5, 14). But if you want to understand this truth about the teaching of Christ the way Paul understands it, inasmuch as it is opposed to the shadows and the legal types, this truth is said to be "according to piety" also because it alone "teaches us that, having rejected impiety and worldly desires, we should live soberly, piously, and justly in this world" (Tit. 2:12). Indeed, those legal rites in it were only certain bodily exercises, and did not teach piety except typologically. Therefore, the passage here can also include that word of the Apostle in 1 Tim. 4:8, "Bodily exercise is useful to a point, but piety is useful for all things."

Question 6

Why is it said of God that He would not lie (v. 2), but it is not said likewise about angels and men, although they may also be zealous for the truth?

Although Paul does not say that *only* God would not lie, the sense

---

23   Up to this point, this Jerome quotation appears in the *Glossa Ordinaria*.

still conveys that exclusive particle, just as He is said elsewhere to be alone powerful and alone to have immortality (1 Tim. 6[:16]). Now these things are attributed to God alone, although some men are also powerful and angels and the souls of men are also immortal, because God has all those things by nature, but creatures by participation in grace. But it is one thing to have through oneself, and another for what you have to be in the power of a giver, says Jerome on this passage. So also, God is the only one who does not lie because He is true by nature. Nay rather, He is truth itself, as Christ is called in John 14:6, and the God of truth (Ps. 31:5), who cannot lie (Heb. 6:18). But the angels have this gift given by God, that they do not lie, and have been so confirmed by Him in the good that they cannot lie. Men, however, are corrupt by nature and prone to lying, which is why every man is called a liar in Ps. 116:11 and Rom. 3:4, and even when they strive for the truth, still they do not always reach it. For a threefold reason, then, does Scripture attribute only to God things that also belong, by a certain measure of His, to creatures: (1) because He is such by nature as the creatures are through grace, and what things are accidents in creatures, in God are pure essentials, for no accidents belong to God, as Cyril[24] writes in book 2 of the *Thesaurus*, chapter 1. (2) Because creatures have these things from Him, since "every best gift and every perfect gift" descends from God (Jas. 1:17). Now He who gives to others what He has from no one, is said by no means undeservedly to be the only one who has it. (3) Because all those things are in God immutably and constantly, which in creatures vary by easy alteration, and are not always found. Hence Augustine in book 1 of *de Trinitate*, chapter 1, writes of the Apostle's words "who alone has immortality," "He would not say 'alone has,' except that true immortality is immutability, which no creature can have, since it is a trait of the Creator only."

---

24 St. Cyril of Alexandria (c.376–444).

Question 7

What does Paul mean by "the times of the world," before which he writes that eternal life was promised (v. 2)?

Answer: There are those who think that "the times of the world" here means "ancient times," as one reads in Ps. 77[:5], "I have considered the ancient days and have kept the eternal years in mind," and in Acts 15:7, "From ancient days, God has chosen among us that the nations should hear the word of the Gospel through my mouth," *etc.* This is how Thomas Aquinas understands it, and also Johann Piscator in his analysis of this text. That is, he says that "before the times of the world" means "before many ages," namely from the beginning of the world, there is a promise, doubtless of the kind that was made to our first parents, "the seed of the woman would crush the head of the serpent," *etc.* But in the Greek it is not πρὸ χρόνων ἀρχαίων (from *ancient* times), but αἰωνίων (*eternal*), which nowhere signifies "ancient," but always "eternal." And Paul writes, "the promise made before those eternal times," so it cannot be taken to mean those promises that were made in time.

Some take it to mean some eternity preceding the creation of the world, during which God existed with the angels and without mutability. Thus Augustine writes on this passage, "It should be believed that before these times of the world there was some eternity of times that is called 'eternity' because it is not varied with changes."[25] Jerome seems to have been of this opinion, because he writes on this text, "Not yet six thousand years are completed of our time, and it should be pondered how many eternities existed beforehand, how many origins of worlds, in which angels, thrones, dominions and the other powers served God, and remained without the alternations and measurements of time, God thus commanding." But Scripture knows nothing of such an age in which angels existed before the world was created. This was the error of Origen, condemned in time past at the Lateran Council under

---

25 This seems to be a paraphrased summary of an excerpt from Augustine's *De diversis quaestionibus octoginta tribus*, qu. 72, in the *Glossa Ordinaria*.

Innocent III.[26] Lombard reckons in book 2 of the *Sentences*, chapter 1, that Jerome is speaking here from the mind of Origen, and Cornelius à Lapide[27] writes on this text, "Whenever the angels may be, they are part of the world, as is established from Col. 1:16. It is certain that they did not have their own age in which they existed before the world was created."

Others, among whom is Augustine in book 12 of *De civitate Dei*, chapter 16,[28] think that there were eternal times beforehand, which nevertheless were not coeternal with God, and Augustine proves it from this text of our Apostle, because before those eternal times there was only God, and he did indeed promise eternal life. But it is certain that time is a measure of motion. Therefore, where there was no motion as of yet, there could be no time; but just as motion begins with the world, so also does time. And the same Augustine also writes correctly in *contra Priscillianistas*, chapter 6, that "eternal times" are named thus in Pauline diction because they do not have any time before themselves; for it is customary in the Scriptures to use τὸ αἰώνιον ("eternity") sometimes without an end, sometimes with an end, in which sense Rom. 16:25 uses it: the Gospel is called "a mystery silent χρόνοις αἰωνίοις (from eternal times)." We judge that the simplest thing of all is to take "αἰώνια (eternal) times" to mean "all the ages that have ever flowed by from the beginning of the world." For the ages, or the world created by God, are called αἰῶνες (eons, ages) in Heb. 1:2, and Jerome writes on Matthew chapter 21, "עולם, αἰών means both 'age' and 'forever.'" Therefore, before those ages were created, that is, during all eternity, which in Sirach chapter 1:4 is ἐξ αἰῶνος, "from eternity," and in 24:14, πρὸ τοῦ αἰῶνος ἀπ' ἀρχῆς, "before eternity, in the beginning," and as

---

26 The Fourth Lateran Council, 1215. And indeed, Jerome did write his commentary on Titus in the years 387–88, ten years before he began writing against Origen, back when he was very much under Origen's exegetical influence. Balduin is right to make this connection.

27 A Roman Catholic (Jesuit) scholar who wrote Scripture commentaries (1567–1637).

28 This is the other work of Augustine's quoted in the *Glossa Ordinaria* on this question.

it is expressed in Ephesians 1:4, "before the foundation of the world," He promised eternal life to the elect. In this sense it is said to be their inheritance, "prepared from the foundation of the world" (Matt. 25:34).

Question 8

How could God promise eternal life "before the times of the world," or from all eternity, when men did not yet exist?

Answer: Because it seems harder to promise something from eternity, there have been some who think that this πρὸ χρόνων αἰωνίων (before eternal times) is the same as "before many ages," or from that, "from the beginning of the world," just as the Gospel is said to have been promised beforehand through the Prophets in the Holy Scriptures (Rom. 1:2). This is Piscator's opinion in his notes on this text. Others say that God promised the faithful from eternity that He was going to give life, either to His Son, His Wisdom that was with Him before the creation of the world, or to future men, whose fall He had formerly foreseen, and thus wished also to take care of their restitution in time. These are the words of Andreas Hyperius[29] in his *Commentary* on this passage. But it is better to recognize metonymy here in the word for promising, so that the sense is, "He has promised, that is, He has decreed before the times of the world that He promises to give eternal life to His faithful ones." And thus that promise has reference to the decree of God that He has made from eternity in His Son, concerning our salvation. Anselm adds two final opinions on this passage: He promised in this way, he says, because He made the promise especially to men who did not yet exist "before the times of the world," except that it had already been fixed by predestination in His eternity and in His Word, coeternal with Himself, what was going to be in His time. Or, to whom did He make the promise, if not to His Wisdom, promising that all those who were going to believe in Him were going to have eternal life?

---

29 Theology professor at Marburg, lived 1511–64; not squarely in either the Lutheran or Reformed camp.

Theological Aphorisms from this Part of the Chapter

1. The peculiar property of ministers is the ministry (*munus*) of the Word, if not to make his hearers learned, at least to lead them to faith and the knowledge of the truth, by the example of Paul in verse 1. For faith is not a trait of all (2 Thess. 3:2), nor is the knowledge of divine truth natural, but both are kindled through the Word. Thus it is written that faith is from hearing (Rom. 10:17), and God is said to sanctify us in truth through the Word (John 17:17). Also the Lord uses the works of ministers in this way, which is why men are said to believe through their word (John 17:20). Therefore he has discharged his office (*munus*) properly who teaches in such a way that faith in Christ is born and grows in the souls of his hearers, and the end of faith, which is the salvation of the soul, ensues at last.

2. Faith is a trait of the elect (v. 1). From this there are two πορίσματα (corollaries). One is that not all men are elect, because faith is not a trait of all, but "however many were ordained to eternal life" are said to believe (Acts 13:48). The other is that anyone can be certain of his salvation as long as he holds fast faith and a good conscience, for these are the marks of the elect, by which they are distinguished from those who are false. This is why Paul commands Timothy to hold fast "faith and a good conscience" (1 Tim. 1:19).

3. Saving faith consists in the knowledge of the truth (v. 1). Thus Paul in another passage connects the salvation of men and the knowledge of the truth (1 Tim. 2:4). Now that knowledge of the truth is the knowledge of Christ; that is why Christ is said to justify many by means of His knowledge (Isa. 53:11). Elsewhere it is called "knowledge of salvation" (Luke 1:77). It follows from this that they do not have saving faith who have not been properly instructed concerning Christ, or who go astray in other chief doctrines pertaining to celestial truth. For faith is one connective thing that requires knowledge of all the articles of the faith. From this it is easily settled, what should be concluded concerning the salvation of the Sacramentarians, the Anabaptists, the

Papists, and the like, who think correctly in certain areas, but stray from the truth in very many.

4. Theological wisdom surpasses all the arts and sciences because it has an object that is by far the noblest, namely "the truth that is according to piety" (v. 2). Dialectic, Astronomy, Geometry, Music, Jurisprudence, and indeed, any skill or discipline you like, has its truth, and first principles of the kind that require no extended demonstration, but nevertheless have nothing about piety, that is, nothing about faith in Christ, nothing about the love of the perfect God and your neighbor. For piety consists in these two things. Only Theology teaches these things from the prophetic and Apostolic Scriptures, and from this teaching alone is the hope of everlasting life. It behooves us, then, as we are commanded elsewhere to strive after the better gifts (1 Cor. 12:31), accordingly to choose the better and more useful sciences in which our zeal may be employed. So then, let us be wary of the truth of the other arts and disciplines, lest we should be infants in that celestial wisdom which is occupied with piety, and outmaneuvered by the wiles of the heretics. And because of this threat, let no one at all, in whatsoever walk of life, be so estranged from piety that he devotes no time or labor to the recognition of this truth.

5. The celestial teaching does not consist in the subtlety of disputations, but in true piety; thus is it called "the truth that is according to piety." Therefore anyone may make progress in this study, with the result that his whole life testifies concerning his growth. For they are surely unworthy whose life suggests nothing of piety, who make any boast about their understanding of this truth. For St. Paul writes about them below, that they confess that they know God, but deny it with their deeds (Tit. 1:16), and he shows that men are theologians not by words, but by deeds, men who know the experience of virtues more than the vaunting of virtues, who do not say great things, but live as servants and worshipers of God, as Cyprian once said of the philosophers in his sermon on the good of suffering [*De bono patientiae*].

6. The reward of true piety is eternal life (v. 2), for it has the promise of this life and the future life (1 Tim. 4:8). For although eternal life is the gift of God (Rom. 6:23), nevertheless God permits no one to be

pious by grace, but has made the most abundant promises to piety, that He might hasten to assist our sluggish flesh toward the study of piety. But Paul calls it "the *hope* of eternal life," because in this world we do not yet have it, but instead the piety of the faithful has been exposed to many adversities; and yet they have the hope of life and everlasting happiness; but they have "hope, which does not confound." So because Paul is able to "glory in his tribulations," they "know that tribulation works patience, and patience approval, and approval, indeed, hope, and hope does not confound" (Rom. 5[:3–5]).

7. The foundation of our hope, the hope we receive concerning eternal life, the reward of faith and piety, is the promise of God who cannot lie (v. 2). Having rested upon this, our hope confidently awaits eternal life in the midst of all the miseries of this world. For He who promises is also able to do it, because He is God, and He wants to show that He does not deceive in His words, and that it is impossible for Him to lie (Heb. 6:18). Furthermore, this promise has been made "before the times of the world," when men had as of yet done nothing, either good or bad, and so there is nothing that might void God's promise. This is that firm foundation, leaning upon which we are able to shatter all the devices of doubts that Satan mobilizes amidst the many hardships of this life, and to believe with Abraham in hope against hope, because God is faithful, and will not deny Himself (2 Tim. 2:13).

8. The teaching about the salvation of men has been comprehended in the eternal decree of God, but was removed from human eyes until it was manifested through the Prophets and Apostles. Hence it is called "the mystery of God, silent for eternal times, but now made plain through the Scriptures of the Prophets, according to the command of the eternal God" (Rom. 16:[25–]26). So just as we marvel at the fatherly will of God toward us, that He was concerned about the salvation of men before they were born, the Prophets and Apostles have to be loved in the same way, as confidants and interpreters of the divine will and decree, whose teaching Paul held to be of such great value that He laid it as the foundation of the Church (Eph. 2:20). Therefore we inquire from them what things pertain to our salvation. For God entrusted His word and decree to them, and committed to them the care of His

church. To know more than them in these divine mysteries is to act foolishly.

9. God does not lie, Paul says (v. 2), because it is impossible for God to lie (Heb. 6:18). For He is true, but every man false (Rom. 3:4). Therefore they fetter themselves with the most serious crime, who accuse God in any way of a lie. This happens (1) when His word is called into doubt because it has exceeded our understanding, because God is nevertheless greater than our understanding, and in this kind of thing one ought to believe in order that he might understand, not understand in order that he might believe. Thus we are commanded to "take our understanding captive in obedience to Christ" (2 Cor. 10:5). (2) When we do not have faith in His promises. For he who does not believe the Son makes Him a liar (1 John 5:10). "Nor is God like a [man] that He should lie, nor like a son of man, that He should be changed" (Num. 23:19). "The word of the Lord is right, and all His works [are] in faithfulness" (Ps. 33:4), and "He who receives His testimony witnesses that God is true" (John 3:33). (3) When His threats are disdained on account of the delay in their execution, which scoffers do, of whom Peter speaks in 2 Pet. 3:3ff. (4) When prophetic oracles are mocked, which some used to do, about whom Isa. 28:10 speaks. This is to mock God Himself, who "spoke through the mouth of His holy Prophets" (Luke 1:70). "But the vision will not lie; if it makes delay, wait for it, because coming it will come, and will not be late" (Hab. 2:3). (5) When the decree of our election and salvation is held to be changeable, as Huber once taught. For "the counsel of God remains forever" (Ps. 33:11), and "His gifts are ἀμεταμέλητα" (not-to-be-repented-of, Rom. 11:29). So let this be the Apostolic aphorism: God does not lie, like a holy anchor against any doubts from which our flesh is accustomed periodically to cause problems.

10. Christ is true God, which can be proven in different ways here. First, because Paul calls himself the servant of God, but in the Epistle to the Romans, chapter 1, he calls himself the servant of Christ. Next, Christ is here expressly called God our Savior (vv. 3–4). Third, because Paul received from Him the command to preach the Gospel, because it is not a trait of a mere man, but of God, to send the Apostles and

to commit the Church to them. For Paul received this command to preach from Christ twice: the first in his conversion (Acts 9:6, 15, 17 and 22:10, 14, 15), then when he was in a trance of the mind among the prayers in the temple (Acts 22:17, 18, *etc.*).

11. The faith of all the pious is in common (v. 4), of whatever station they may be and at whatever time they have lived. Therefore the faith is said to be one (Eph. 4:5) because one Christ is Lord and Savior of all. This communion of faith joins us with the fathers of the Old Testament, for on both sides is the one teaching about Christ, and the same path to life, which is why Peter said in the council at Jerusalem, "We believe that we are saved through the grace of our Lord Jesus Christ, just as they are" (Acts 15:11). It also joins those who by reason of their status and condition are different in some other way, as parents and children, magistrates and those who are subject, the rich and the poor. Thus Paul has Titus, whom he has called his son by reason of his spiritual generation, for a brother according to their common faith. The passage Matthew 22:10 refers to this.

12. We have grace and peace, in which two things our blessedness consists, from God the Father and Jesus Christ our Savior (v. 4). Therefore, he who does not know Christ will not have true peace, and they are beyond grace, because Christ alone is that εἰρηνοποιὸς (peacemaker) reconciling Jews and Gentiles to God in one body through the cross (Eph. 2:16), in whom also God receives us into grace (Eph. 1:6). He is the throne of grace, to which we draw near with confidence that we will attain mercy and grace by His timely aid (Heb. 4:16).

The Second Part of the Text [Titus 1:5–16]

Τούτου χάριν κατέλιπόν σε ἐν Κρήτῃ, ἵνα τὰ λείποντα ἐπιδιορθώσῃ, καὶ καταστήσῃς κατὰ πόλιν πρεσβυτέρους, ὡς ἐγώ σοι διεταξάμην.	5. For the sake of this thing I left you behind in Crete, that you might continue to correct what things were lacking, and appoint presbyters in every town, as I had commanded you,

Titus 1

Ἔι τις ἐστὶν ἀνέγκλητος μιᾶς γυναικὸς ἀνὴρ, τέκνα ἔχων πιστά, μὴ ἐν κατηγορίᾳ ἀσωτίας, ἢ ἀνυπότακτα.

Δεῖ γὰρ τὸν ἐπίσκοπον ἀνέγκλητον εἶναι, ὡς Θεοῦ οἰκονόμον, μὴ αὐθάδη, μὴ ὀργίλον, μὴ πάροινον, μὴ πλήκτην, μὴ αἰσχροκερδῆ.

Ἀλλὰ φιλόξενον, φιλάγαθον, σώφρονα, δίκαιον, ὅσιον ἐγκρατῆ.

Ἀντεχόμενον τοῦ κατὰ τὴν διδαχὴν πιστοῦ λόγου, ἵνα δυνατὸς ᾖ καὶ παρακαλεῖν ἐν τῇ διδασκαλίᾳ τῇ ὑγιαινούσῃ, καὶ τοὺς ἀντιλέγοντας ἐλέγχειν.

Εἰσὶ γαρ πολλοί, καὶ ἀνυπότακτοι, ματαιολόγοι, καὶ φρεναπάται, μάλιστα οἱ ἐκ περιτομῆς.

Οὓς δεῖ ἐπιστομίζειν, οἵτινες ὅλους οἴκους ἀνατρέπουσι διδάσκοντες ἃ μὴ δεῖ, αἰσχροῦ κέρδους χάριν.

Εἶπέ τις ἐξ αὐτῶν ἴδιος αὐτῶν προφήτης Κρῆτες ἀεὶ ψεῦσται, κακὰ θηρία, γαστέρες ἀργαί.

6. if anyone is blameless, the husband of one wife, having faithful children who are not liable to the charge of debauchery, and who are not insubordinate.

7. For it is necessary that a bishop be blameless, as God's steward, not stubborn, not irritable, not given to drink, not a striker, not shamefully given to wealth,

8. but hospitable, zealous for good works, sober, pious, temperate,

9. holding fast to what is according to teaching, to the faithful discourse, that he might be able also to exhort through sound teaching, and refute those who contradict it.

10. For many are insubordinate, and babblers, and seducers of minds, especially those who are from the circumcision.

11. It is necessary to shut their mouth, for they subvert entire houses, teaching things it is not right to teach, for the sake of filthy riches.

12. A certain man from among them, a prophet who was one of their own, said, "Cretans are always liars, evil beasts, lazy gluttons."

Ἡ μαρτυρία αὕτη ἐστὶν ἀληθής. Δι' ἣν αἰτίαν ἔλεγχε αὐτοὺς ἀποτόμως ἵνα ὑγιαίνωσιν ἐν τῇ πίστει.

Μὴ προσέχοντες Ἰουδαϊκοῖς μύθοις, καὶ ἐντολαῖς ἀνθρώπων ἀποστρεφομένων τὴν ἀλήθειαν.

Πάντα μὲν καθαρὰ τοῖς καθαροῖς τοῖς δὲ μεμιασμήνοις καὶ ἀπίστοις οὐδὲν καθαρὸν, ἀλλὰ μεμίανται αὐτῶν καὶ ὁ νοῦς καὶ ἡ συνείδησις.

Θεὸν ὁμολογοῦσιν εἰδέναι, τοῖς δὲ ἔργοις ἀρνοῦνται, βδελυκτοὶ ὄντες καὶ ἀπειθεῖς, καὶ πρὸς πᾶν ἔργον ἀγαθὸν ἀδόκιμοι.

13. This testimony is true. For that reason, one must refute them severely, that they might be sound in the faith,

14. not paying attention to Jewish fables and the precepts of men opposed to the truth.

15. Indeed, all things are pure to the pure. But to the polluted and unfaithful, nothing is pure, but their mind and conscience have been polluted.

16. They profess that they know God, yet they deny it by their deeds, because they are abominable, and heedless of what has been said, and disapproved with respect to every good work.

Notes from text.[30]

Analysis and Explanation of the Second Part

After the illustrious introduction, in which the Apostle has expressed a summary, as it were, of the teaching that ought to be set forth in the church, he comes to the thing itself, and describes at length the duty (*officium*) of the good pastor, to whom the teaching of faith and life eternal has been committed. First, though, he reminds Titus of his office (*munus*), that he might remember for what reason he has been left by the Apostle on the Island of Crete. *"For the sake of this thing I left you behind on Crete, that you might correct the things that are lacking, and that you might appoint presbyters throughout the cities, just as I*

---

30 Verse 15 (Greek): μὲν is absent from WH and NA28. WH and NA28: μεμιαμμένοις.

also arranged for you" (v. 5).[31] It is like what he wrote to Timothy, "I asked you," he says, "to remain at Ephesus when I went into Macedonia, that you might denounce certain men, so they would not teach otherwise," *etc.* (1 Tim. 1:3). The Jesuit Benedict Justinian[32] points out that the translator has neglected the rules of Latin Grammar here, as he does, not infrequently, in other places, for "*in Creta*" should have been said, not "*Cretae*," because in the Greek it is ἐν κρήτῃ, and Crete is not the name of some town, but of the whole island.[33] Now if the Latin is Jerome's version, as is commonly supposed, it seems to have been said in this way out of his own familiar custom. So in the Eusebian Chronicle:[34] "he was slain *Istriae*",[35] meaning "*in Istria*," and in his Letter against John of Jerusalem:[36] "You are asked a question *Palestinae*, and you reply *Aegypto*,"[37] and "He lives *Cypri*,"[38] that is, "*in Palestina*," "*in Cypro*." In his Letter to Geruchias:[39] "*Bythyniae* he met his death by poison," for "*in Bythynia*." Also, "the Jews rebelling *Macedoniae*," that

---

31 Balduin is quoting the Vulgate now, not his own translation of the Greek, which accounts for some differences.

32 Wrote commentaries on all the Pauline Epistles; died 1622.

33 "*Cretae*" is the locative case, which would be good Latin for a city or a *small* island, but since Crete was considered to be a *large* island, the locative should not have been used for it.

34 Jerome's *Chronicon* (or *Temporum Liber*), composed c. 380. He translated the chronological tables from the second half of Eusebius's history into Latin, and then extended the chronicle from 325 to 379.

35 This comes from the first item that Jerome lists for A.D. 354, and concerns the death of the Emperor Gallus.

36 *To Pammachius against John of Jerusalem*, written by Jerome in 397 or 398, unfinished and probably unsent, but well-known after his death.

37 Section 4 of the letter.

38 Section 41 of the letter. The text erroneously has "*versari in Cypro*" here, but Jerome actually wrote "*versari Cypri*" (Migne, PL 23.410D), using the locative for a large island, contrary to the classical rule—exactly the behavior that Balduin is documenting here. Note how, with this error in place, the text has Balduin informing us that "*in Cypro*" means "*in Cypro*."

39 Letter 123, written 409. The text names the recipient "Gerontias."

is, "*in Macedonia*,"⁴⁰ which is the observation of Joseph Scaligeri⁴¹ in *Animadversionibus Euseb.* p. 233 & p. 234, and Johann of Drusius⁴² in the aforementioned investigations, p. 324. But Crete is the noblest island situated in the midst of the sea, spacious with one hundred cities, named thus either from the nymph Creta, daughter of Hesperus, or from the king Cucretum, as Pliny has it (book 4, *histor. nat.*, chapter 12),⁴³ where he also describes its position and names its nobler cities. Others add that no harmful animal is found in it. Today it is under the power of the Venetians, and on account of the fruitfulness of its best noble vine is often and commonly called Candia. The Apostle reached this island twice: the first on his long journey through Greece, when he stayed for three months (Acts 20:3), the next on the nautical journey when he was led captive to Jerusalem (Acts 27:7), on which occasion, at the same time, he laid foundations like a wise architect of the church, and softened the hard hearts of the Gentiles, so that they believed in the true God who is the Father of our Lord Jesus Christ, their idols having been abandoned. But because he himself could not remain always in that place, he left his faithful disciple Titus there, that he might strengthen the beginnings of the nascent church, and build the edifice of the church upon the foundation laid by Paul. Now to this end, two things were laid on him as necessary to be taught: (1) that he might correct the things that were lacking. In Greek this is ἐπιδιωρθώσῃ, as if he said, "that you might correct further," or "that you might continue to correct," those things, that is, that have been corrected by me, and that as long as these things have not been recalled to the full line of the truth, they might be corrected by you, and might attain the pattern of uniformity. This is how Jerome explains it, and Erasmus from him,

---

40 This citation does not come from the Letter to Geruchias, and Balduin does not tell us which of Jerome's works it does come from.

41 Joseph Justus Scaliger (1540–1609), French Huguenot, pioneering historian and textual critic.

42 Johann Clemens van der Driesche (1550–1616), Dutch theologian, Hebraist, and exegete who taught at Oxford University.

43 That is, Pliny the Elder, since he was the one who wrote the *Natural History*.

because Chrysostom also agrees with him (Homily 2 on this Epistle). (2) That he might appoint presbyters for each town in that island, lest some village should be cheated of the celestial teaching. By the word "presbyters" he means any teachers of the church, whether they be bishops or priests or deacons, for these titles are applied indiscriminately in Acts 20, where those who are called presbyters in v. 17 are later in v. 18 called bishops; or in v. 5 of this chapter [Titus 1] they are called presbyters who in verse 7 are called bishops. Thus in Phil. 1:1 all the ministers of that church are called bishops, for in one city there could not have been many bishops.

The requirements of the bishop are enumerated in the same way in 1 Tim. 3:2, and in this chapter it is the things that befit all the ministers of the church. Therefore Titus ought to appoint such ministers of the church through all the towns of that island, just as if he were the highest president and inspector of those churches, and this appointment should be done (1) by instruction in the true faith, (2) by calling, (3) by ordination, (4) by inspection or governance. And all these things were to be done just as Paul ordered, for Paul established in each of the churches what things were in conformity with decorum and edification, as is clear from 1 Cor. 7:17. And the apostolic ordination, that which concerns the appointment of ministers specifically, is read in 1 Tim. 5:22, namely "do not lay hands quickly on anyone," and also is read specifically in Acts 14:23, that the Apostles left the churches they had planted to their own pastors, whom they made not rashly, but with prayers and fasts preceding, and did not force on the churches by domineering power and a price, but appointed presbyters by the approbation of the whole assembly.[44] Therefore Paul wants Titus to act in this matter not from private judgment, but according to the apostolic arrangement, for it is a great matter, to commit the salvation of souls

---

[44] Or "by the votes of the whole assembly," but not in such a way as to mean that the decision was made by secret ballot, or that the winning candidate always somehow got 100% of the votes. The "*suffragiis totius coetus*" would be voices raised generally by the assembled congregation in approval of the man proposed by the Apostle. Acts 14:23 does mention the prayers and fasts explicitly, but not the approbation.

to others. And the Apostle also adds a remarkable description of the true teachers of the Church, lest Titus should err in choosing pastors, and indeed in almost the same words that he had used to Timothy (1 Tim. 3). *"If anyone is without reproach, he says, the husband of one wife, having faithful children, not under accusation of riotous living or insubordinate"* (v. 6).[45]

Three things are required here of a minister of the church: (1) that he be ἀνέγκλητος (blameless); in Timothy he wants him to be ἀνεπίληπτον, irreproachable, one whose life is free from guilt. Now he is ἀνέγκλητος who cannot be accused or summoned to court, but it is not required of a bishop that he should be free from all sin, but to the extent that nothing may be faulted in this external conduct. For as Augustine says in book 1 *Contra duas Epistolas Pelag.*, chapter 14, "No one could rightly be ordained a minister in the church if the Apostle had said, 'if anyone is without sin" where he says 'if anyone is without reproach,' or if he had said 'having no sin' where he says 'having no reproach.' For in fact, many baptized faithful are without reproach, but you have said that in this life no one is without sin." Nor is it required that a bishop not be accused at all, as if a man who had once been accused, for example, were unfit for the ministry, but that the accused not be convicted, or that he not be summoned to court by reason of his own conscience, the law accusing *him*. And another thing, if it were sufficient to have made an accusation, who will be innocent? Christ and the Apostles were accused, but nothing was detracted from their ministry, because they were not convicted. Finally, it is not enough that someone be ἀνέγκλητος at the time of his ordination, but it is necessary that all his life be without guilt, lest he should be tormented by any conscience of sin, or at any time he should commit a deed worthy of accusation.[46]

(2) The minister of the church should be the husband of one wife, as is also held in Timothy, where we have made many observations about

---

45 Balduin is quoting the Vulgate again, not his own translation.
46 That is, lest he should remember such a sin from his past or commit such a sin in the future.

this subject. The meaning is that the bishop should not be πολύγαμον (polygamous), or one who has many wives at the same time, whether they are all receiving his intercourse, or some have been divorced, because among the Jews it was not uncommon, when they would often give their wives a writ of divorce for a trivial cause and, when those had been thus dismissed, would marry others. Paul did not admit a man of this sort to the ministry of the Word, on account of the scandal and the example that the Gentiles could easily have imitated. What some of the Fathers and the pontifical writers think, that second marriages have been prohibited for the ministers of the church by this precept, we are not able to approve, and we have dealt with this at length in chapter 3 of my previous work on Timothy, part 1, question 2. We do not want to do it here. And neither do we grant that married men, having been admitted to the ministry, should abstain from their spouses afterwards, for our Paul does not require such a thing as a bishop who was not married, but who is "the husband of one wife," because the use of marriage, if they handle the other things rightly, does not impede the ministry, but as Theophylact writes on this text, "Thus marriage is a precious thing, that with him it can ascend to the holy episcopal throne and see."

(3) The bishop should have faithful children, not immoderate, not obstinate. For it is right that the whole family of these men should be without offense. Therefore the children of presbyters (a) should be faithful, that is, brought up in the right faith, (b) should not be debauched or immoderate, or prodigal, given to gluttony, scorn, gambling, and lust; for ἀσωτία (profligacy) includes all these things. And some consider that the Apostle is here thinking of the turpitude of the Cretans, who were impurely involved in the impure habits of the young. For Strabo reports of the Cretans in *Geography* book 10 that it was customary among them to be mad for boys, and it was even lawful there for nobles to abduct any number of them, and keep them with themselves for two months, and after thus giving them gifts for their services, to send them home; and it was decreed by the ancient laws of the Cretans that

from puberty all Cretans should immediately enter marriage[47] and this infamous pederasty, of which they finally began to be ashamed, for this reason: that they might extinguish adulteries and promiscuous lusts. See Caelius Rhodiginus,[48] book 15 of *Antiq. lect.*, chapter 9. The Apostle does not want the children of presbyters to be like that. (c) They should not be ἀνυπότακτοι (unrestrained)—unmanageable, rebellious, and contumacious fellows who shake off every yoke of discipline, and are elsewhere called children of Belial [*e.g.*, Deut. 13:13; 1 Sam. 2:12]. The good education of their children, then, is required of presbyters. For if they are indolent in this respect, how will they rightly care for the salvation of others?

(4) Now follow the other requirements of a bishop, down to v. 10. The fourth is, let the minister of the Church be a steward of God. *"It is necessary* (he says) *that a bishop be without offense, as God's steward"* (v. 7). Here the reason seems to be given *why* the minister of the church should live blamelessly: doubtless because he is not the lord of the family, but its household manager (as it is in Greek), who is going to give an account to his Lord sometime, to which pertains Christ's analogy in Luke 12:42ff. But surely nothing hinders you from understanding the bishop's new virtue as faithfulness, for nothing else is required of stewards than that they be found faithful (1 Cor. 4:2). Therefore, since ministers are stewards of the mysteries of God, they should be faithful in teaching, warning, reproving, consoling, neglecting no one, and accommodating themselves to the customs, abilities, and need of all.

5) *He should not be proud,*[49] μὴ αὐθάδης (stubborn), who must depend so greatly on a judgment not his own, and must not please himself too much, or be stubborn in his own opinion, whence arises

---

47 Strabo says this too, in the same chapter, but explains that these betrothals, while *arranged* when the boy reached puberty, were not actually *consummated* until the girl was deemed capable of keeping her own house. In the mean time, the boys lived a communal life at public expense, and were preyed upon in the manner described.

48 Caelius Rhodiginus (Lodovico Ricchieri, 1469–1525), a Venetian classicist who published his *Antiquarum Lectionum* in 1516.

49 Balduin continues to quote from the Vulgate in his comments, though he has provided his own translation of the Greek above.

Titus 1

insolence and contempt for others, but must listen to others willingly, and if he has erred anywhere out of weakness, must listen to the one who corrects him. Certainly αὐθάδεια is the obstinacy and impudence of a mind that yields to no one, which Aristotle in his great *Ethics*[50] opposes to σεμνότητι (solemnity), or gravity in conduct.

(6) *He should not be irritable*, μὴ ὀργίλος (irascible). The disposition to anger, or irascibility, is prohibited here, not the feeling, or anger itself. For anger happens to the good man also, and is sometimes necessary by reason of his office [*officium*]. But irascibility is from an excessive perturbation of the mind, without legitimate cause, often on account of something trifling, a vice that should be far from all teachers—especially of the church, because it ruins the wise and causes many disorders, for it "does not work righteousness" (Jas. 1:20).

(7) *Not drunk with wine*, μὴ πάροινος, as in the Epistle to Timothy, who would not willingly sit at wine, and would not be troublesome to others out of winebibbing or intoxication, for this is παροινεῖν (to be drunk with wine). To do anything from wine or intoxication, that is, to brawl, to make false accusations, to rave, to shout, to indulge the lusts, and the like is ἀσωτία (profligacy), which Paul writes is in wine (Eph. 5:18).

(8) *Not a striker*,[51] that is, not one who would fight with others, nor cause harm, either by insolence of language or bad example. For πλήκτης includes these three things: (a) the hand, (b) the tongue, (c) a perverse example; for in these ways, your neighbor can be struck. See more about this in Timothy.

(9) *Not greedy for shameful wealth, not one who looks only to things that make for profit, who longs only to grow rich, which makes matters such that many things that should have been corrected are silently passed over.* To this vice, αὐτάρκεια (self-sufficiency) has been opposed,[52] when a man lives content with his own lot. Prohibited here, then, are

---

50 The *Nicomachean Ethics*.

51 A note in the book's margin here reads, "In law, a striker [*percussor*] is one who is hired to strike."

52 By Aristotle, that is.

excessive frugality, manual labor,[53] and similar illicit and disgraceful exertions aimed at getting rich, which greatly dishonor the ministry of the Word. That is why the Apostle calls it αἰχροκέρδιαν (i.e., αἰσχροκέρδεια, base covetousness), not prohibiting profit *per se*, that is, not thinking it foreign to the minister of the Word if he should accept from his grateful hearers a compensation for his labors, but attacking illicit means and the intention of getting rich.

(10) *He should be hospitable*, φιλόξενος (loving strangers), which is said on account of the necessity of those times, when there were many travelers and exiles whom the church was obliged to feed, and the Apostle wanted the ministers to arrange its work in this area. Today it should be done when the ministers of the churches have diligent care of the ecclesiastical treasury, so that from it provision should be made for the poor, and so that they might not refuse hospitality to travelers and exiles, if there should ever be such a need. Jerome writes on this text that the bishop's house should be the common guesthouse of all, and at one time, in fact, this was such a frequent kind of service [*officium*] that the bishops seemed to vie with each other for this reputation, and held "the bond of hospitality," as Tertullian says in *De praescript.*, chapter 20,[54] as a symbol of Christian love. Today, with ministers' reduced resources, no more can be imposed on anyone than his shoulders could bear.[55]

(11) *A lover of good things*, φιλάγατος[56] (loving the good), which

---

53 In Aristotle, αὐτάρκεια is not just the virtue of moderation (not being driven to accumulate wealth), but also freedom from need, which assumes that the man who has this virtue is sufficiently well-off to have a lot of time for leisure and contemplation (*Ethics* X.8), which in Aristotle's context would mean that he was a landed citizen, not a manual laborer of even the most skilled kind. How this principle translates to the life of a pastor, or how manual labor could be a "get rich" scheme, is not easy to see.

54 *De praescriptione haereticorum (On the Prescription of Heretics*, or *The Prescription Against Heretics*).

55 When Balduin speaks of "reduced resources," he is comparing the situation of pastors of his day to that of bishops in the days of Jerome and Tertullian, not to that of pastors in Paul's day.

56 The correct form of this verb is φιλάγαθος, with a theta, as it appears above in the text.

can refer as much to things as to a person, namely that he should praise and pursue things that are good and honorable, and show favor to good men, and envy no one, and increase their good things[57] as much as he is able.

(12) *Temperate*, σόφρων (prudent), sober and discrete, one who does all things with moderation and circumspection, for this virtue should be referred to temperance of the mind rather than the body, for which reason it also has the name σοφρωσήνη (prudence), as if it were σόφουσα τὴν φρώνησιν, "what might make the mind wise," that is, lest he should relax the reins on his emotions.

(13) *Just*, δίκαιος (just), one who harms no one himself, and gives of his own to anyone, and by his example urges others to justice and equity.

(14) *Pious*, ὅσιος (holy), worshiping God and living in a holy way.

(15) *Self-controlled*, ἐγκρατὴς (self-controlled), abstaining from all illicit impulses and disturbances of the mind, by which he could be hindered in his office (*officium*).

(16) *Embracing that which is according to teaching, the faithful discourse*, that is, he must be orthodox in religion, and constant in orthodoxy, for in the Greek it is ἀντεχόμενος (holding on), tenacious and clinging faithfully and firmly to sound teaching; for to ἀντεχεσθαι is to hold on with your teeth, and to be affixed. This description, then, requires three things: (1) an agreement with sound teaching, in which there must be no impurity; (2) the gift of setting it forth, for he calls it "discourse, which is according to teaching," that is, which can be taught among others; (3) constancy in that teaching, to which Paul wants the minister of the Church to cling with his teeth.

(17) "That he might be able both to exhort in sound teaching, and to refute those who contradict it." With this circumlocution, he expresses what it is to be διδάκτικος *apt to teach*, which he required of the bishop in 1 Tim. 3:2. This consists in exhorting and refuting. Exhortation pertains to those who are more sluggish in the pursuit of truth

---

57 "Probably meaning 'good works' (see Balduin's translation above), but the Latin leaves it vague here."

and piety, who must be roused that they might hold on to what they have, lest anyone should snatch their crown away; or to the weak and afflicted, who must be cheered with consolations, for to παρακαλεῖν (exhort) is also to console. Refutation consists in the refuting of false teaching and in the reproving of bad morals, for ἀντιλέγοντες (those who contradict) are found on both sides. It is necessary for the minister of the Word to be δύνατος (capable) of all these things, one who both has learning, that he might be able, and greatness of heart, that he might be willing. For many *could* refute others, but are not willing, because they fear their animosity. So this whole ninth verse pertains to the minister's teaching, about which he adds the reason why he wants him to be δυνατὸς ἐν λόγῳ (capable in discourse): *because there are also many who are disobedient, babblers and seducers, especially those who are from the circumcision* (v. 10). He designates three types of bad men here: (1) the ἀνυπότακτοι (insubordinate), who cannot bear the yoke of discipline, but as Jerome writes, "pervert with a certain amazing impudence the sowing of good minds, which naturally have the knowledge of God, by means of their own foolish opinion"; (2) the ματαιόλογοι (talking-at-random), the babblers, prating uselessly about vain things; and thus as long as theologians want to give heed, they become babblers; (3) the φρεναπάται (soul-deceivers), the seducers, who deceive minds and delude men who have been led away from the truth. There are very many of this sort, he says, especially the Jews, whom he calls "from the circumcision," because they were set apart by this from the other peoples, and also they placed the greatest confidence in it. *It is necessary that these be refuted, who subvert entire houses, teaching things it is not right to teach, for the sake of filthy riches* (v. 11). This is the reason why Paul wants the bishops who have to be appointed in each town to be δυνατὸς ἐν λόγῳ (capable in discourse), obviously so that they might be able to refute bad men of this sort—in the Greek it is ἐπιστομίζειν, to shut the mouth and to impose silence, that they might stop causing harm, because (1) they subvert entire houses, which is the greatest injury, to seduce not one man only, but a whole family; nor even one family, but many. (2) They have useless and destructive teaching, namely about the Jewish distinction of foods, about the necessity of circumcision, about Sabbath observance and the like, which do not bind Christians. (3) They have the worst object, namely filthy riches, because they are eager to please the rest of the Jews, and they hope they will obtain for themselves a reward that is not to be taken lightly. He has refuted these morals in the same men with the testimony of a certain Cretan: *A certain man from among them, a prophet who was one of their own, said, "Cretans are always liars, evil beasts, lazy gluttons"* (v. 12).

Jerome refers these words either to Epimenides[58] or to the poet Callimachus of Cyrene.[59] This whole verse is in Epimenides: κρῆτες ἀεὶ ψεῦσται, κακὰ θηρία, γαστέρες ἀργαί. Callimachus repeats but the beginning of this verse, and it could have been that he was alluding to that verse of Epimenides, just as Hesiod in the *Theogony* has a similar verse about shepherds: ποίμενες [ἄγραυλοι] κακ' ἐλέγχεα, γαστέρες οἶον (Field-dwelling shepherds, worthless disgraces, bellies only). Or it was a proverbial saying, κρῆτε, ἀεὶ ψεῦσται, borrowed by Callimachus from common usage. Now Paul calls Epimenides a prophet of the Cretans, although he was a poet and a philosopher, (1) because poets are called prophets, who were thought to sing their songs by some divine inspiration, whom they called ἔνθεος (inspired/possessed by a god). Thus Plato called poets daughters of the gods in book 2 of *The Republic*, and Ovid's saying is well known: "There is a god within us, and dealings with heaven. / This inspiration comes from celestial places."[60] Hence the poet was said to be Μουσοπατακτὸς, smitten by the madness of the Muses, and φοιβόληπτος (possessed by Phoebus Apollo) and Μουσόληπτος (possessed by a Muse), one who was inspired by the divinity of Phoebus and the Muses, according to Gyraldus, *History*

---

58 Epimenides of Knossos (lived some time in the 7th or 6th century B.C.) was a poet and a philosopher, and appears as a seer in Greek myths.

59 Callimachus (d. 240 B.C.) was born in Cyrene (in Libya), married a wife from Syracuse (Sicily), and ended up in Alexandria (Egypt). He does not seem to have been a Cretan at any point in his life.

60 "*Est Deus in nobis, sunt et commercia coeli, / Sedibus aethereis Spiritus iste venit.*" Ovid, *The Art of Love* III. 549–550.

of the Poets dialogue 1, p. 5.⁶¹ And even Origen thinks in book 3 of περὶ ἀρχῶν (*On First Principles*), chapter 3, that there is a certain special ἐνέργεια (operation) and power that inspires Poetry, for which reason so very many of the Greeks were of the opinion that the poetic art cannot exist without madness, and it is reported several times in their histories that those whom they call prophets were suddenly filled with the spirit of a certain madness. (2) Epimenides in particular was thought to have a god, several of whose oracles Diogenes Laërtius recites, and writes that because of this reputation, not only was he sought by the Athenians for the sake of purifying their city,⁶² but also sacrifices had been offered to him, as to a god, by the Cretans themselves,⁶³ that they might be the ones to declare that he had been endowed with a certain singular power of discerning future things. Cicero also mentions this Epimenides in book 2 *De divinat.*, among those who have prophesied through madness. (3) Some think that he is called a prophet because this verse is cited from Epimenides' book, which is entitled περὶ τῶν χρησμῶν, *On Oracles*.⁶⁴ (4) Others perceive irony here, as if Paul called a poet a prophet because such prophets were fitting for such Christians as the Cretans were. (5) Others think that "prophet" here is the same as "teacher of ethics," one who teaches morals, which Epimenides did, since in this verse he is primarily censuring the morals of the Cre-

---

61   The *Historiae poëtarum Graecorum ac Latinorum* (*Histories of the Greek and Latin Poets*) of Italian scholar Giglio Gregorio Giraldi (1479–1552).

62   Diogenes Laërtius records (*Lives of Eminent Philosophers* I.10.110) that the city of Athens was struck with a plague, and sent for Epimenides so he could tell them which god had been offended. He came to Athens and let loose a flock of white and black sheep in the city, telling the Athenians to mark where each lay down, and to build an altar there to the divinity of that place. The plague ended when they had done this and executed two men involved in a recent coup attempt, which Epimenides diagnosed as the root of the problem. Diogenes Laërtius added that many of these altars still existed in his day, still blank, "with no name inscribed upon them." The altar St. Paul discovered in Acts 17:23 "to an unknown god" may have been one of these.

63   Diogenes Laërtius attributes this claim to "some writers" (I.10.114).

64   According to Erkki Koskenniemi, this title, περὶ τῶν χρησμῶν, never appears in ancient sources. "The Famous Liar and the Apostolic Truth," *Filología Neotestamentaria* 24 [2011]). The article can be found at https://www.bsw.org/filologia-neotestamentaria/vol-24-2011/the-famous-liar-and-the-apostolic-truth/637/

tans. Now, the morals of the Cretans were most corrupted, of whom Polybius writes that in land and sea battles, they were most inclined to ambushes, artifices, pillaging, nocturnal assaults, and all kinds of deception, but in battle were sluggish, timid, and utterly useless. We have heard above about their infamous pederasty. Coelius Rhodiginus adds from Strabo, in book 18 of *Lection. antiq.*, chapter 26, that this monstrous vice existed among them without any disgrace, and that it was lawful to abduct boys for this purpose even by force, and that he who would interfere with these attempts would not be free from the stain of disgrace, and that the beloved was called κλεινὸς, that is, distinguished, but the lover was called *philethora*, that is, passionate. See similar things in book 15, chapter 9.[65]

Moreover, three prominent vices are noted in this race by Epimenides, by means of this celebrated verse: (1) that they are ἀεὶ ψεῦσται, always liars. This arose from the fact that they feigned that Jupiter was buried on that island, and inscribed these words on his tomb: "Here lies Jupiter," and yet they took him for an immortal god. Calimachus decries this especially in his praises of Jupiter. But there are also other lies of theirs, for instance, about Rhadamanthus, about King Minos and his minotaur, about Daedalus and his labyrinth, which are indeed ascribed to the poets who concealed their wisdom under these figments, about which see Natalis Comes,[66] in *Mytholog.* Book 6, chapter 5. Nevertheless, the vice peculiar to this race, and thence innate, is that the Cretans were called liars, and prominent architects of fables,

---

[65] A note in the book's margin here reads, "The Proverbs of the Greeks: the three worst kappas: Cappadocians, Cilicians, and Cretans. Augustine understands it in book 3 *De Grammat.* concerning three Corneliuses." The Augustine reference is to his *De Grammatica: Regulae*, in which he writes (I.4): "*Inde est illud,* τρία κάππα κάκιστα, *id est tria cappa pessuma, de Cornelio Sylla, de Cornelio Cinna, de Cornelio Lentulo. Hi enim per tres litteras designati sunt in libris Sibyllinis.*" "Thence is that τρία κάππα κάκιστα, *i.e.,* the three worst cappas, of Cornelius Sulla, of Cornelius Cinna, of Cornelius Lentulus. For these were designated through three letters in the Sibylline Books."

[66] Natali Conti (Noël le Comte in French) was an Italian humanist who lived 1520–1582 and published a ten-book *Mythologiae* in 1567. He believed that classical myths contained allegorized philosophical meanings that enlightened readers were expected to understand.

just as the Carthaginians, for instance, were called treacherous, the Scythians violent, the Persians vain, the Thracians given to drink, the Sybarites and Campani haughty, the Milesians and Regini effeminate, the Arcadians dull, the Gauls petty and vain, the Spanish boastful, the Carians base; concerning these see Erasmus in *Adagiis* (chil. 1, cent. 8, ch. 27) and Alexander of Alexander,[67] book 4 of *Genial. dier.*, chapter 13. Other authors also have noted the fickleness of the Cretans and their facility for lying, for instance Ovid, in book 1 of *De arte amandi*: "Note what I sing. Crete, who supports a hundred cities, cannot deny this, liar though she be."[68] And Statius[69] in book 1 of the *Thebaidos*: "and your false goddess, Crete."[70] From this come the proverbs, "to κρητίζειν" (to Cretanize) for "to lie," "One must Cretanize with a Cretan," and "to be Cretan to a Cretan"; that is, one cheats when one's peers are agreeable to deceptions and frauds. (2) Another vice is brutishness, for they are called κακά θηρία, evil beasts, who live with the morals of wild animals, focused only on profits, given to frauds and deception without regard to person, and as Jerome adds, thirsting for the blood of deceivers. That is, they both freely deceive, and carry out vengeance on those who deceive. This is why "to κρητίζειν" (to Cretanize) is sometimes the same as "to cheat," and "to deceive." And Polybius writes in book 7,[71] "In general, the pursuit of shameful gain and avarice has attained such a place among them, that among all morals, only to the Cretans does no acquisition seem to be shameful."[72] Now this vice arises from the previous one, for people who are not ashamed to lie are prone to deceptions. (3) The third vice is sloth and excess, for they are called γαστέρες ἀργαί, lazy bellies. It is customary to call men who are given to the gullet and

---

[67] Alessandro Alessandri (1461–1523), a lawyer of Naples who published a learned miscellany entitled *Genialium dierum* (*Of Pleasant Days*) in 1522.
[68] I.296–7.
[69] Statius (c. 45–c. 96), Roman poet, author of a 12-book epic called the *Thebaid*.
[70] I.278–9.
[71] Book 6 in modern editions.
[72] Polybius, *Histories*, VI.46.

the paunch "bellies," as in Terence, in *Phormio*, and in Lucilius,[73] whom Tully[74] quotes in his *Orat. pro Caelio*: "Live, O Bellies!" In other places, our Paul too describes such men in this way, saying that they have as God their belly (Phil. 3:19). The Cretans are called by the epithet "lazy bellies" because they were given to leisure, and hence were free for dances and other pleasures and exercises of the body, on which subject see Rhodiginus, book 5, chapter 3. Phavorinus,[75] when he recounted this plausible recollection,[76] calls the Cretans γαστριμάργους, gorgers and gluttons, for μάργος is "gluttonous." And Canterus[77] thinks in book 1, chapter 5 of *Novar. lect.*,[78] that Epimenides, when he had wanted to say γαστεραμάργην, and the poem's meter would not allow it, substituted ἀργὴν in its place, which he intended to mean the same thing.

Now it should be known that these vices are noted in the Cretans, as others are in other provinces, not because they were observed in individual sojourners, but because they were common, and remained almost uncorrected. Elsewhere, the Cretans are commended for the pursuit of wisdom, of justice, of good laws, and the like, in which areas they had the most outstanding of the Greeks, especially the Spartans, as their imitators and followers, as is found in Strabo, Aristotle, Plato, and others: see Rhodiginus book 15, chapter 9, and book 18, chapter 1. Now our Apostle introduces this verse of Epimenides about the vices of the Cretans in order to agree with him by his own reckoning: *This testimony is true*, he says, *for which reason, rebuke them, that they might be sound in the faith* (v.13). The Apostle shows that he has done no injury to the Cretans when he called them disobedient, babblers, and seducers, because both they and their worst moral characteristics had

---

73 Gaius Lucilius (c. 180–c. 103 B.C.), early Roman satirist, whose works survive only in fragments.

74 That is, Cicero: Marcus Tullius Cicero.

75 Or Favorinus (c. 80–c. 160 A.D.), Roman sophist and philosopher.

76 Balduin probably speaks of Phavorinus *remembering* something because he is citing his Ἀπομνημονεύματα (Memoirs).

77 Gulielmus Canterus, or Willem Cantor (1542–75), Dutch humanist and philologist.

78 *Novarum Lectionum Liber* (Book of New Readings).

already been most justly censured long ago by their own countrymen.

For this reason, he wants Titus to carry out the office [*officium*] of a good pastor, whose responsibility it is to recall the wandering sheep, not only by the shepherd's pipe, but also by the staff. That is, he commands him to rebuke such people sternly. In the Greek it is ἔλεγχε αὐτοὺς ἀποτόμως, reprove them concisely, severely, without respect of persons. For ἀποτόμως, strictly speaking, is "truncatedly" and "cut-shortly," from τεμνῶ, which means "cut," "cut into." Metaphorically it is the same as "to the quick," "sharply," "severely," the metaphor having been taken from surgeons, who cut wounds to the quick, all the way, not without pain for the patient, that they might be able to heal him. So Titus is told to be similarly unsparing with the babblers and seducers, that they might both think rightly and teach others rightly, for this is what it is "to be sound in the faith." For ἑτεροδοξία (heterodoxy) is compared to a disease in 2 Tim. 2:17. For those whom he accuses here, labor under such a disease. Therefore he adds, *not paying attention to Jewish fables and the commandments of men who turn themselves away from the truth* (v. 14). These commandments of men are called Jewish fables because things that do not have God as their author are rightly held, in matters of faith, to be useless fables. Such fables of the Jews were those δευτερώσεις (secondary traditions) that Christ prohibits as the ἐντάλματα (commandments) of men (Matt. 15, Mark 7:7). Among these, certain commandments were taken away from the Law of Moses, certain ones added to it, and certain ones erroneously explained, as for example the tithing of dill and cumin (Matt. 23:23), the return of Elijah the Tishbite (Sir. 48:10, Matt. 17:12), the ignorance whence the Messiah would come (John 7:27), the violation of the Sabbath through works of necessity and charity (Luke 14), and the washings of the hands (Matt. 15:2). But they insisted above all on the Mosaic ceremonies, the distinction of days and foods, and the like, precepts that at one time were indeed in the law of Moses, but were abrogated by Christ, as Paul taught in Col. 2:16. When they insisted that these things were necessary for Christians, they were teaching fables, and were opposed to the truth, for which reason Christ also at one time accused the Pharisees, that the commandments of God were transgressed by their traditions (Matt.

15:3), and Irenaeus mentions the Pharisaic law, which was plainly opposed to the law of God (book 4, chapter 12).[79] Because of the closeness of the sea, such patrons of Jewish fables inhabited Crete in the greatest numbers possible. Thus Josephus testifies in his *Life* that nobles dwelt in Crete who were descended, he thought, from the Jews, and were called Idaeans, as if from Mount Ida, which is in Crete.[80]

The Apostle adds a reason why he called those commandments of the Jews "fables," namely because they do nothing toward the purity and sanctity of Christians, which consists not in ablutions and similar ceremonies of the Jews, but in purity of heart and conscience: *To the pure, all things are pure,* he says, *but to the polluted and unfaithful, nothing is pure, but their mind and conscience have been polluted* (v. 15). He teaches that observance of the Levitical ceremonies is useless if the heart is not pure in the sight of God, and that for those who do have a pure heart, it is not necessary. For it does nothing toward that purity of heart that consists in true faith, by which hearts are purified (Acts 15:9). Thus to the faithful, all things are pure. They cannot be contaminated by the use of foods or days, or by discontinuing the Jewish washings, nor yet are they offended by any rites, because they understand in what Christian liberty consists; and those who are destitute of faith in Christ, the kind of man those babblers among the Cretans were, for them that external washing and observance of foods and days shall have profited nothing, but their mind is impure, because they believe nothing rightly about God, they live without Christ and faith, they understand nothing of Christian liberty, nothing of the true way of attaining salvation. Their

---

79 In *Against Heresies*, that is. Balduin cites IV.25, but that chapter does not even mention the Pharisees, let alone a "Pharisaic law." IV.12 does, and fits perfectly into this context.

80 In Book 1 of his *Life* (section 427) Josephus says that his fourth wife, "though she had settled in Crete, was by ancestry a Judean, of parents who were the most noble and most distinguished in that region." Beyond this, he tells us nothing about a Jewish community in Crete, nor does he mention the name "Idaeans," which according to a theory related by Tacitus (*Histories* V.2) was the original name of the Jewish race, and proved that Crete was their primeval homeland (add a 'u' to "Idaeans" and it becomes "Judaeans"). The citation is exceedingly weak evidence for Balduin's claim that Jews inhabited Crete "in the greatest numbers possible" (*quam plurimi*).

conscience also is impure, because they contaminate themselves with the most serious sins, by which their conscience is wounded, and yet they seek salvation in that external observance of Levitical ceremonies. Therefore he adds, *They confess that they know God, but they deny it by their deeds, because they are abominated and unbelieving, and disapproved with respect to every good work* (v. 16). These are clear evidences of an impure conscience. For with the voice, indeed, they profess themselves to be true worshipers of God, children of Abraham, disciples of Moses, but if you look at their life, they are devoid of all religion. Now, note here the Latin translator's solecism: he calls them "abominated and unbelieving," who in the Greek are called βδελυκτοὶ καὶ ἀπειθεῖς. Jerome skillfully renders it "detestable and disobedient," from which it is plain that the old version, full of solecisms and canonized in the Council of Trent, is not Jerome's. Now, βδελυκτοὶ are buffoonish men, sharp enough, but inexperienced and accordingly disagreeable to the wise. Pliny and Horace call them "abominated," or devoted to all horrible things, and detestable. The ἀπειθεῖς are inflexible men, who in no way suffer themselves to be persuaded, or who have faith in no admonitions, for which reason this word is used (1 Pet. 3:20). There were such men among the Cretans, who while insisting on the commandments of men, were not obeying the commandments of God, and besides this were also performing certain abominable deeds, and yet wished to be worshipers of God. But they were disapproved even when they seemed to be doing something good, for the goodness of a deed should be judged not from the substance but the quality of the work.[81]

---

[81] That is, not from what has objectively been done, but from the state or disposition of the deed, i.e.,, from *how* and in connection to *what* it has been done.

Questions from this Part of the Chapter

Question 1

Because Titus was left in Crete in order to correct the things Paul had left unfinished (v. 5), it is asked whether bishops have the power of establishing new laws in the Church?

Answer: The Jesuit Benedict Justinian furnished the occasion for this question, since he writes in his commentaries on this passage, "From this, let the reformers conclude that it is right for the bishops to add new canons to the ancient constitutions and arrangements of the Apostles, and to cut away the evils that daily creep in through recent laws, *etc.*, for as I show more fully elsewhere, all things are not included in the writings of the divine prophets and Apostles, whether those that should be believed, or those that pertain to the right administration of the church." But indeed, there is nothing in our text about new laws having to be established by Titus, but only about the building that Paul began in that island, as a wise architect, having to be continued into the future, something that could be done by means of teaching and ecclesiastical discipline. Nor is there even a reason discovered in this passage why new laws should have been given. The reason is added by Justinian. For the things that must be believed as necessary to salvation had been delivered in full by the Apostle, as he says to the bishops of the Ephesian church in Acts 20:27, "For I have not been evasive, so as to announce to you less than the full counsel of God." These things were only to be repeated by Paul's disciples; surely they were able to add nothing new. As for the things pertaining to the right administration of the church, they indeed had not all been prescribed by the Apostle, although in this event, they would freely accommodate themselves to what he had prescribed in similar cases. However, what pertains generally to ecclesiastical laws and constitutions, whether it is permitted to add new canons or laws to the ancient constitutions of the Apostles, is not in question, for we readily grant that the Apostles could not foresee all the particulars of the churches, whose laws and circumstances are prone to variation from the variety of times and men. But this is inquired: which laws, and what kind, and how should one establish them? On these three points, with respect to this question, the Papists disagree with us. They teach that the Roman Pontiff can give laws not only concerning a certain outward adornment of the church, but also concerning articles of faith and the worship of God, and that these laws bind the conscience and have the power of punishing transgressors, as one can see in Bellarmine,[82] *De Rom. Pontif.*, book 4, chapter 15. But about this subject, the Apostle has not a word in this passage, so how does Justinian order us to conclude from it something of which no traces are present? But our opinion is this, that not the Pontiff, nor only the bishops, but the whole church has the power of giving ecclesiastical laws; not, however, laws about articles of faith, or about inward or outward worship (since such things are already either expressly contained in the Word, or able to be drawn from it through the analogy of faith), but such laws as concern the external εὐσχημωσύνη (decorum) of the church, meaning those that do not directly bind consciences. Transgressors cause either schism or scandal, and therefore must be coerced by ecclesiastical discipline. I will prove all these things with a few words. (1) First, then, that it is not only in the power of the bishops, but in the power of the whole church, that is, in the power of the people and the magistrate, is established from the practice of the Apostolic church, where, when a canon had to be made concerning the administration of ecclesiastical goods, not only the Apostles but also the multitude of disciples, or all Christians without distinction, made their votes known publicly, and chose the seven deacons (Acts 6:2). In the Council of Jerusalem, when laws had to be given for the Gentiles who had converted to the faith of Christ, τὸ πλεῖος also, or the multitude of the people, come together as one with the Apostles and unanimously made the decree about this matter (Acts 15:12, 25, 26). (2) Concerning the magistrate, the matter is expounded specifically, for since every soul has been subjected to him (Rom. 13:1),

---

[82] Robert Bellarmine (1542–1621), Italian Jesuit (Roberto Bellarmino), one of the most prominent controversialists of the Counter-Reformation.

and since it is his responsibility to guard the laws of the church, and he will undoubtedly have the right of giving these laws, he should do so not only by virtue of his authority, but according to the command of Scripture, and to right reason. (3) Next, that it is not in the power of the church or of any man to make laws about articles of faith or divine worship, is established from this, that God does not want to be worshiped by the commandments of men (Matt. 15:9). Nor does it belong to man or angel to make articles of faith. Indeed, it is God's alone to prescribe to us what we must believe as necessary to salvation, and He has done this sufficiently in the word of the Prophets and the Apostles, which is accordingly called the foundation of the church (Eph. 2:20). Also, God Himself wants nothing to be added to His Word, and nothing to be taken away (Deut. 4:2, 12:32). Things that pertain to good order and discipline, however, when they need to be established, the church is rightly discharging its duty in accordance with the condition of each place. For all things in the church should indeed be done in order, and decently (1 Cor. 14[:40]), yet every rite and law cannot be adapted to every particular church, nor yet does this dissonance of rites destroy the harmony of faith. (4) Finally, ecclesiastical laws of this kind do not bind the conscience directly and of themselves; laws of that kind are those that have been given directly by God, who alone is the Lord of consciences, and alone is that lawgiver "who can destroy and deliver" (James 4:12). Hence not even the Apostles were willing to throw men into fetters with their constitutions, nor to lord it over the faith (1 Cor. 7:35, 2 Cor. 1:24). And ecclesiastical laws are not about articles of faith, as we have heard, but about ceremonies and other *adiaphora*,[83] in which a yoke should not be placed upon the disciples' shoulder (Acts 15:10). See 1 Cor. 7:23 and Gal. 5:1. Nevertheless, it can happen indirectly, that a violation of laws of this kind causes scruples for the transgressors, for instance when someone resists returning to ecclesiastical ordinances without just cause, after a proper investigation and when just decisions have been rendered concerning the cases. Because this is done with

---

83 *Adiaphora* are "indifferent things," meaning that they are neither required nor forbidden.

contempt for the magistrate and the word of the ministers and unity in devotion, and not without schism and scandal for the weak, for this very reason, this case does wound the conscience and incur ecclesiastical penalty.

Question 2

Because Paul makes separate mention of presbyters and bishops in verses 5 and 7, it is asked how presbyters should be distinguished from bishops?

Answer: "Presbyter" is not a term of age, but of dignity, common to all who serve the holy ministry. Thus a presbyter is called a bishop in Acts 20:17-28, Phil. 1:1, 1 Tim. 3:2, and in this text, where those whom Paul commands to appoint as presbyters he later, when he is enumerating their requirements, calls bishops. In fact, it is inferred from 1 Tim. 4:14 and 2 Tim. 1:6 that even the Apostle Paul reckoned himself among the presbyters. And when Paul requires the same things from the presbyters that are necessary for the bishops, it is clear that Scripture does not know so exact a distinction between presbyters and bishops; yet afterwards, the church by its free disposition distinguished between bishops and presbyters in certain secondary duties (*officiis*) for the sake of order, until it committed to the bishops the ordination of ministers, the primary oversight of the churches (from which they have the name),[84] the deciding of doubtful cases, and the like; and to the presbyters the administration of the holy things, the visitation of the sick, absolution from sins, and the like. And because this distinction is only one of order, not of necessity, therefore in the absence of a bishop, the presbyters could carry out his duties (*partes*), and in the absence of a presbyter, a bishop could carry out his duties (*partes*), as is in Augustine, in *Quaest. ex utroque testamento*,[85] Question 101, and Ambrose on Ephesians chapter 4. Concerning this distinction, Jerome writes on this passage, "The same man who is a bishop, is a presbyter; and before

---

84 A bishop is an *Episcopus*, that is, an "overseer."

85 The *Quaestiones ex utroque testamento (Questions from Both Testaments)* is a 4th century work of unknown authorship. Modern scholars have determined that it was not written by St. Augustine.

studies in religion were being done by the inspiration of the devil, and it was being said among the people, 'I am of Paul, I am of Apollos, I am of Cephas' [1 Cor. 1:12], the churches were governed by the common counsel of the presbyters. But as soon as each one was considering those whom he had baptized to be his own, not Christ's, it was decreed in all the world that one of the presbyters should be elected and placed over the others, and that the care of the whole church should belong to him, and the seeds of schisms would be removed." As one time followed another, because the tyranny of the Antichrist was striving for monarchical rule of the Church, such a distinction between bishops and presbyters was devised in the Papacy—one that concerns power and jurisdiction—that Episcopacy has become a particular grade in the ecclesiastical hierarchy, and the bishop has authority and power over the presbyters by divine right. That is what the Council of Trent decreed in session 23, chapter 7, but Scripture knows absolutely nothing of such a distinction, nor are grades of this kind discovered in the ministry when the ecclesiastical hierarchy was described in 1 Cor. 12:28 or Eph. 4:11, nor did Christ confer on one of the Apostles so great a prerogative over the others, nor did He confer on all of them together so great a prerogative over the lesser ministers, but He commands the greater one among them to become the servant (*minister*) of the other one; nor do the Apostles concede to the bishops a domination that they do not assume for themselves (1 Pet. 5:3). And Jerome, writing on this text, calls it a custom of the church, that the bishops have been set over the presbyters. "Just as the presbyters know," he says, "that they have been subjected to the one who has been placed over them by the custom of the church, so also the bishops know that they are greater than the presbyters more by custom than by the truth of the Lord's arrangement, and that they ought to rule the church together." Bellarmine recognizes this passage in book 1 of *De Cler.*,[86] chapter 15, but he writes that Jerome spoke doubtfully, although no indication of doubt is apparent. Cornelius à Lapide, in his commentary on this passage, warns that Jerome should be read cautiously, because he wants

---

86   *De Clericis* (*On the Clergy*).

only to show that the presbyters had ruled the church not by hierarchical order, but by spirit and zeal, with the consent of the bishops. But Jerome does not say this, nor did he ever know that hierarchical order that the Papists fashion. Also, he has nothing about the consent of the bishops, but simply contrasts the custom of the church, according to which the bishop is said to be over the presbyters, to the Lord's arrangement, which makes bishops and presbyters equals, insofar as grade of power and jurisdiction is concerned. Thus in his Letter to Evagrius he writes that "at the time of the Apostles, there were not distinct grades of bishops and presbyters, but afterwards, as a remedy for schism, one of the presbyters was elected and placed in a higher grade and called the bishop, although he differed from the presbyters only by the function (*officium*) of ordaining." See more about this question in my commentary on the Epistle to the Philippians, chapter 1, question 2.

Question 3

Can it be rightly inferred, from the fact that Paul orders Titus to establish presbyters through every single town, that the election of ministers of the Word is in the power of the bishops alone?

Answer: Indeed, Justinian[87] does infer thus from this fact, where he adds, on this passage, that the bishops could not have been placed over the churches by any vote of the people, and not even of the churches' ministers, for most of the bishops were placed over those cities in which scarcely two people had received the Christian mysteries. Bellarmine also has this proposition in book 1 of *De Cleric.*, chapter 7. [He says:] The right of electing the pastors and ministers of the church is, by divine law, not suited to the people. But if the people ever had any power in this matter, they had it entirely by the agreement and allowance of the bishops. We oppose to this assertion (1) the practice of the primitive church, where the people also were consulted in the election of the first seven deacons (Acts 6:5) and not even in the election of the Apostle Matthias were they excluded (Acts 1:15 and 26). (2) The power given by

---

87 That is, the Jesuit interpreter Benedict Justinian, mentioned above.

Christ to the church, for the keys have been given to the whole church, not to one rank, at least (Matt. 18:17). Therefore, neither the election nor the calling of ministers has been restricted to any rank, and Christ also wants everyone to beware of bad teachers (Matt. 7:15). John bids them to test a spirit, whether it is from God (1 John 4:1), and by this very command, the right of discerning and electing is given to all the ranks. (3) The authority of the Fathers, for Cyprian writes expressly in book 1, Letter 4,[88] that the people especially have the power, either of electing worthy priests, or rejecting unworthy ones; and he proves that it is of divine law from the fact that in old times a priest was selected with the people present, under the eyes of all, and was verified as worthy and suitable by public testimony (Num. 20 and 26, Acts 1[:15–26]). Thus it was decreed at the Council of Nicaea and the Council of Carthage that the whole council [senatus] of the church should elect men that have been set before the people and called to ecclesiastical offices [munera]. And they wanted great care to be taken, in old times, that a pastor should not be thrust upon an unwilling people. Concerning this matter, see [Corpus Iuris Canonici,] distinction 3, can. Nosce, and Tertullian, Apolog.[89] chapter 39. Now, when Paul confers on Titus the right of establishing presbyters, this is done with regard to carrying out [the duty], because it is the job of a bishop to know the attainments and the gifts of the ministers, and to commend these things to the people, and it can by no means be inferred from this that Titus alone thrust presbyters upon the churches without the consent of the people. Nor does it matter that there were few Christians at the beginning, for even that fewness makes a kind of multitude, and does not give Titus the power to act alone, without informing the people.

---

88   I.e., Letter 67 in modern numeration.

89   *The Apology.*

Question 4

Why does Paul require of a bishop that he be the husband of one wife (v. 6), although elsewhere he writes, "I want you all to be like myself," that is, celibates (1 Cor. 7:7)?

Answer: Benedict Justinian ties this knot, but does not untie it. He says that Paul could not have commanded marriage for priests because he said elsewhere, "I want you all to be like myself." But neither do we say that Paul commanded it, but that he did not exclude married men from the ministry, and therefore that he nowhere commanded celibacy for the ministers of the church. That wish of the Apostle in 1 Cor. 7:7 in no way takes marriage away from priests. For (1) it does not pertain directly to marriage, but to continence, which can exist even in the married. This is known from the fact that (a) it is uncertain whether Paul had a wife or not when he was writing these things. Of the Fathers, Ignatius (Letter 6) and Clement of Alexandria (book 3 of the Στρωμάτων [the *Stromata*])[90] affirm that he did have one, and Eusebius in book 3 of his *Hist.*, chapter 30.[91] (b) It is clear from the context that Paul is talking about married people whom he wants to abstain sometimes from the conjugal act, that they might be free for prayers and fasting, lest Satan should tempt them on account of their incontinence, as he says in v. 5. To these people he proposes his own example in v. 7: "I want you all to be like myself," namely continent, not celibate, for he is speaking with the married. [2] Next, Paul does not want to lay a yoke on them because of his own wish, as the Papists do by the law of celibacy. Even though he desires those who do not have the gift of continence to contain themselves, he in no way constrains them. Thus he says in v. 6, "I say this according to indulgence, and not according to precept," and in v. 7 when he has said, "I want you all to be like myself," he then adds, "but each one has his own gift from God: one in this way, the other in that way." It is therefore a wish of

---

90 *Stromata* III.6.

91 In this passage, Eusebius is quoting the aforementioned passage from Clement, *Stromata* III.6, so it is not an independent source.

possibility, namely: if they should be able to contain themselves. It is in accord with this wish of Paul's that they be able, but if they are not able, he commands them to use marriage: "But if they do not contain themselves," he says to marry. "It is better to marry than to burn" (v. 9). (3) If he was talking especially about marriage there, and not about continence, it would nevertheless be only a wish in keeping with the condition of those times, when all things were full of dangers and persecutions, and therefore it was better to be celibate than to be married, if it could be done without danger of burning, "on account of the present necessity," as v. 26 says. Therefore that wish, if it could be altogether attained, still does not derive from the opinion of perfection (the way the Papist priests want to be celibate), but from the teaching of a more tranquil life.

Question 5

The Apostle requires of a bishop that he have faithful children, not wanton or disobedient (v. 6). It is therefore asked whether someone might be unfit for the ministry on account of evil children?

Answer: What Jerome held in this area on this text is rather harsh. Granted, he says, that it happens not rarely that children who were well educated by their parents, and were ennobled with right discipline and good morals, relax the reins because of lusts and vices; still he says that the vices of one's children justly bar one from the priesthood, in order that he who presides in the church might be able freely to correct the vices of others, and not fear their censure on account of the shameful deeds of his children. It is true that this should be given attention in the election of ministers, I do not deny it, and accordingly, if we can consider the case of a man being elected, I would say that he should not easily be used for the ministry if he labors under bad repute on account of the vices of his children, for it is fitting that the household of a minister of the church should be like Caesar's wife, free of all evil suspicion, and as it is written to Timothy, "He who does not know how to preside over his own household well, how shall he govern the church of God?" (1 Tim. 3:5). But if children lawfully acquired and liberally educated during his ministry have departed from their upbringing, as happens sometimes, their parent nevertheless cannot abdicate his office on that account, since it would not be right that a parent should bear the iniquity of a child in this way, and similar examples are not lacking among holy men, even as Samuel was not deposed on account of his disobedient sons (1 Sam. 8:4). But when parents conspire with their children, and increase their malice with leniency, then there is sufficient just cause why they should no longer be accepted in that holy office, which does not allow a failing of this sort, even as we read that the High Priest Eli was deprived both of his life and his priesthood for this cause (1 Sam. 2:28ff).

Question 6

How does Paul say in v. 13 that the testimony of the Cretan poet Epimenides is true, when in v. 12 this same Epimenides has named all Cretans "liars"?

Answer: The Greeks call this kind of speech τό ψευδόμενον (falsified), when someone seems to contradict himself, as when Epimenides says that Cretans are liars although he himself is a Cretan, and by this very fact seems to have spoken a lie, since Cretans will consequently be truthful. In Dialectics, it refers to the fallacy of *Ignoratio elenchi*,[92] which can be easily explained. For that proposition ("Cretans are liars") is either particular, and thus it does not necessarily include Epimenides, or it is said concerning an innate vice of that race, about which any one of them can testify, for instance, a German testifying about the Germans' fondness for drink, a Parthian about the Parthians' vanity, *etc.*; for even one who is accustomed to lying can sometimes speak the truth. Some prattle that the Cretans are called liars by the poet because they say the tomb of Jupiter is with them, although Jupiter is immortal, and therefore that, because Paul says this testimony is true, it follows

---

92 The fallacy is called "ignorance of refutation" because (in its original definition by Aristotle) it consists in trying to refute a position by proving an argument that does not actually contradict the position you are ostensibly disproving. The connection to Balduin's subject seems to be that Epimenides' quotation appears to contradict itself, but does not actually.

that he proves the immortality of Jupiter. But Chrysostom answers, and Jerome, that the Apostle is not confirming the whole poem of that poet, but only the part in which he calls the Cretans liars for their innate readiness to lie. Theodoret too answers in the same way: he called the testimony true, not confirming the poetic fables, but proving the inconstancy of the Cretans' mind.

Question 7

Why does Paul call the observance of the Levitical ceremonies "Jewish fables," although they had been commanded by God?

Answer: This would be done for two reasons. (1) Because those precepts of the ceremonial law were supposed to continue only until New Testament times, and to have their end in Christ, as the Apostle testifies in Col. 2:16. Therefore whoever extends them further is forcing not God's commandments, but his own fables on the church. For not observing the commandments of God is the same as observing them wrongly. (2) Because only the external use of those ceremonies was being urged, without the faith of the heart in Christ. This external worship could not please God without faith, and insofar as that use was perverse, it changed the precepts of God into fables. Chrysostom replies in this way in homily 3 on this epistle: "All the Jewish observances can be called fables in two ways," he says, "either because they are done in pretense, or because they are done at the wrong time. For if they are done when they ought not to be done, and the deeds cause injury, they are a useless and harmful fable, *etc.*" Jerome demonstrates this answer with examples: "If anyone," he says, "after the coming of Christ is mutilated and not circumcised,[93] he is serving Jewish fables and the commandments of men opposed to the truth. 'For he is not a Jew who is one in the open, but who is one in secret, and the circumcision of the heart is in the spirit, not the letter' [Rom. 2:28–29]. If anyone keeps the Passover, not 'in the unleavened loaves of sincerity and truth' that he might drive out of his soul all 'the old leaven of malice and wickedness'

---

93 These are similar words in the Latin: "*conciditur et non circumciditur.*"

[1 Cor. 5:8], he is attending to fables and following shadows, having neglected the truth. If anyone, not rising again with Christ, not seeking those things that are above, but that are below (*cf.* Col. 3:1–2), says, 'Do not touch, do not taste, do not handle, which things are in corruption by that very use, according to the precepts and doctrines of men' [Col. 2:21–22], he is following righteousnesses that are not good and precepts that are not good." From these last words, Jerome turns his attention to the passage in Ezekiel 20:25, "I have given them precepts that are not good," where Jerome understands the ceremonial laws to have been practiced by the Jews neither rightly nor at the right time, but badly, as we have shown elsewhere. See the commentary on 1 Timothy, chapter 2, part 1, question 7. In the same way, the Israelites are said to have "multiplied altars for the purpose of sinning" (Hos. 8[:11]). For although they did not multiply them for this purpose, in order to sin, yet because they thought that they were worshiping God in this way, they were said to sin, because their worship was without the Word, and God could not approve of it.

Question 8

Because Paul writes that to the pure all things are pure (v. 15), ought one to contaminate oneself even with things that are impure in themselves?

Answer: Cornelius à Lapide writes on this text that Luther taught thus. "Luther concludes," he says, "therefore fornication also has been purified for the pure, that is, for the faithful. For as he says, 'Nothing justifies but faith, so nothing contaminates but unbelief.'" But the Jesuit lies most shamelessly, and so he does not dare to cite the passage where Luther wrote these things. In fact, he has this in his commentary on Galatians, chapter 2: "Only faith is necessary for us to be righteous, everything else is most free, neither commanded anymore nor prohibited." And again, "I have nothing to do with the law, because I have liberty." And in the book *On Christian Liberty*, "For the Christian man, there is need of no work, no law, because he has been freed from the law through faith." Bellarmine too censures all these things in book 4 of *De Justif.*,⁹⁴ chapter 1. But he never taught that fornication is pure to the pure. Indeed, in the cited passages he is speaking of the Christian liberty that the faithful have, not saying that they may live as they please and throw off the yoke of the law completely, but that they have been freed from the compulsion and curse of the law, as also from the use of the ceremonial law. In that quotation that "everything else" besides faith "is most free, neither commanded nor prohibited," he is speaking about liberty from the ceremonial law, for he is dealing there with Peter's error, when by abstaining from the foods of the Gentiles, he compelled the Gentiles to Judaize [Gal. 2:11ff.], as if the Jewish observance of foods were necessary to salvation. Luther is saying there, Paul is fighting for liberty against necessity, for "only faith in Christ is necessary for us to be righteous, everything else (the things, that is, that pertain to the rites of the Jews) is most free, neither commanded anymore nor prohibited." And to this pertains our Paul's dictum, "To the pure all things are pure": all things, that is, that at other times were forbidden to the Jews as unclean.

For faith in Christ has freed us from those Jewish rites. In the other quotation, [Luther] is dealing with liberty from the compulsion of the law: "I have nothing to do with the law, because I have liberty," that is, the law cannot compel me to obedience, but by the free Spirit I do the things that are of the law, "for where the Spirit is, there is liberty" (2 Cor. 3:17). Therefore liberty is being compared not to an Epicurean license of the flesh, but to the compulsion of the law, he says in his book *On Christian Liberty*, when he says that we are freed from the law through faith, doubtless so that it might not be able to condemn us, as Paul says clearly: "The law of the Spirit of life," that is, of faith, "has set me free from the law of death and sin" [Rom. 8:2], that is, from the law, which increases and works death and sin, as Luther explains in his commentary on Galatians, chapter 2. And in this way Luther declares his mind in the same book *On Christian Liberty*: "It is clear," he says, "that faith suffices the Christian man for all things, and that he will have no need of works in order to be justified. If faith has no need of works, and has

---

94 *De Justificatione*, On Justification.

no need of the law, if it has no obligation, surely he is free from the law, and truly 'the law has not been made for the righteous man,' *etc.*" [1 Tim. 1:9]. But that Luther taught that a faithful man is thus already free from sins, so that fornication or whatever other sin becomes allowed to him, can be proven by no word. But the contrary is clear from the things that he has written on Chapter 3 of Genesis: "Man does not have such liberty that if God commanded, he could do it or not do it. For because it has to do with the commandments of God, man is not free, but must obey the voice of God or endure the sentence of death." Thus he writes concerning Christian liberty.

This is Christian liberty, our faith, which makes it not that we are at leisure, or that we might live evilly, but that no one needs the law or works to attain righteousness and salvation. And in the book *On Monastic Vows*, "It is not Evangelical liberty to be able to omit the commandments of God,"[95] nor are we free from having to do works. And in the Preface to the Epistle to the Romans, "Liberty or liberation from the law is not a carnal liberty of doing nothing, but is a spiritual liberty that does not remove the law, but bestows and offers that which is required by the law, namely that we should do good works with delight and love, without legal coercion."[96] This is the invariable opinion of Luther, which we firmly cite against the lies of the Jesuits.

Question 9

Is the Papistic distinction of foods, with which they embellish their fasts, rightly refuted by these words, "To the pure all things are pure"?

Answer: These words are appropriately cited against all those who invent necessity for things indifferent in themselves, so that also when the images, having been retained in the churches on account of such long familiar usage, were overthrown unseasonably, and as if under the law of necessity, then we rightly say, "To the pure all things are pure," that is, they can be retained with a good conscience by those

---

95   WA 8:606.

96   WA DB 7:21. This is a translation of the German, rearranged a little.

who know that an idol is nothing (1 Cor. 8) and that the demolition of images accomplishes nothing towards salvation. And we use this Apostolic dictum especially rightly against the Papistic fasts, in which they abstain from certain foods as if they were unclean or not lawful to eat, and in which abstinence (this is especially impious) a good portion of the righteousness before God is made to consist, such that others who do not abstain are condemned. But Scripture in many places rejects abstinence of this kind. Christ says, "What goes into the mouth does not defile a man" (Matt. 15:11). Paul in fact says, "To the pure, all things are pure," and "Foods should not be forbidden, which God has created to be used with thanksgiving by the faithful" (1 Tim. 4[:3]), and that "Nothing is common or unclean of itself, except to him who thinks that something is unclean, it is unclean" (Rom. 14:14). And because some were insisting on a legal distinction of foods as if it were necessary, to the extent that they thought that those who were eating whatever foods they liked were sinning, and offending God, and defiling their conscience, he set against them the distinction of the Old and the New Testament, and the rejection of the Levitical rites in the New, saying, "Let no one judge or condemn you on account of food and drink, for these were the shadows of future things, but the body is of Christ" (Col. 2:16[–17]). Included in his estimate of these men are the Papists also, who insist just as much on the distinction of foods as necessary, according to which they institute their feasts, and locate in it both righteousness and the worship of God; which is nothing else than to deny *ipso facto* that Christ has been revealed. For in this passage the Apostle testifies that this distinction has ceased. Indeed, Cornelius à Lapide writes on this text that "this passage of the Apostle does nothing against the fasts appointed by the Church, which are not appointed on account of the uncleanness of the foods, but for moderation, the correction of the flesh, and to practice obedience; to placate the wrath of God, better to devote oneself to prayer, and for other holy ends." But he cannot escape by this reasoning, for they make certain foods unclean by the very fact that they prohibit their use, even though they consider them clean by nature. In the same way, none of the Jews has supposed (as Cornelius thinks) that certain foods are unclean by nature, but because it was not permitted to eat such things, therefore they became unclean strictly with respect to use—or as Peter calls it, common. Thus when that Levitical distinction of foods was abrogated at the time of Christ, that very abrogation was called the purification of foods, and common foods were reckoned as clean: "What God has purified, do not call common" (Acts 10:15). And so that distinction of foods customary in Papistic fasting is said to have been instituted to placate the wrath of God, and is exceedingly Judaic, for Paul censures this very thing in a number of Judaizers, against whom he stated his admonition, "Let no one judge you in food or drink, *etc.*" [Col. 2:16]. The other ends of fasting are indeed honorable, but there was no need at all, on their account, for a fixed law binding the conscience, nor indeed has the institution of fasts for the sake of moderation and prayers been restricted to any time, nor to certain kinds of foods, but it can be undertaken at all times, and is free to each person, according as the devotion of his heart shall have advised him. For Scripture, especially the New Testament, nowhere prescribes laws concerning certain or fixed times for fasts. In the primitive church also they were not in use, but finally around the year of the Lord 400, at the same time as the monastic life, laws for fasts were also introduced, because of the opinion of necessity and of merit, just as Chemnitz has at great length deduced from history in part 4 of the *Examen*,[97] folio 135, where he also faithfully relates and explains the history about Spiridion of Tremithus, Bishop in Cyprus, which Cornelius mentions in this passage.

Theological Aphorisms from this Part of the Chapter

1. It is the role of a faithful teacher of the church to correct the defects of his hearers, for the Apostle wants his Titus to correct the things that were lacking in the Cretan church (v. 5). For no church is so pure and perfect, and the diligence of no teacher so great in extirpating

---

97 *Examen Concilii Tridentini* (1565–73), *Examination of the Council of Trent*, by Martin Chemnitz.

errors or vices, that nothing of this labor will be left to his successors. Christ Himself reformed the Jerusalem temple for the third time [cf. 1 Kings 15; 2 Kings 22], and left to His disciples in the church enough that had yet to be purged, and there is always something left, down to the present day, that the diligence of one's predecessors could not completely remove. The vestiges of these things must be faithfully suppressed in order that the church might press on more and more towards perfection, and "that he who sows and he who reaps might rejoice together" (John 4:36).

2. Lest the ministers of the church should take it badly if they have labored and others share in the reward and the honor, let it be done in a way with utility for the church. For our Paul also laid the foundation of the Cretan church, which was a matter of the greatest labor, and so he himself, while present, was working with the matters in which there was most danger and difficulty, but he committed to his disciple the things which had more honor than labor. He "laid the foundation like a wise architect, but another built on it" (1 Cor. 3:10). This has the greatest importance to the concord of the ministers, lest any should envy the labors of another, if by chance one shall have labored with greater praise and fruitfulness than others, that they should in all things give greater attention to the common good. For thus a pastor must be disposed, says Chrysostom on this passage, and must not seek his own honor, but pursue the common utility.

3. It is a matter of great labor to restore a corrupted church, not the work of one year, nor of one man, so Paul joins Titus to himself as a co-worker in establishing the church of the Cretans, and joins to Titus other fellow-priests, but acknowledges that all the vices have not yet been cut to the quick, but leaves to his successor too something that needs to be corrected. Let no one marvel, then, if churches that have collapsed are not immediately restored in a brief time. It is easier to erect a new building than it is to rebuild a collapsed one from its ruins into a sound structure. And this was prefigured of old in the building of Solomon's temple, for which seven years were needed, although 153,300 artisans were laboring daily in that work (1 Kings [5:15–16; 6:38;] 8). Thus it is not surprising that the Reformation of the church, begun

through Blessed Luther, did not have its completion in one year, but he made progress by laboring, and left to others enough that they should do in rooting out old errors and defects from the church.

4. It is necessary that each town in each province should have its own pastor, that the Word of God might dwell in us richly (Col. 3:16), which if it comes to any region must be considered of great benefit to the place. In like manner, there is need of schools where men of this kind are educated. It was truly the most lamentable thing that, as in the first days of the Reformation, churches had to be entrusted to workmen who were sometimes or in some ways fairly unskilled, to the detriment of the schools from whence learned men could have sprung. The magistrate should therefore be warned so that he has the conservation of the schools commended to him, because if they should fail, it must be feared that the church would also suffer damage.

5. The ministry should not be easily entrusted to just anyone who pursues it, but he should be of the most proven morals, and as our Paul says, ἀνέγκλητος (blameless, v. 6). For as Jerome writes on this text, "How can a leader of the church remove evil from its midst if he has fallen in a similar transgression? Or by what boldness will he reprove the sinner when, even silent, he must answer himself that he has committed the same deeds that he is reproving?" This is why the Apostle wants us, in another place, not to quickly lay hands on anyone (1 Tim. 5:22), and writes about deacons, "Let them be proven first, and so let them minister, having no crime" (1 Tim. 3:10). Also for this reason he wants the bishop "to have a good testimony from those who are outside" (1 Tim. 3:7).

6. It is permitted to the ministers of the church to live in marriage, because Paul wants the presbyter to be "a man of one wife" (v. 6). It can in no way be concluded from this that no one should be initiated in the holy order of Episcopacy who has *not* taken a wife, a piece of foolishness that Benedict Justinian foists on us by way of calumny, but experience itself refutes him, because many among us live in the ministry, both celibate and widowers. But this text teaches clearly that it is possible for a bishop or teacher of the church to live in marriage and to beget children, as does that other text also in 1 Tim. 3:2. And

the Lord's ordinance in the Old Testament agrees with this, the one He gave the priests, that they should indeed take wives, but not a prostitute or a divorcée (Lev. 21:7). Their High Priest also was married and gave attention to begetting children, and nevertheless stood daily at the altar in the temple of God (Ex. 29:38, Num. 28:3). What is read of Enoch (Gen. 5), Noah (Gen. 6), and Abraham (Gen. 25, *etc.*) is similar. Nor in fact is there some other rule in the New Testament, because the law of marriage is the same in both, and it is known from Matt. 8:14 that Peter, the chief of the Apostles, was married, as was Philip (Acts 21:9), and the prohibition of marriage in general is expressly called a "doctrine of devils" (1 Tim. 4:1). So it is amazing that the Papists, contrary to Scriptures so clear, insist so much on the celibacy of priests that they write that priests sin gravely if they contract marriage, as if they were fornicating or keeping a concubine in the house, as Coster[98] has it in *Enchir.* Chapter 19, proposition 9. Their obtuseness in this respect should be noted also, along with their manifest impiety, because they deny that this celibacy is a matter of divine law, *e.g.*, in Bellarmine, book 1 *De cler.*, chapter 19. But the Council of Trent, session 24, canon 9 calls it an ecclesiastical law. And yet they dare to defend it from divine law, that is, from the Scripture of the Old and the New Testament. More on this elsewhere.

7. The good education of children is indeed required of all parents in general (Eph. 6:4), yet it is especially necessary for the ministers of the church, whom our Paul wants to have faithful children, not wanton, not obstinate (v. 6). For how can he be free to correct the vices of others if he fears the reprimands of others on account of his children's shameful deeds? But because even properly educated children nevertheless sink below their parents' level, which the example of Samuel's sons testifies (1 Sam. 3[:13]), the children of priests also should accordingly take care not to spatter some stain upon their parent's office. For Satan is cunning, and when he can contaminate someone's ministry neither

---

98 Francis Coster (1532–1619), Belgian Jesuit who wrote the *Enchiridion controversiarum præcipuarum nostri temporis de Religione* (*Handbook of the Chief Controversies of Our Time Concerning Religion*, first ed. 1585, final ed. 1608).

by ungodly doctrine nor by a reprobate life, he attempts to do this in the ministers' children and family. Therefore "resist the devil, and he will flee from you" (Jas. 4:7).

8. Because the life of ministers of the Word ought to be distinguished by many virtues (which our Apostle enumerates with an extended catalog, vv. 7–8), the price of the work is that those who aspire to the ministry be especially accustomed to those virtues from youth. Let them not be αὐθάδεις (stubborn), men who are excessively pleasing to themselves and admire their own opinions, a vice that is too familiar in our youth. For in youth we come into the times when one who does not understand on his own seems to lack understanding. Hence others are not heeded, and if anything has an appearance of uniqueness, it is preferred to the judgments of all the wise. This is the most harmful disease in the church, to which must be opposed that statement of the Apostle Paul in Rom. 12:3, "μὴ ὑπερφρονεῖν παρ' ὃ δεῖ φρονεῖν ἀλλὰ φρονεῖν εἰς τὸ σωφρονεῖν ἑκάστῳ, ὡς ὁ θεὸς ἐμέρισε μέτρον πίστεως" ("Do not think more highly than it is right to think, but think according to sound judgment, as God to each man has assigned a measure of faith"). Let them not be irritable, men who are easily incited to wrath, or even who hold fast to wrath; for "the wrath of man does not work righteousness" (Jas. 1:20). And especially when correcting the morals of his hearers, there is need of gentleness, because "the servant of the Lord should not quarrel, *etc.*" (2 Tim. 2:24). Let them not be given to wine, that is, out of control, the kind of vice that is quite characteristic of youth, but in wine is ἀσωτία (prodigality, Eph. 5:18). Let them not be contentious and ready to fight, so that they can bear the insults of their hearers. "For the teacher is a physician of souls," Chrysostom says, "and a physician does not strike at all, but even if the sick man should have happened to strike him, he corrects and mends and cures."[99] Let them not be φιλάργυροι (fond of money), but readier to give than to receive, that they might be able to be content with a small ministry; let them not seek moneys by illicit or base means. For as Jerome says, "The bishop who desires to be an imitator of the Apostle, having food and

---

99 Homily 2 on Titus, *NPNF* 1st Ser., vol. 13.

clothing, should be content with these things only [1 Tim. 6:8]. Those who would serve another should get their living from the other [1 Cor. 9]. Let them get their living; let them not become rich."[100] Let them love the poor and true pilgrims, that they may be able to be in some way hospitable. Let them give attention to honor, to justice, to piety, and to moderation, that they may attain a habit of virtues. In all these things, indeed, the bishop must be the image of the faithful (1 Tim. 4:12). For unless his life accords with his teaching, he is tearing down rather than building up. For this reason, bad teachers of the churches are most severely reproached in Scripture (Ezek. 13:3ff., Zech. 11:17, Ps. 50:16, Rom. 2:21, *etc.*).

9. As far as teaching is concerned, three things are required of a minister of the church (v. 9): (1) Constancy in the profession of the Holy Scripture, for Paul wants him to ἀντέχεσθαι (hold fast), to cling tenaciously to the faithful discourse, lest he should forsake it in a time of danger. This virtue is preferable to all learning, which consists to so great an extent in subtle speculations that accomplish little toward piety; and yet it is not without learning, but with the kind of learning that has as its end truth, not victory. And thus it does not depart from the holy teaching that it has once embraced, although it be pressed with many sophistries, although useless disputants, in turn, be carried away by any "wind of doctrine" [Eph. 4:14], although it is too true that the truth is lost by quarreling. (2) The gift of teaching, so that he is able to set forth sound doctrine for others in a useful way, for Paul wants the minister to be δυνατὸν (able) to relate sound doctrine to others, whether it be by information for the more unlearned, or in admonishing the wandering, or in exhorting to the pursuit of virtues, in all of which things there is need of discernment, that the Scripture may both be rightly explained and skillfully applied, that is, in time and place, for an opportune word profits much, concerning which Solomon speaks in Prov. 25:11. "Golden apples on silver beds, one who speaks a word in its time." (3) The gift of refuting adversaries, for the Apostle wants a minister of the church to τοὺς ἀντιλέγοντας ἐλέγχειν (refute those

---

100 PL 26.567CD.

who contradict). An accurate understanding of the controversies is necessary to this business, so that things are not condemned when they have simply been heard by others, but when they have been read in the writings of the adversaries, pondered, and examined according to the rule of the holy Scripture. From all these things it is understood that he who wants to discharge these parts of the ministry correctly must not conduct his studies in a way that is simply perfunctory, but with the highest exertion of the mind and an earnest plea for divine aid. For excellent teaching is necessary along with the highest wisdom, as is also an understanding of the arts that heretics use to disguise their deceptions, as is the study of philosophy and languages, without which nothing excellent is accomplished in theological study. Here, then, the mind must be especially directed. For the other things that pertain to life, he can have in common also with the laymen, but the things that concern teaching are peculiar to the teachers of the Church.

10. The Church is never entirely cleansed of false teachers, concerning whom the Apostle speaks in v. 10. For ματαιόλογοι (babblers) are always found, who teach foolish things, and yet listen to no one but themselves or those like themselves, the sort who are not even heretics, concerning whom Paul writes to the Corinthians, "It is necessary that there should be heresies among you" (1 Cor. 11:19). And indeed, they profess ὀρθοδοξίαν (orthodoxy) of teaching among them, and yet they perform the business of the church with their empty talking. It is always necessary for sincere teachers of the church to be instructed against these men, for their business will not always be with open heretics, but with admirers of self-satisfied men of this sort, such as the Jews were at the time of Paul, who were wonderfully pleased with their own ἐθελοθρησκείαις (self-chosen services), whom he called babblers and φρεναπάτας (soul-deceivers), for they thrust upon men the vanities of their own brain in place of true theology, to the deception of very many minds, since they may always find those by whom they might be heard, to those people's most immediate destruction.

11. The principal duty of the ministry is to reprove, to shut the mouth of the one who contradicts, and sternly to rebuke seducers (vv. 9, 11, 13). Nay, rather, it is the office of the Holy Spirit, who first dis-

puted with the world (Gen. 6:3). Christ also says the Holy Spirit "will accuse the world concerning sin" (John 16:7–8). Hence the ministers of the Word are like instruments of the Holy Spirit. They are commanded to "separate the precious from the worthless" (Jer. 15:19), to discern between the clean and the unclean (Ezek. 22:26), to inquire into those who seduce the people with idolatry (Deut. 13:1–2), to "watch those who make causes of offense contrary to doctrine" (Rom. 16:17), to "correct those who resist" the truth (2 Tim. 2:25, 4:2), to "attend to themselves and the whole flock" (Acts 20:28). In this vein we have the examples of the Prophets (Ex. 32:21, 1 Kings 18:17, Isa. 56:10–11, Jer. 23:15, 29:8, 21), of Christ (Matt. 7:15, 15:14, John 10:8), of Paul (2 Cor. 11:13, Phil. 3:18, 1 Tim. 1:20), of Peter (2 Pet. 2:2), and of John (1 John 2:18, 1 John 4:3, Rev. 3:9). Canon 13 of the Council of Constantinople, the Fifth,[101] says: "If anyone does not anathematize things most impiously composed, and those who have thought or think things like them, but also all who have written against the right faith, such men are anathema."[102] All these things ought to be set against the πολυπραγμοσύνη (officiousness) of some of the civil authorities, by which they dare to shut the mouth of the ministers of the church with princely edicts, lest *they* should shut the mouth of the babblers, according to our Apostle's admonition; and also in part against the negligence of certain ministers, who turn a blind eye to ungodly teaching by remaining silent, lest they should be disturbed in their ministry, or forced to experience the hatred of the world and the devil. Augustine wrote about them a long time ago in *Epistol. 148 to Valerian*.[103] "In this life and especially in this time, there is nothing easier and more cheerful, and more acceptable to men, than the office of Bishop or Presbyter or Deacon, if the thing be done perfunctorily and flatteringly; but nothing is more wretched and lamentable and damnable in the sight of God."

---

101 That is, the Fifth Ecumenical Council (553), which was the Second Council of Constantinople.

102 The canon deals specifically with the errors of Theodoret, Nestorius, and Theodore of Mopsuestia. Balduin quotes selectively to make it a general statement.

103 Letter 21 in modern numeration, written in 391 to his bishop before he succeeded to that position.

12. The goal of ecclesiastical refutation is soundness in the faith (v. 13), and it is as much for the sake of the false teachers themselves, that they might recognize their own errors and come to the knowledge of the truth, as it is for the sake of their hearers, that they not be entangled in errors and lose purity of doctrine. For it is of great interest to the church that purity of doctrine be conserved in her, without which she can neither exist herself, nor profit others to salvation. For as Paul writes in Romans 16:17, "Those who cause dissensions and causes of offense contrary to sound teaching do not serve our Lord Christ, but their own belly, and through sweet speeches and blessings they seduce the hearts of the innocent" (v. 18 too). So also in our text, he says that those who are to be refuted teach things it is not right to teach for the sake of filthy riches (v. 11). He calls them "evil beasts and lazy gluttons" (v. 12), and elsewhere "enemies of the flesh of Christ, whose end is destruction, whose God is the belly, and whose glory is in their shame, who think on earthly things" (Phil. 3:19).

13. Occasionally to mingle some things from the writings of the pagans with sacred sayings is both licit and useful, by the example of our Paul, who intended by references of this kind more easily to convict the Gentiles to whom he wrote of their error, and to lead them to knowledge of the truth. For sometimes he refutes them by their own testimony, as he proved in this passage, from the verse of a Cretan poet, that the morals of the Cretans were sufficiently corrupted. Sometimes he moves them with a proverbial saying, and even a commonplace among the pagans, as in 1 Corinthians 15:33, with the verse of Menander, "Perverse communications corrupt good manners," concerning which Jerome writes in his Letter to Demetrias,[104] "The Apostle, taking up a secular verse, made it ecclesiastical." Sometimes he seeks, from a witty saying or some maxim of a pagan writer, an opportunity for Christian instruction, as when in Acts 17:28, from the half-line of the poet Aratus, τοῦ γὰρ καὶ γένος ἐσμεν (for we are indeed his offspring), he speaks of the true God, whose honor the Athenians conferred on the unknown God, or on gold, silver, and stone sculptures, gods painted and shaped.

---

104   Letter 130.

In morals, we usefully employ the maxims of pagan writers, in order that it might be made clear that these things were known by nature even by the pagans, and therefore that they should be observed more diligently, lest we should seem to be doing anything against the commandment of nature. For then, that saying of Jerome to Nepotian should hold precedence instead: "Let a Presbyter's speech be formed by the Scriptures."[105]

14. Almost any nation has its own peculiar vices. For the Cretans, a lust for lying is noted, and laziness (v. 12). For the Athenians, a zeal for novelty (Acts 17:21); for the Jews, a proneness to idolatry (everywhere in Scripture); for others, other vices. These are not so much to be censured as mourned, for they remind us of our common condition, that no one may live without offense, and "all flesh has corrupted its way" [Gen. 6:12]. They teach how much depends on a good education from youth. For many things are drawn from parents and first instructors, that pass at length into habit, nor can they so easily be set aside. Also they restrain pride and contempt for other men, because anyone may find in himself and in his race something that should be corrected. So then, let us consider the vices of other nations, lest we forget our own.

15. Things that are good and laudable in themselves are assigned harsh and disagreeable names when abuse occurs. Thus Paul calls the Levitical rites, instituted by God Himself, "Jewish fables" (v. 14) because the Jews even after the abrogation of that Law impose them as necessary to salvation. Thus Paul calls his righteousness σκύβαλα καὶ [ζημίαν] (dung and loss, Phil. 3:8)—that is, if an opinion of merit should have occurred. And Isaiah compares all his righteousness and that of his people to the rag of a menstruating woman (Isa. 64:6), partly because of an opinion of merit, partly because of clinging impurity. Therefore it should not be ascribed to Blessed Luther as a fault that he called the good works of the righteous "sins," for he did not say that they were such from their nature, but as it is written, he declares in *Assert. artic.*[106]

---

105 Letter 52, section 8.

106 *Assertio omnium articulorum M. Lutheri per bullam Leonis X novissimam damnatorum* (*Defense of All the Articles of Martin Luther in Leo X's Latest Bull of*

31 that "A righteous man sins in every good work," and in article 32, "A good work, done in the best way, is a mortal sin according to God's judgment." But he is teaching nothing else than what Solomon taught in Ecclesiastes 7[:20], "There is not a righteous man on earth, who does good and does not sin," and Isaiah and Paul in the passages that have been mentioned, and Augustine in book 9 of the *Confessions*, chapter 13, "Woe even to the laudable life of men, if You should investigate it in the absence of mercy!" And Gregory in chapter 9 on Job: "Holy Job saw that all our good works are mere sins, if they are judged by God; therefore he says, 'If a man wanted to contend with Him, he could not answer Him one thing in a thousand'" (Job 9:3).[107] But elsewhere Luther preached the good works of righteous men rather magnificently, inasmuch as they are considered in their nature. For thus he writes on Galatians chapter [3], "Apart from the motive of justification, truly no one can commend good works magnificently enough. Or who could sufficiently preach the usefulness and fruitfulness of a single good work that a Christian does from faith and in faith? It is more precious than heaven and earth," etc.[108]

16. No creature is unclean in itself, but "to the pure all things are pure," (v. 15). For "God sees all the things that He has made, and they were very good" (Gen. 1[:31]). "Because every creature is good" (1 Tim. 4:4). For although Leviticus 11 established the distinction of clean and unclean things, nevertheless this was not done on account of the things, because they could have polluted themselves with some food *per se*, but only because [God] wanted to restrain the luxury of foods, as Chrysostom explains in homily 3 on this Epistle: "For what reason does He prohibit the pig," he says, "and certain others from among living

---

Condemnations), written 1520 to rebut Pope Leo X's bull *Exsurge Domine*, WA 7:94–151.

107 Gregory the Great, *Moralia in Job*, commenting on 9:1–3 (*PL* 75.859). Balduin is paraphrasing here ("*Sanctus Job videbat, omnia nostra bona opera esse mera peccata, si judicantur a Deo: ideo dicit* [verse 9:3]" for "*Sanctus autem vir, quia omne virtutis nostrae meritum esse vitium conspicit, si ab interno arbitro districte judicetur, recte subjungit* [verse 9:3]."

108 Comment on Gal. 3:22, cf. *American Edition* 26:334.

things? He did this not because they were unclean, but He sought to curtail the greatest part of luxury." Others add that the animals considered unclean by God may have other characteristics in their body or their nature that reminded men of vices, and hence were prohibited. For that reason those were prohibited that live by plundering, that are cruel and savage, that love easy living and squalor, in order that men might learn to call themselves back from robbery, avarice, lusts, baseness, and ferocity to temperance, righteousness, chastity, purity, and gentleness.

17. After the Levitical Law is abrogated, we are certainly not bound to a fixed distinction of foods, of days, and similar rites, for all things are pure to the pure, or to the faithful, and that distinction has been borne through Christ (Col. 2:16). Neither is anything impure in itself, except to the one who judges the thing to be impure (Rom. 14:14); yet to one who judges that it should be classed with the things that are lawful and pure in themselves, it is not a cause of offense. Thus it is lawful to eat meats, although Paul wants to abstain from the eating of meats if he should see that a brother is made to stumble (1 Cor. 8:13). Scripture permits marriage with an unbeliever, although it does not conceal the danger to those who do this (1 Cor. 7:12, 16). It is permitted a pious man to dwell among the impious, for Christians can live even "in the midst of a crooked and perverse nation" without blame, upright, and can live as the lights of the world (Phil. 2:15). And as Ambrose says in book 2, *De virginibus*, "Brothels do not defame chastity, but chastity destroys even the infamy of that place."[109] Yet in all these things one must act cautiously, for not all things that are lawful are always beneficial [cf. 1 Cor. 6:12]. For experience testifies that even some of the most honorable men have been corrupted by reason of perverse companionship or unclean places. For "he who touches pitch is stained by it" (Sirach 13:1). To this pertain the Apostolic exhortations in 1 Corinthians 7:16 and elsewhere.

18. Unbelief especially contaminates a man, in such a way that he cannot enjoy even lawful things beneficially; for to the unbelieving, nothing is pure, but their mind is stained, and their conscience (v. 15).

---

109 *On Virgins*, 2.26.

For they make, from their use of things, either a merit or a cause of offense. They thrust at both sides: there at love for God, which cannot stand with the merits of men, here at charity for the neighbor, before whom a cause of offense must not be placed. For the sake of example, to abstain from certain foods at certain times, in order that we can be free for prayers and pious meditations, is a lawful thing and pure in itself, but since the Papists add the opinion of merit, and think that because of their fasting, they are closer to God than others who do not fast in this way, that thing lawful and pure in itself becomes unlawful and impure to those unbelieving fellows. In the same way, to take away the images in temples is in itself a lawful and pure thing, but if it be done because of an opinion of necessity, and with offense for the weak, it becomes impure. This is the reason unbelief alone is said by blessed Luther to condemn, because it also alone repels Christ, and is the prolific mother of all the other sins.

For where faith is found, there is no sin against conscience, nor can other sins condemn, unless they are joined with unbelief. See Luther in his German treatise against the King of England, volume 2 of the Jena edition, folio 144.19.[110] It is the abominable sin of hypocrisy when someone professes knowledge with the mouth, and nevertheless conducts himself by his deeds as such a one who has cast off all concern for God (v. 16). Psalm 14:1 says concerning them, "The impious man says in his heart, there is no God." The world is full of these men, whom our Paul calls βδελυκτοὺς καὶ ἀπειδεῖς, abominable and rebellious, because God abominates hypocrisy and they suffer themselves to be led by none of God's laws. Athanasius says of them that they feign Christianity and engage in battle against Christ. Their condition on the last day will be far worse than that of the heathen, who have not learned about God, and yet have lived honorably by the guidance of the natural law. For the servant who knows the will of the Lord and does not do it will be flogged with many lashes (Luke 12:47). Therefore "do not come to God with a double heart, nor be a hypocrite in the sight of men, nor make them stumble with your lips" (Sir. 1:36–37).

---

110   Luther, *Antwort deutsch auf König Heinrichs Buch* (1522), WA 10/2:259–61.

Chapter 2

Argument and Division of the Chapter

The next part of the Epistle now follows, in which the Apostle deals with the responsibilities of the hearers, and in this chapter indeed exhorts anyone, in his station of life, to adorn his life with manners and pursuits befitting the teaching of the Gospel, the sum of which he expounds on this occasion with magnificent words. For it is not enough to set forth sound teaching in general, but it must also be rightly explained to hearers of every age or station. There are two parts of the chapter.

I. *In the first, down to verse 11, are contained moral precepts, according to men's different stations.*

II. *In the second, from verse 11 down to the end of the chapter, Christ's coming into the flesh is treated, and His coming for judgment, between which boundaries the whole life of Christians is situated.*

The First Part of the Text [Titus 2:1–10]

Σὺ δὲ λάλει ἃ πρέπει τῇ ὑγιαινούσῃ διδασκαλίᾳ.	1. But you, speak things that befit sound teaching.
Πρεσβύτας νηφαλίους εἶναι σεμνούς, σώφρονας, ὑγιαίνοντας τῇ ὑπομονῇ.	2. Old men, that they be sober, dignified, temperate, sound in faith, charity, patience.
Πρεσβύτιδας ὡσαύτως ἐν καταστήματι ἱεροπρεπεῖς, μὴ Διαβόλους, μὴ οἴνῳ πολλῷ δεδουλωμένας καλοδιδασκάλους.	3. Old women, in like manner, that they be of an appearance that befits their religion, not slanderers, not being slaves to much wine, that they might teach honorable things.

Ἵνα σωφρονίζωσι τὰς νέας, φιλάνδρους εἶναι, φιλοτέκνους,

Σώφρονας, ἁγνὰς, οἰκουργοὺς, ἀγαθὰς, ὑποτασσομένας τοῖς ἰδίοις ἀνδράσιν, ἵνα μὴ ὁ λόγος τοῦ Θεοῦ βλασφημῆται.

Τοὺς νεωτέρους ὡσαύτως παρακάλει σωφρονεῖν.

Περὶ πάντα σεαυτὸν παρεχόμενος τύπον καλῶν ἔργων ἐν τῇ διδασκαλίᾳ ἀδιαφθορίαν, σεμνότητα, ἀφθαρτίαν.

Λόγον ὑγιῆ ἀκατάγνωστον ἵνα ὁ ἐξ ἐναντίας ἐν τραπῇ μηδὲν ἔχων περὶ ὑμῶν λέγειν φαῦλον.

Δούλους ἰδίοις δεσπόταις ὑποτάσσεσθαι ἐν πᾶσιν εὐαρέστους εἶναι, μὴ ἀντιλέγοντας.

Μὴ νοσφιζομένους, ἀλλὰ πίστιν πᾶσαν ἐνδεικνυμένους ἀγαθὴν, ἵνα τὴν διδασκαλίαν τοῦ σωτῆρος ἡμῶν θεοῦ κοσμῶσιν ἐν πᾶσιν.

Notes from text[111]

4. By which they might be able to make the young women temperate.

5. That they might love their husbands, that they might love their children, that they might be sober, pure, keepers of the home, kind, subject to their own husbands, lest the Word of God be badly spoken of.

6. Urge the young men likewise to be sober.

7. Offering yourself in all things as an image (*forma*) of good works in teaching, in integrity, in seriousness.

8. In sound, irreproachable speech, that he who resists might be suffused with blushing, having nothing bad to say about you.

9. Exhort slaves, that they obey their own masters, that they be pleasing to them in all things, not arguers.

10. Not purloining, but showing all good faith, that they might adorn the teaching of God our Savior in all things.

---

111   Verse 4 (English): The second half of this verse has been moved to the beginning of the next verse.

Titus 2

Analysis and Explanation of the First Part

At the end of the preceding chapter, the Apostle had said concerning the false teachers that they teach things it is not right to teach, and that they confess that they know God, but deny it by their deeds. He sets Titus against them, as a genuine teacher of the Church, whom he wants to teach his hearers in such a way that every one of them might respond with an Evangelical profession. *"But you, speak things that befit sound teaching"* (v. 1). Jerome distinguishes in this passage between sound teaching and τὰ πρέποντα (the fitting things) of sound teaching. Those things consist only in theory and the understanding of sacred matters; these things consist also in *praxis*. In that is only simple education; in this is also the correction of life. Therefore, since the False Teachers of the Cretans both are teaching false things (for they were saying things that it was not right to say) and were living impiously by professing to teach divine doctrine, the Apostle wants Titus to form his hearers in such a way that in them, life might match teaching. Therefore he prescribes rules for each age of men and station of life, by beginning with the elders:[112] *"Old men, that they be sober, chaste, prudent, sound in faith, in love and patience"* (v. 2). He requires at least four virtues of old men. (1) Sobriety, for he wants them to be νηφαλίους, a word that means both sober and vigilant. Therefore because old men are by nature slower, duller, and sleepier he wants them to flee drunkenness, lest by sleep or wine they should exhaust what is left of life;[113] but they should be circumspect, on guard especially against things that ill befit their age. (2) Seriousness, for he wants them to be σεμνούς (august), which the old translator rendered *pudicos* (chaste),[114] but σεμνότης is gravity of manners, which is opposed to the levity that is connected to

---

112   A note in the margin here reads, "The vices of old age: sluggishness, slowness, forgetfulness, dullness of the senses, irascibility."

113   A note in the margin here reads, "Plutarch writes in book 1 of *Convivial Questions*, question 3, 'Old men are easily corrupted by drunkenness.'"

114   A note a little further down in the margin reads, "Jerome translates *pudicos* (chaste) so that they might not give themselves over to lust in an unseasonable time of life."

shameless manners and talk, such as are sometimes heard in the time of youth. But old men should be venerable in manners and conversation,[115] and thus in their whole life, lest they should indulge in an unseasonable time of life, lest when their blood is already cooled, they should be examples leading the youths to ruin, as Jerome says. (3) Prudence: he wants them to be σώφρονας, which Chrysostom understands as having to do with moderation of the affections, for σῶφρον signifies that one is more moderate. But this virtue follows a little later. Here, he requires the prudence in counsels and circumspection in all actions that is in most cases the distinctive trait of old men, but because they sometimes become boyish, he wants them to be excited by the ministry of the church, lest they should neglect the adornment characteristic of their age. (4) Constancy in good: the Apostle calls it "soundness," for sound men are steadfast and robust, and do not fall easily. Old men are accustomed in most cases to be tenacious in their purpose, and not to change their mind easily. The Apostle teaches in what activity they should therefore demonstrate that firmness of opinion, namely: (a) in faith, lest they should be easily "carried off by any wind of doctrine" [Eph. 4:14], but should tenaciously embrace the Apostolic teaching that once they drank in; (b) in love, lest they should lightly conceive a grudge against other men, lest they should be mistrustful, lest they should love only for the sake of utility, which are vices familiar to old men; (c) in patience, for old men are disposed to anger, fretful, severe, and peevish. Thus it is necessary that they secure their mind with patience, since all things will not be done to their liking. Therefore soundness in faith is needed by old men on account of God, soundness in love on account of the neighbor, soundness in patience on account of themselves. The one thing pertains to religion, the next thing to conversation, the last thing to both.

From old men the Apostle proceeds to old women. "*Old women likewise,*" he says, "*of a holy appearance, not slanderers, not being slaves to much wine, teaching well in order that they might teach the young*

---

[115] A note in the margin here reads, "A foolish old man is an abomination to the Lord, Sirach 25[:3–4]."

women prudence, that they should love their husbands, love their children, be prudent, be chaste, having care of the house, kind, subject to their own husbands, that the Word of God might not be blasphemed" (vv. 3–5). That ὡσαύτως, that "likewise," pertains partly to the things that he said about old men, since old women, just as much as old men, should be honorable, sober, chaste, sound in faith, *etc.*, and partly to the things that befit sound teaching, in this sense: that the things that are required of old women pertain equally to having to adorn the genuine teaching of the Gospel, and to the things that have already been prescribed for the old men. Theophylact understands "old women" in this passage to mean the wives of the presbyters,[116] because they are called πρεσβύτιδες (feminine form of "presbyters") in the Greek, but in this passage this word does not have to do with rank, but with age. It is dealing, then, with all women of more advanced age. He wants them (1) to be in a holy appearance, doubtless so that their interior adornment might be shown from all their outward covering. In the Greek it is ἱεροπρεπεῖς ἐν καταστήματι, that is, of such an appearance as befits their religion. Let it not be scurrilous, or heathenish, or wanton, but Christian, so that signs of the Christian religion might appear in all their appearance, bearing, motion. He wants them (2) not to be slanderers or accusers, for in the Greek it is μὴ Διαβόλους (not slanderers), not to detract from others' reputation. For they are wont to be talkative and inquisitive, talking about things it is not right to talk about, as they are depicted in 1 Timothy 5:13.

Especially if they are more mature, they discuss the manners of the younger ones, and they accuse them, although as Jerome says, "they should teach them privately not to do, rather than accusing publicly what they have done."[117] (3) *"Not being slaves to much wine,"* for as Jerome says again, "What lust is in the young, drunkenness is in the old,"[118] and little old ladies are quite prone to the vice of drunkenness. But he does not forbid them all use of wine, for this time of life, when it

---

116 Or "the wives of the elders."
117 Jerome, *Commentary on Titus*, PL 26.580C.
118 Ibid. 581A.

has weakened, has need of wine; but it requires moderation at least, lest they should be slaves to wine, that is, lest they should be overcome by wine, from which many things follow later that are not at all fitting for that age or that sex. For the senses are occupied with drinking, so that they are not hers, but wine's. (4) He wants them to be καλοδιδασκάλους, that is, good instructresses of young girls, whom they should teach to be honorable. Therefore it is necessary for them also to live honorably.

Now, they should teach prudence. That's ἵνα σωφρονίζωσι in the Greek, *i.e.,*, [teach] to be sober, modest, and chaste, to behave circumspectly, so they will not be deceived by cunning people. They should therefore teach these girls to love their husbands—nothing contributes more to conjugal tranquility than this—and to love their children, which has reference to the education of children, in which mothers are chiefly occupied as long as the children are of tender age; to be σώφρονες, which some render "prudent," and others "sober"; to be chaste and blameless in propriety; to be οἰκουροί, keepers of the home, not running around here and there outside, but to take care of their affairs at home; to be good-natured, lest they should trouble their whole family with bitterness; to be subject to their own husbands, for it is shameful for a woman to exercise dominion in the home, for the woman is called ὕπανδρος (married, but etymologically "under a man") (Rom. 7:2), and is under the power of the man by the ordinance of God (Gen. 3:16). The Apostle adds a reason for this precept: that the Word of God might not be blasphemed, which some apply to all the things that he has thus far prescribed to old women, and some just to the thing that came immediately before it, namely that the younger women should be subject to their husbands, lest the Word of God should be blasphemed. By "Word of God" Jerome understands God's first judgment, by which the woman was put under the power of the man. We more correctly understand it to mean the teaching of the Gospel, to which Christians have pledged allegiance. All those virtues with which the Apostle has so far dealt are required of these Christians, who when they neglect them, wash away the stain by means of the Gospel that they profess. Also supporting this opinion, he elsewhere wants Christians to live in a manner worthy of the Gospel (Phil. 1:27), and worthy of their calling

(Eph. 4:1). Consequently, the Apostle has thus far instructed the old women. Now in the third place, he turns his attention to the young men: *"Urge the young men likewise to be sober"* (v. 6). He wants them to σωφρονεῖν (to be sound of mind), a word that includes many things: temperance, chastity, circumspection, vigilance, and the moderating of all affections, in order that the things that are usually abundant in young men might be repressed: wildness, impudence, wantonness, arrogance, and similar vices. Titus should require these things of the young men, but he has appointed the old women as shapers of the younger women, because he wanted even the appearance of evil, and every suspicion that could come from frequent contact with girls and women, to be far from the bishop. Fourth, he instructed Titus himself, and under his name all the teachers of the church. *"In all things,"* he says, *"offer yourself as an example of good works, integrity in teaching, seriousness, a sound irreproachable word, that he who is against you might be ashamed, having nothing bad to say about you"* (vv. 7–8). This is, as it were, a declaration of that which he desired above, that bishops be blameless, which he here explains piece by piece. And indeed, if a minister of the church cannot be ἀναμάρτητος (blameless), he can at least live in such a way that he is not as a cause of offense to others, but rather an example in faith and life. Therefore he wants him to be a τύπον, a form or exemplar, for others (1) in life, or good works; (2) in teaching, in which he should show integrity in order that his teaching might be sound; and seriousness, that he might conduct himself not frivolously, but with due reverence, for this teaching is the sound word; therefore it should not be corrupted by ἑτεροδιδασκαλία (different teaching). It is the irreproachable word, therefore it should be handled reverently, and this not only on account of hearers who are pious and desirous of learning, but also on account of enemies of the truth who diligently pry into his faith, teaching, and life, who are confounded by the manner of pastors of this kind, and even after the most diligent investigation still find nothing of which they can accuse him. Fifth, he adds also some things concerning slaves: *"Slaves,"* he says, *"are to be subject* (that is, I exhort them to be subject) *to their masters, pleasing them in all things, not contradicting, not cheating, but showing good faith in all things, that they might adorn the teaching of God our Savior in all things"* (vv. 9–10). Here he requires four things of slaves: (1) the subjection and obedience owed their masters, (2) that they be pleasing in all things, which some understand in this way, that the slaves should be pleasing to themselves, that is, that they should be content with their condition, lest out of indignation or disgust for their lot, they should do what does not befit pious men. Others think that they should please their masters in all things that have been commanded them. (3) Patience, so that when they have been rebuked by their masters, they do not contradict or talk back, but remember that they are subject. (4) Faithfulness, so that they do not cheat their masters and furtively break off a piece of the things that have been committed to them, for that is what the Greek word νοσφιζομένους means. For νοσφίζειν is the same as to take away furtively, since you cannot carry off the whole thing. But instead let them attend with a good faith to the things that have been entrusted, and administer them. The aim of this precept is that they might adorn the Savior's teaching, that is the Gospel, in all things. It is the same reason that he added a little earlier to the women's precepts: *"that the Word of God might not be blasphemed."* For integrity of life accomplishes much toward the decoration of teaching. So much for the precepts about morals in different stations of life.

Questions from this Part of the Chapter

Question 1

What does the Apostle mean by "a holy appearance," by which he wants old women to be adorned (v. 3)?

Answer: In the Greek text, women of this kind are called ἱεροπρεπεῖς ἐν καταστήματι, as if you might say, "dressed in the vesture that befits women dedicated to God." The Greek word κατάστημα has reference not only to clothing, but to the whole appearance, motion, and progress of the body. But if you should refer it specifically to the clothing of women, this passage seems as if it were concerned with the clothes of religious women, whom they call nuns in the Papacy. Thus Ambrose translates, "a habit[119] worthy of religion," which, it is known from Athanasius's book on virginity and Jerome's Letter 15[120] to Marcella, is of a dark color. But our Paul is not dealing with a certain order of women, but with old women, or women of a more advanced age in general, to whom he commends a holy appearance, which adorns women of whatever age. For this reason he gave all women a similar command in 1 Tim. 2:9. Now, the holy appearance of a woman is (1) modest, not a wanton or light appearance, which would expose a half-naked body to the lusts of other men, and invite lustful eyes. For what holiness can there be in that which is an incentive to lusts? Thus Gyges said to Herodotus that a woman takes off her modesty along with her tunic.[121] Eusebius censures in Plato, that having followed the Constitutions of Lycurgus in his books *The Republic* and *The Laws*, he mentions that women, not only young but also old women, wrestle naked along with men in the gymnasiums, and that naked young women dance along with naked young men.[122] Ignatius also gives attention to this in the Letter to the Philippians [ch. 6]. But who now will reprove those voluptuous younger women, with older women who, lightly clad, model the shape of the body by the baring of some parts? The natural simplicity of those peoples who have never used clothes averts the mind from wandering lusts more than precious garments mixed with the baring of members. Thus Lerius affirms, in his description of America,[123] that American women in their simplicity and natural nakedness, although they are not inferior in beauty to our women, are less wanton in their

---

119 *Habitus*, which I have been translating "appearance," due to its broader meaning in this passage, but in this sentence, the *habitus* is said to be "of a dark color." This passage explains why a nun's distinctive dress is called a "habit."

120 In modern numeration, Letter 24 is to Marcella, and includes this detail of a virgin putting on a dark dress when she determined to take a vow of chastity (section 3).

121 Gyges said this to Candaules, not to Herodotus, in Herodotus's *Histories* I.8.

122 *Republic* book 5 and *Laws* book 7.

123 16th century Brazil, that is. Joao Lerius, *Historia navigationis in Brasiliam, quae et America dicitur* (*History of a Voyage to Brazil, which is also Called America*), first Latin edition 1586.

manners than French women, who because of their elegant and exquisite garments and adornments (add also, because of the baring of certain parts of the body) are accustomed to be proud. See Camerarius, book 1 of *Historical Meditations*,[124] chapter 34. (2) The holy appearance of women is what is appropriate for this sex. For in the Law of the Lord is it expressly prohibited that women should use the garments of men, and men the garments of women, and the one who should have done otherwise is an abomination in the sight of the Lord (Deut. 22:5). This is a natural thing, so that the dignity and distinction of sex might be retained, and wandering lusts, betrayals, and murders might be averted. For this reason, even among the pagans, who have changed the garments, they have lessened the damage by all ages' memory of the disgrace, as the examples of Hercules[125] and Sardanapalus[126] testify, among others.[127] Among women, Semiramis is infamous for this reason. When her husband was dead, she impersonated a man in order to take possession of the kingship, as Justin testifies in book 1 of his histories.[128] Berenice, the mother and sister of Olympians, who attended the games in the clothing of a man, as Pausanias testifies in his entries

---

124 Philippe Camerarius, *Operae horarum subcisivarum, sive meditationes historicae* (Frankfurt am Main: Peter Kopf, 1601).

125 Referring to an episode in the Hercules legend in which the hero has to serve a woman named Omphale for a year as her slave. Later versions had him doing women's work and wearing women's clothing during this period.

126 Legendary last king of Assyria, according to the Greek writers Ctesias and Diodorus, who portrayed him as a transvestite and extreme hedonist.

127 A marginal note here reads: "Hercules served Omphale in altered dress. Clodius [Publius Clodius Pulcher, Roman Senator of the 1st century B.C.] attended the rites of the good goddess dressed in women's clothing [because men were banned from them, and he wanted to seduce Julius Caesar's wife Pompeia]. Sardanapalus, having abandoned the majesty of his rule, spent his life among women."

128 Justin was a Latin historian (c. 2nd century A.D.) who was confused in the Middle Ages with Justin Martyr. In the story he refers to, Semiramis impersonates her son upon the death of her husband, so as to succeed to the throne of the Assyrian empire.

on Elis.[129] Such was Hypsicratea, wife of Mithridates;[130] Joan Anglicus, who in men's clothing hid among the Cardinals, and was elevated to the Papacy, as Sigbert testifies, and Platina, and others.[131] And among Christians this thing has always been known as an especially great stain of infamy, for which reason also in the Council of Gangra, Canon 13,[132] a woman who uses men's garments is anathematized. Ambrose also, in book 4 of his *Letter to Irenaeus*,[133] talking about this Law of the Lord, says, "If you investigate truly, that which nature itself abhors is incongruous. For why do you not want to be seen as a man, which you were born? Why do you assume an appearance alien to yourself? Why do you impersonate a woman? Or you, woman, a man? Nature clothes each sex with its own garments."

In short, there is a differing use, a differing appearance, motion, gait, differing strength, a differing voice in a man and a woman, and a

---

129 Pausanias (2nd century A.D.), *Description of Greece*, book 5. The story tells how Berenice (or Pherenice) coached her son for the Olympic Games and disguised herself as a man in order to attend as his trainer, since married women were forbidden to spectate under pain of death. She was discovered in her celebrations when her son won, but the judges spared her since her father and brothers and son had all been victorious Olympians.

130 The sixth wife of Mithridates VI, the King of Pontus, who resisted the Roman Republic for a time in the 1st century B.C. She disguised herself as a man and learned to fight so as to accompany her husband on campaigns, and then later into exile.

131 According to a 13th century account widely regarded as fictional today, Pope Joan reigned from 855 to 857, and was discovered when she gave birth in the middle of a procession. Sigebert of Gembloux was an earlier authority (he died 1112), but the "Pope Joan" passage has been proven to be a later interpolation to his *Chronicle*. Bartolomeo Platina did include the story in his 15th-century *Lives of the Popes*, but he presented it as dubious hearsay. See S. Baring-Gould and Margot H. King, "Pope Joan," *Vox Benedictina: A Journal of Translations from Monastic Sources* 3, no. 3 (1986): 240–253, at https://monasticmatrix.osu.edu/commentaria/pope-joan.

132 The synod of Gangra (modern-day Çankırı, Turkey), held in 340, was a local anti-Manichaean council. Its canons were later ratified by the ecumenical Council of Chalcedon (451). One of them targeted women who wore men's clothing as an ascetic method.

133 Ambrose, Letter 69, actually one of many letters Ambrose wrote to Irenaeus (not the famous bishop of Lyons, who lived two centuries earlier), and far too short to be divided into books. Perhaps in Balduin's day several such letters were considered to be parts of the same letter.

lie is disgraceful in word, much less in dress. Now, these are women's garments, far and wide: a flowing toga falling to the ankles, and the stole[134] and the *flammeum*,[135] and chaplets and the net (*reticulum*) with which they cover their heads, as Alexander of Alexander[136] writes in book 5 of *Genialium Dierum*, chapter 18. And Ulpian's words are in the sixth law on clothing, women's, some pages into "On Gold and Silver, Dress":[137] "Women's garments are those that have been prepared for the sake of the *materfamilias*, which a man cannot easily use without censure, like stoles, *pallia*,[138] the tunic, head coverings, girdles, turbans, which have been prepared more for the sake of covering the head than adorning it, breadths,[139] *penulae*.[140]" The stole is a woman's garment, which is why it is called στολὴ ἀπάνθρωπος (the far-from-man stole) by the Greeks, unworthy of a man, and in Suetonius, in chapter 23 on Caligula,[141] Livia is called "Ulysses in a stole," because she was a most clever woman. The toga was a garment common to men and women, but women who were accused of adultery, or discovered at it, set aside the stole and wore the toga, as clothing fit for a prostitute, as appears in Juvenal, Satire 2:

"If you like, let Carphinia also be condemned;
Even condemned, she will not don a toga like that."[142]

---

134 The *stola*, that is, a kind of long gown that was the traditional dress of the Roman matron.

135 The *flammeum* was a flame-colored veil worn by brides and Vestal Virgins.

136 Alessandro Alessandri (1461–1523), *Genialium dierum* (*Of Pleasant Days*) in 1522.

137 The reference is to Justinian's Law Code, *Digest* 34.2.23.2, a paragraph of laws taken from the jurist Ulpian (c. 170–223). "Gold and Silver, Dress" are the first three topics from the list that heads section 34.2.0.

138 The pallium was a Greek-style cloak, which is probably why it was considered unmanly in Ulpian's day for a Roman male.

139 Pieces of cloth sewn onto a dress to add embellishment or make the skirts fuller.

140 The *paenula* was a woolen full-body traveling cloak. The lexicons know nothing of its being a feminine garment.

141 In *The Lives of the Twelve Caesars*, book 4.

142 Lines 69–70. Juvenal is criticizing the lawyer Creticus for wearing a delicate, unmanly toga as he conducts cases accusing women of adultery. "Fabulla is

and Martial, book 2, Epigram 39:

> "You give your shapely adulteress dresses of scarlet and violet.
> Would you give her the gifts she has deserved? Send a toga."

The *flammeum* is a mantle for the head, or rather a veil for the face, of linen, or at one time it was of a saffron color, which is why it was called κρόκεος πέπλος (saffron mantle), and it was worn by new brides as a sign of indissoluble wedlock, as is clear from Lucan, who writes concerning Marcia when she was married again to Cato, "[No] saffron *flammea* veiled her downcast features."[143] Chaplets were garments of honorable matrons, virgins, and even Vestal Virgins, with which they covered their heads. Prostitutes did not deserve them. Hence Ovid, in book 2 of *de Tristibus*,[144] because he wished to show that he had not written his amorous books for dignified matrons, says, "Be far away, chaplets!"[145] And the chaplets are quite often paired with the stole as the distinguishing marks of honorable matrons, as is clear from that passage of Tibullus, book 1, elegy 6:

> "Only teach her to be chaste, although no chaplet
> Holds her hair bound, nor long stole her feet."[146]

The *reticulum* is a covering of the head that holds the hair. Sometimes it is adorned with interwoven gold and pearls, which is why it is a "gilded *reticulum*" in Juvenal, Satire 2. The *palla* is also a garment

---

an adulteress; if you like, let Carphinia also be condemned." That is, even condemned adulteresses, forced by law to adopt men's clothing, will not wear a toga as effeminate as the one Creticus has on.

143 Lucan's *Pharsalia*, book 2, lines 361. The [No] is added from context, from the preceding line. If both lines are translated, this is what they say: "No saffron *flammea* veiled her downcast features, lightly to cover the timid modesty of a bride." It is possible that Balduin misremembered the source and did not intend the "No" to be understood, but he has just said that "*new* brides" wore the *flammeum* as a sign of "*indissoluble* wedlock," neither of which stipulations applied to Marcia's case, as she had been married to Cato, then divorced and married to Hortensius, and was now being "married again to Cato," as Balduin has noted.

144 *On His Sorrows*, a collection of poems Ovid (43 B.C.–17/8 A.D.) wrote while in exile from Rome. Today this collection is commonly called *Tristia*, "Sorrows."

145 Line 247. Ovid here quotes lines from his own *The Art of Love* (I.31–34) to prove that he was not trying to corrupt Roman wives with that scandalous work, but had warned them from the start to avoid it.

146 Albius Tibullus (c. 55 B.C. – 19 B.C.), lines 67–68.

of the honorable woman, or with a tunic, the *pallium*, as in Nonius Marcellus.[147] Thus the Roman Senate sent as a gift to Queen Cleopatra "an embroidered *palla* with a purple cloak," as appears in Livy, decade 3, book 7.[148] Similar garments of honorable matrons are the *cyclas*,[149] the *ricinius* or *ricinius*,[150] the *crocoton*,[151] the *supparum*, the *toga praetexta*,[152] the *strophium*,[153] wet stomachers,[154] turbans and things of this kind, of which mention is made even in Isaiah chapter 3, verse 19 and following.

About these things see Alexander of Alexander, book 5 of *Genialium dierum*, chapter 18, (3) The holy appearance of women is also moderate, not extravagant, something to which this sex is especially inclined. For as Jerome says in Letter 12,[155] "The feminine race is φιλόκοσμον (ornament-loving), and we know that many even of noted chastity are happily adorned, though not for any man, nevertheless for themselves." Thus from time to time, even among the Gentiles, laws have been made concerning clothing, and for a long time at Rome it was prohibited to wear a varicolored garment by the *Lex Oppia*, as appears in Livy, chapter 4, decade 4.[156] Also Nero forbade the use of the amethyst and Tyrian

---

147 Nonius Marcellus was a Roman grammarian and encyclopedist who probably lived in the 4th or early 5th century A.D. His work *De compendiosa doctrina* is a dictionary that illustrates word usage with quotations from Latin literature. As such, it is a major source of fragments from works that are otherwise lost to us. I have not been able to discover which passage in this work Balduin is referring to.

148 I.e., book 27.

149 "A state-robe of women, with a border running round it" (*Liddell and Scott*).

150 Probably the *ricinium*, "a small veil thrown over the head by the early Romans, esp. by mourners and women" (*Liddell and Scott*).

151 Probably the *crocota*, a saffron-colored court-dress.

152 The kind of toga worn by high-born children before they came of age.

153 A band worn under a woman's breast for support.

154 A *fascia pectoralis* is a fancy garment mentioned in Isaiah 3:24, rendered "stomacher" in the KJV and Douay-Reims. A stomacher was a heavily ornamented center panel for a bodice, worn by men and women in the 15th and 16th centuries, but by Balduin's day only by women.

155 In modern numeration, Letter 128.2.

156 *History of Rome* 34.1. The *Lex Oppia* (Oppian Law) was an austerity measure instituted by Gaius Oppius during the Second Punic War (215 B.C.) and repealed

color,[157] so that it might perchance be more precious, as Suetonius testifies in the *Life of Nero*, chapter 32.[158] God Himself censures that luxury in garments by way of Isaiah, in the passage previously cited. And because women are accustomed to take pride even in their hair, it was at one time decreed that matrons and women of proven chastity might use nothing but black for their hair, but prostitutes might use blonde, as is known from Juvenal, who speaks of Messalina, wife of the Emperor Claudius, who wore black hair, a woman's matronly chastity, and yet when she went to a brothel to sate her lust, covered her head with a blonde wig, lest she be recognized. He writes thus in Satire 6:

"And hiding black crime with a blonde wig,
She entered a brothel, stuffy with old rags."[159]

Yet if it was natural, even the blonde hair color was praised in honorable matrons. Thus Ovid, in book 2 of *De Fastis*, writes of Lucretia, a most chaste matron:

"Her form pleases him, and her snowy color, and blonde hair,
And the color was there, produced by no art." [160]

St. Peter also censures the luxury of women's hair and garments, when he writes in 1 Peter 3:3[-4] that the ornamentation of women should not be "external—the hair, or encircling with gold, or of the donning of garments—but the hidden man of the heart, in the incorruptibility of a quiet and modest spirit, which is rich in the sight of God." But let these things suffice concerning the appearance of women in this passage.

Question 2

The Apostle requires of old women that they teach well (v. 3). Why then does he write elsewhere, "I do not permit a woman to teach"? (1 Tim. 2:12),

---

in 195 B.C..

157 The city of Tyre was renowned in the ancient world for the purple dye it produced.
158 In his *Lives of the Twelve Caesars*.
159 Satire 6, lines 120–121.
160 *On Festivals*, book 2, lines 763–4. The preferred modern name is *Fasti*.

and again in 1 Cor. 14:34, "Let the women be silent in the church, for they are not permitted to speak."

Answer: In our text the Apostle wants the aged women to be καλοδιδασκάλους (teachers of virtue), which some have taken to mean that they are not to be madams[161] and accomplices to another woman's wickedness. Thus Beza even changes it to "instructresses of respectability," and Erasmus, "that they might teach honorable things." But Jerome has correctly observed that the Apostle allowed them the liberty of teaching. Others have extended this liberty even to public gatherings. Licinius, the bitterest enemy of the Christian name, did not permit men to take part in prayers with women, in order that the bishops might not interpret the sacred things for the women, but women might have women as instructresses of these things, as Eusebius reports in book 1 of *de vita Constantini*, chapter 46.[162] The Quintillianist heretics took women into the Episcopate or Diaconate for the sake of Eve, as Epiphanius testifies, heresy 49.[163] The Cataphrygians, or Pepuzians, granted the priesthood to women whom they called deaconesses, and as men ordained deacons, so women ordained the deaconesses, as Augustine mentions in *de haeresibus* chapter 27 and Epiphanius, heresy 79.[164] But the public office (*munus*) of teaching in the church was plainly prohibited by the Apostle in the passage cited, lest this should be practiced in the primitive church.

For Tertullian writes, *de velando virginum*, chapter 9, "It is not per-

---

161 That is, procuresses, female pimps; *lenae*.

162 Chapter 53 of *The Life of Constantine* in modern editions. Licinius was Constantine's eastern co-emperor until Constantine invaded the East and deposed him in 324. He jointly issued the Edict of Milan (allowing toleration for Christianity) with Constantine in 313, but later persecuted the churches in various ways.

163 This is the 49th sect mentioned in Epiphanius of Salamis's (d. 401) comprehensive anti-heretical treatise *Panarion*. According to him it was a sub-group of the Montanists that followed a Montanist prophetess named Quintilla.

164 "Cataphrygians" is another name for the Montanists. They are no. 27 in Augustine's list (*On the Heresies, to Quodvultdeus*), and the Pepuzians, a Montanist offshoot, are no. 28. In the *Panarion* the Phrygians/Montanists come right before the already-mentioned Quintillians/Pepuzians at no. 48, but Epiphanius does mention them again under no 79, the Collyridians (*PG* 42.742).

mitted a woman to speak in church, but neither is it permitted to teach, or baptize, or offer, nor to claim a part for herself in any masculine function (*munus*), much less the priestly office (*officium*)."[165] And Clement of Rome says in book 3 of the *Constitutions*,[166] chapter 6, "We do not allow women to teach in the church, but only to pray and to hear the teachers, for our Master, the Lord Jesus Christ, when He sent us twelve to teach the People and the Gentiles, never sent women to preach, although women were not lacking." Also, in the Fourth Council of Carthage, the Fathers proposed the law, "A woman, even if she is learned and holy, should not presume to teach men in the assembly." See chapters 98 and 99 of the Council; also [*Corpus Iuris Canonici*,] distinction 23 in the decrees, ch. 29, *mulier*.[167] Moreover, these things were not so instituted by the Apostle and the holy Fathers without cause, "because it is against nature and divine order for women, who have been subjected to men by Genesis 3:16, to teach publicly in the presence of men. It is contrary to their modesty and humility, to speak in public. Also, discretion is greater in men, and rational discourse better."[168] "The female race is unsteady and prone to error, and provided with a humble intellect," says Epiphanius, heresy 79.[169] "The woman is also commanded by law to be silent, Anselm says on chapter 2 of 1 Timothy,[170] since when she

---

165 *On the Veiling of Virgins*, ch. 9.

166 *The Apostolic Constitutions*, traditionally attributed to Clement of Rome (died c. 100), are dated c. 375 by modern scholars.

167 This canon does not come from any Council of Carthage, but rather from the *Statuta ecclesiae antiqua*, a collection of rules on church discipline attributed by modern scholars to Gennadius of Marseille in the second half of the 5th century A.D. The *Collectio Hispana*, and therefore the later *Pseudo-Isidorean Decretals* and *Decretum* of Gratian, attributed it to "the Fourth Council of Carthage," supposedly in 389.

168 Balduin has taken the preceding three reasons almost verbatim from Cornelius à Lapide's commentary on 1 Cor. 14:34–35. I have added quotation marks accordingly.

169 The Epiphanius quotation does not come from Cornelius à Lapide, but is added by Balduin, *PG* 42.742A. The unattributed borrowing resumes immediately afterwards.

170 Anselm of Canterbury wrote no commentaries on Scripture. The reference may be to Anselm of Laon (d. 1117), who composed (or began composing?) the standard interlinear gloss for the Vulgate. This opinion does not appear in that gloss,

spoke, she recommended sin to her husband. And finally, a rein should be put on feminine talkativeness,"[171] which Chrysostom considers in homily 9 on the First Epistle to Timothy. Now, the fact that our Paul wants women to be καλοδιδασκάλους (teachers of virtue), and what things they should teach well, pertains to private instruction. For it has not been forbidden them to teach younger people in the ways of the Lord, for in this manner Priscilla, the wife of Aquila, more accurately explained the way of the Lord to Apollos (Acts 18:26), and Timothy was instructed from childhood in the true faith of Christ by his grandmother Lois and mother Eunice (2 Tim. 1:5), and the women at Christ's sepulcher are commanded to announce the Lord's resurrection to His disciples (Mark 16). This private instruction also pertains entirely to the right education of children, which is equally the responsibility of mothers, as parents (Eph. 6:4). So Chrysostom resolves the apparent ἀντιλογίαν (contradiction) in Paul this way (homily 4 on this Epistle): "Teaching by men and women is permitted," he says, "but he permits the woman a word of exhortation only at home, nor ever allows her to be in command, nor to make her speaking long at all. Thus he adds, 'nor to be over a man,' so they might teach the young women."

Question 3

The Apostle wants slaves to please their masters in all things, and not to contradict them (v. 9). Should everything then be done to please the superiors to whom we have been subjected, such that it would be wrong to contradict them?

Answer: It is a mark of hypocrites to do all things for the approval of their superiors. That's why in another passage the Apostle does indeed want slaves to obey their masters, but not to "serve in order to be seen, as if pleasing men, but in simplicity of heart, fearing God" (Col. 3[:22]).

---

but Anselm of Laon did write other commentaries. Cornelius à Lapide cites Anselm here, but Balduin adds the detail that it comes from a commentary on 1 Timothy 2.

171 The borrowing from Cornelius à Lapide's commentary on 1 Corinthians 14 ends here.

Therefore slaves obey their masters badly, and children their parents, and subjects their magistrate, in matters that are contrary to the obedience that they owe God, as when impious things are commanded, and things that are contrary to good morals; when the magistrate exercises compulsion either to idolatry or to strange worship, or rashly changes something in the church's rite, whence arises manifest scandal. Here, to consent is not virtuous, but it is permissible to contradict, for "one ought to obey God rather than men" (Acts 5[:29]), and nothing should be done against conscience, nor yielded in such a way that Christian liberty, by which we have been freed from the yoke of human traditions, is in any way violated, and the yoke of servitude thrust upon consciences. Nor is it even in the power of the magistrate, by himself, by his own authority, to change anything in the worship or rites of the church; but here the consent of the whole church is required, for what affects all is governed by all, with no injustice at all. Therefore in such a case nothing should be done to please one's superiors, but they should be entirely contradicted, because on such an occasion the superiors are abusing their power and authority, and thus that contradiction is made not so much against the superiors' office as against the abuse of it. Thus Eleazar would not even pretend to eat of the swine's flesh to please the tyrant (2 Macc. 6:24). Daniel would not even pray with the windows shut to please his king (Dan. 6:10). Moses would not leave even a hoof in Egypt to please Pharaoh (Ex. 10:26). Saul's servants would not slay David to please their king (1 Sam. 19:1). According to the imitation of these examples, nothing that is contrary to conscience and the obedience owed to God should be done to please superiors, but it is just and right to contradict. Moreover, that contradiction should be made not only with words, but also by action, not only so that things that are evil might not be done, though ordered by superiors, but so that we might dissuade by instruction those who are defiled with perverse opinions, or "drawn away by their lust" [James 1:14] to unlawful things; that is, that we might press them hard with petitions to spare both their own consciences and those of others, especially the tender ones, and fervently pray to God to hinder those impious attempts.

But if one be permitted to obtain nothing, the matter must be commended to God, and whatever dire penalties must be borne, rather than consent to something that in any way wounds the conscience and piety. Certainly impious mandates must by no means by rescinded by open force and an armed hand, for here that passage of the Apostle always holds, Romans 13:2, "He who resists the power resists the ordinance of God." This is most true, whether children resist their parents, or servants their masters, or subjects violently resist the magistrate. Moreover, our Apostle wants slaves to please their masters in all things, and not to contradict. This should be understood in this way: either that they should be content with their condition, so that it is pleasing to them even though it is servile, or that they should strive to please their masters in all things that are pious and honorable, the way he wanted them to "obey in all things" in Colossians 3[:22], doubtless in the things in which they owe obedience to their masters. Moreover, the contradiction that is prohibited here should be understood as that fretful response to masters' orders, even fair and just ones, that the Apostle wanted to be far removed from the slaves of Christians, for it contends with the obedience and subjection by which they are obligated to their masters. Therefore one must distinguish between lawful and unlawful contradiction. The lawful has a place with commands that are impious and violate the conscience, and is allowed to servants who can seek to turn the danger away from their masters by their frequent warnings. Thus Jonathan contradicted his parent Saul (1 Sam. 19:4). Thus Elijah contradicted Ahab (1 Kings 18:18) and the Apostles the High Priests and elders (Acts 4:19), and Ambrose the Emperor Valentinian when he demanded that basilicas be handed over to him: "It is neither right for me to hand it over," he said, "nor profitable for you, O Emperor, to receive it. By no law are you able to violate the home of a private citizen, and do you consider the house of God something to be carried off?" (Letter 33 to Marcellina).[172] And Hosius, Bishop of Cordoba, con-

---

[172] Letter 20 (section 19) in today's numeration. The confrontation between St. Ambrose and the Emperor Valentinian II occurred when Empress Justina, the young Emperor's Arian mother, demanded through her son that Ambrose designate the Portian Basilica in Milan for use by the Arians in her court. Ambrose refused, and with the support of the populace prevented the Emperor's troops

tradicted the Emperor Constantine:[173] "Desist, I ask, O Emperor, lest you mix yourself up with ecclesiastical affairs, nor command us in this kind of thing, but rather learn from us yourself. God has committed the empire to you, but to us He has entrusted the things of the church" (reported by Athanasius in his *Letter to those living the solitary life*).[174] It is customary to touch on these things, even if obedience might be refused also to good and useful commands, as the Jews contradicted the prophet: "We will not hear from you the word that you have spoken to us in the name of the Lord" (Jer. 44:16). Or when those who are justly reproving are answered as Sarah's handmaid replied to her mistress (Tobit 3:9–10).[175] Or finally when even good words are calumniated, the way Peter contradicted Christ (Matt. 16:22). Our Paul prohibits this latter kind of contradiction, but the former sometimes has great utility.

Aphorisms of the Commonplaces[176] from this Part of the Chapter

1. It belongs to a teacher of the church to say things that befit sound doctrine (v. 1). Therefore he should not propose impious things, nor scandalous things, nor fables composed to excite mockery, but "the one who speaks, let him speak the utterances of God" (1 Pet. 4:11). For "The word of the Law is perfected without falsehood" (Sir. 34:8). Then let him not pass the time only by disputing, but let him teach things that form morals and the life of men, for in the church, "all things should

---

from entering the church.

173 Hosius wrote this letter not to Constantine, but rather Constantius II, in 353.

174 Athanasius quotes this letter in his *History of the Arians* (ch. 44), not in his first or second *Letter to the Monks*.

175 Sarah, who had lost seven husbands in succession to the demon Asmodeus, had this thrown in her face when she had to chide a servant. "So when she reproved the maid for her fault, she answered her, saying: May we never see son, or daughter of thee upon the earth, thou murderer of thy husbands" (Tobit 3:9).

176 Commonplaces (*loci communes*) were the topics by which a systematic treatise was arranged, particularly one on theology. In other places in the commentary, Balduin uses the phrase "Theological Aphorisms from this Part of the Chapter."

be done for edification" (1 Cor. 14:12). For on this account does God bestow gifts on the teachers: not for destruction, but for edification (2 Cor. 10:3). And this the fruit of Christian teaching, that it makes sound men, who both believe rightly and live well. That is why it is called "sound doctrine" by metalepsis.[177]

2. Christians of all stations and ages must be directed by the ministry of the Word. For that reason, Paul himself prescribed rules of life for older and younger, and parents and children, and slaves and masters (Eph. 6:1ff., Col. 3:18ff.), and enjoined his disciples, Timothy and Titus, also to do the same (1 Tim. 5:1ff. and in this our text). Therefore no one should withdraw himself from the ministry, for it is the common ὄργανον (instrument) of the Holy Spirit, through which by ordinary means He governs our life and promotes our salvation, which is why it is called "the ministry of reconciliation" (which all men need, 2 Cor. 5:18), and the ministers themselves are called leaders and shepherds[178] of souls, who must be obeyed (Heb. 13:17). Indeed, those who murmur against them are said to have murmured against God Himself (Ex. 16:7).

3. All frivolity should be absent from old age. Thus Paul wants old men to be sober, modest, prudent, sound in faith and love (v. 2), men who might be able to guide others by their example, and to provide for their own. Indeed, Sirach 25:4 includes a foolish and senseless old man among the three detestable things. Foolish old men of this sort, who in that time of life still barely know about God and divine matters, who still are inflamed by cups and lusts, drunkenness, quarrels, and follies, offer themselves to be mocked by their juniors. Scripture calls them hundred-year-old children (Isa. 65:20), because they are indeed able to count back many years, but when it comes to piety, understanding, and virtue they are worse than children. Solomon says of them, "Better is a poor and wise boy than an old and foolish king who does not know how to anticipate the future" (Eccl. 4:13). And Chrysostom says, in Homily 7 on the Epistle to the Hebrews, "It is truly a shame, and a ridiculous thing, to be adorned with grey hair on the outside, but have the sense

---

177 Balduin is using the word "metalepsis" more broadly than it is used today.
178 Or pastors (*pastores*).

of a child on the inside, *etc.* I say these things not accusing the old, but the young, for those who do these things are youths to me, even if they have reached their hundredth year."[179] Seneca too complains about these things in Letter 4. "Childhood does not still remain in us, but childishness, which is more serious. And this is assuredly worse in that we have the authority of old men and the vices of boys; and not of boys only, but of infants. The former fear trifles, the latter fear falsehoods, we fear both." Talking about an old man of this sort, Antiochus the Sophist said to Philostratus that he would become ἐν παισὶ μὲν γείρων ἐν δὲ γέρουσι παῖς, "an old man indeed among children, but a child among old men." Old men should be warned, therefore, to perform deeds that befit their age, for it is a delightful thing when grey hair has wisdom conjoined, *etc.* "The crown of old men is to be experienced in many things, and their glory is when they fear God" (Sir. 25:8). Such a man was Simeon, "a righteous man, and devout" (Luke 2[:25]).

4. The more mature wives should be instructresses of the younger ones (v. 3), for whom they should not only carry the torch of an honorable life, but also show by good instruction the reason for living rightly. That they may attain this, let them denounce all frivolity in words, in garments and in gestures, from which Sirach considers the mind to be easily known (19:27). Let them avoid drunkenness, for a drunken woman is an enormous calamity (Sir. 26:11). Let them not be talkative, for in much-speaking is vanity (Prov. 10:19). Let them abstain from revilings and disparagements of others, from which many women have perished, such as Jezebel (2 Kings 9:31ff.) and Athaliah (2 Kings 11:14ff.). And let them live in such a way that the younger women might suffer themselves to be unpleasantly uprooted by them, according to the example of Ruth, who followed her mother-in-law even outside her homeland on account of her piety and respectability (Ruth 1:16).[180]

5. The domestic virtues of women are love for their husbands and children, sobriety, chastity, and the care of the household, concerning all of which things Paul treats in verse 5. The first virtue is the bond

---

179 Homily 7, from sections 8 and 9, commenting on Heb. 6:14.

180 That is, on account of her mother-in-law's piety and respectability.

of conjugal harmony, which is one of the three most beautiful things that Sirach says please God and men (25:2). Thus Paul inculcates mutual love in spouses (Eph. 5:25). The second virtue is the foundation of a good education, for those who do not love children are ἄστοργοι (loveless), and take no care for education, but the commandment of the Lord is: everyone must teach his son while there is hope (Prov. 19:18), and "educate your children in the discipline and instruction of the Lord" (Eph. 6:4). Therefore God put into parents a natural φιλοστοργίαν (affection) toward children, of which there is mention in Isaiah 49:15, Matthew 7:9, and everywhere else. The third virtue, and the fourth, protects reputation, for women who are licentious and fond of drink are held in bad repute. But since "if God should not give it, they cannot be continent any other way," let them ask of God (Wisdom 8:21). The final virtue for women is the peculiar virtue of their sex, for women should be οἰκουροὶ (housekeepers), which is also why they are called matresfamilias,[181] because they ought to keep themselves to their home, and not sally forth here and there about their homes, idle, something that Paul prohibited (1 Tim. 5[:13]), for this is a mark of prostitutes, that they are impatient with tranquil things, and their feet are unable to remain at home—"now out of doors, now in the streets, and now they lie in wait at the corners" (Prov. 7:12). But concerning the prudent woman Lemuel says in the Proverbs of Solomon, "She has considered the paths of her house, and does not eat bread idle" (Prov. 31:27). The ancients also depicted Venus standing on a shell as a symbol of the virtuous *materfamilias*, who always carries her home with her, as appears in Plutarch, in his "Conjugal Precepts."[182]

6. The virtue of young men is σωφροσύνη (soundness of mind, v. 6), and it encompasses many things: temperance in food, lest they should be given to wine and gluttony; chastity, lest they should boil over with lusts and weaken the body before its time; moderation of the affections, that they might act carefully and circumspectly in all

---

181 The plural of *materfamilias*, the maternal counterpart to *paterfamilias*.

182 The "Conjugal Precepts" appear in Plutarch's *Morals*, book 2. Balduin refers to precept no. 32.

things, and there might be no suspicion of baseness in them. The more established all these traits are, during this time of life in which (as Ambrose says on chapter 13 of Job) "the body's heat persists the most, and is inflamed by the ferment of the steaming blood,"[183] the greater praise those youths deserve who are truly σώφρονες (of sound mind) and παιδαριογέρωντες, or "younger old men" which moniker Macarius the Egyptian[184] attained when he was still young, on account of the aged prudence and gravity of his manners, as Nicephorus testifies in book 9 of his *History of the Church*, chapter 14.[185] And Pindar writes of Demophilus in Ode 4, [κεῖνος] γὰρ ἐν παισὶ νέος, ἐν δὲ βουλαῖς πρέσβυς, ἐχκύρσας ἑκατονταετεῖ βιοτᾶ: "Among boys he was a youth, in counsels an old man who had reached his hundredth year."[186]

7. Corrupted morals of the hearers blaspheme the Word of God (v. 5), for when the pagans abstain, by the leading of the natural law, from many vices that are common among Christians, they shrink back from Christian doctrine, and attribute those morals to it, as if it taught us to live wickedly, or at least permitted licentious living, and this is to blaspheme the Word of God. This is why, when the People of God were led away to Babylon on account of their crimes, "the Lord said that His name is blasphemed continually, all day long" (Isa. 52:5), because He has so exceedingly rebellious a people. "They have profaned my holy name," He says, "because it was said of them, 'Behold, this is the People of the Lord, and they have departed from His land'" (Ezek. 36:20). In order to avert this ignominy from His name, He promises them liberation in verse 23. "I will sanctify my great name, which has been profaned among the nations, which you have profaned in their midst,

---

183 St. Ambrose, *De interpellatione Job et David* (*Of the Appeal of Job and David*) book 1, section 21 (*PL* 14.845A).

184 Macarius of Egypt (c. 300–391), abbot of the monastic community in the desert of Sketis for the last fifty years of his life, frequently appears in the *Sayings of the Desert Fathers* (*Apophthegmata Patrum*).

185 Nikephoros Kallistos Xanthopoulos (fl. 1325), Byzantine historian who wrote a history of the church in eighteen books from the birth of Christ down to the year 610, and possibly five more books taking the story to 911, but only a table of contents is extant for those latter books.

186 Pythian Odes, Ode 4, lines 501–4.

that the nations might know that I am the Lord." Thus Paul, when he has reproved the crimes of the Jews—that they teach others, and do not teach themselves—adds, "You who glory in the Law, dishonor the name of God through transgression of the Law, for the name of God is blasphemed among the Gentiles because of you" (Rom. 2:23[-24]). He reproaches the Corinthians also for the same thing, when he writes that such things have been heard among them as are not heard even among the pagans (1 Cor. 5:1). But indeed, abuse of God is included in every shameful deed, partly because the Word of God, which prohibits it, is considered worthless; partly because offense is given to others. Thus Basil writes in the *Shorter Rules*, Rule 4, "Who has dared to say that some sin is small, although the Apostle decides and says, 'You dishonor God through transgression of the Law'?"[187] And in Rule 250: "Through transgression it may come to pass that those who are outside our faith at one and the same time consider the Lord's teachings to be contemptible, and rise against us more confidently because of them, and—as it were—tear the transgressor apart with their reproaches and reprimands."[188] Certain Evangelicals expose the Word of God to the same abuse today, who by their dissolute life offer Turks, Jews, and Papists occasion for blaspheming, as if our doctrine were an instructress of crimes, or permitted the license to do whatever you want. One must beware, therefore, lest he profess the faith of Christ only with the mouth, but let him also prove it by his work, "for faith without works is dead" (Jas. 2:26). "For the hearers of the Law are not righteous before God, but the doers of the Law will be justified" (Rom. 2:13).

8. The ministers of the churches ought to be an especial example of good works (v. 7), that in them might be traced the lines of all the virtues, and the whole life of their hearers might henceforth express them. Therefore Paul not only required of his disciples that they be models for the faithful (1 Tim. 4:12, 2 Tim. 4:5, and in this text), but also writes that he chastises his own body, "lest by teaching others, he

---

187 Basil of Caesarea, from the tractates of the *Shorter Rule* (*Lesser Asceticon*), *PG* 31.1084C.

188 *PG* 31.1249BC.

himself might come to be rejected," (1 Cor. 9:27), and elsewhere he says that "he gives no offense, lest his ministry might be disparaged, but in all things we present ourselves as ministers of God, in much suffering, in tribulations, in necessities, in difficulties, in blows, in prisons, in insurrections," *etc.* (2 Cor. 6:3[-5]). Examples of this kind from pious teachers of the church not only increase in others love for the venerable ministry, but also incite them to imitation, about which Augustine writes in book 8 of *On the Trinity*, chapter 9: "We believe that the ministers of God should live this way, not because we heard it from people, but we perceive it inwardly, within ourselves, or rather above ourselves in the Truth itself. Therefore from what we see, we love him[189] whom we believe to have so lived. And unless we especially loved this form [of righteousness], which we regard as always stable and immutable, we would not love him on account of this—because we hold in our faith that his life, although he lived it in the flesh, was adapted to this form and was congruent with it. But somehow we are excited further to love the form itself, through the faith by which we believe that someone lived in such a way, and through the hope by which, from the fact that some men have lived this way, we who are men do not despair that we can live that way, too, so that we both desire this more ardently and pray for it more faithfully."[190] So let the minister of the church look to these things, that he might not only teach well, but also model by his life the things that he teaches. Let him consider for himself the dictum that Jerome writes in the *Epitaph of Nepotian, to Heliodorus*, "The eyes of all are turned upon you, your house and dwelling founded, as it were, upon a height. It is the mistress of public discipline. Whatever you have done, men reckon it ought to be done by themselves. Beware lest you do something either that those who wish to find fault might seem justly to attack, or that those who are induced to imitate might do wrongly."[191]

9. Three things are required of Christian teaching, of which Paul

---

189   In context, St. Augustine is referring to St. Paul, and specifically to the list of his trials in 2 Cor. 6:3–5.

190   St. Augustine, *On the Holy Trinity* 8.9.

191   Jerome, Letter 60, section 14.

writes in verses 7 and 8: integrity, seriousness, and soundness, by which he denotes the sufficiency of a doctrine that has no need of human additives, for in itself and inasmuch as it is extracted from the Prophetic and Apostolic Word, it is whole and perfect, because "the Law of the Lord is spotless" (Ps. 19[:7]). This excludes from the doctrine of the church all frivolity, fables, and follies, the same as useless questions. Paul has also prohibited these things elsewhere (1 Tim. 1:4; 6:4; Tit. 1:14). This commends purity and honesty of doctrine, and excludes heresy and the figments of one's own ingenuity, and turns a man over to God's eloquence alone. For in the church, whatever is proposed beyond those things is unwholesome and counterfeit. Teaching should therefore be examined according to these κριτήρια (criteria). If one of them is lacking, it cannot be salutary, but where they have all been joined together, the adversaries have nothing that they can censure.

10. The ministers of the church need sound doctrine and an honorable life, not only on account of their hearers, that they might be rightly instructed, but also on account of their adversaries, that they might not be able justly to criticize anything in them (v. 8). For they make a practice of closely watching those they set themselves against, that they might seize upon the appearance either of a bad life or of false doctrine. Because of these men, the minister needs dexterity in teaching and circumspection in living, lest any occasion should be given them for reviling (1 Tim. 5:14). St. Peter's admonition has to do with this: "Such is the will of God, that by doing well you might make dumb the ignorance of imprudent men" (1 Pet. 2:15).

11. Two virtues are prominent in servants: (1) obedience and (2) faithfulness. Paul deals with the former in v. 9, when he does not want slaves to be arguers, but to be subject to their masters and content with their condition, and with the latter in v. 10, when he wants them to be without deceit and to defraud no one, but to act with good faith in all things. These virtues are opposed to the vices of servants, which are common in this class of men, whence come rebellion and theft. For they usually obey their masters unwillingly, and coerced compliance is called servile, and is opposed to filial obedience, for children obey their parents willingly. They also take care of their own things more

than their masters', of whose goods they leave nothing when they can conveniently snatch it. This precept of our Apostle must be repeatedly impressed on them for this reason: that one might not hear bad reports about them, but rather that the Gospel of Christ should be adorned. Indeed, the ones who have been adorned by these virtues are not undeservedly loved by their masters, according to the admonition of Sirach: "If you have a slave, let him be to you as your soul, treat him as a brother, since you have acquired him in the soul's blood" (Sir. 33:31).

12. Great praise belongs to Christian teaching, because it changes men's character in such a way that now they can "adorn the Gospel of God our Savior," as our Paul says—men who at one time had nothing worthy of ornament or commendation. Among the Gentiles, the condition of slaves was the lowest of all, and with good reason the most contemptible of them, to the extent that in the civil law they are held to be nothings, and are commonly said to have no head, that is, no liberty, nor city, nor family (Caelius Rhodiginus, book 25 of *Antiquarum Lectionum*, chapter 23). On account of their infidelity, it was once said of them, "There are as many enemies as slaves," as appears in Seneca's Letter 47[192], and although in the course of time they were able to acquire their liberty with money, many would purchase their liberty with money obtained through plunder and thefts, as Alexander of Alexander reports in book 4 of *Genialium Dierum*, chapter 10. So perhaps it happened that our Apostle intends to command the slaves of Christians not to embezzle from the goods of their masters, but rather by their faithfulness to adorn the Gospel of God our Savior. And this is the nature of the Gospel, that it corrects the most corrupted morals of men. For servants too, when they embrace the teaching of the Gospel, know that piety, faithfulness, obedience, and like virtues are required from those who love the name of our Lord Jesus Christ. Concerning this end of the Gospel, he now continues in the next part.

---

192 Seneca the Younger, *Moral Letters to Lucilius*, Book 5, Letter 47, section 5.

The Second Part of the Text [Titus 2:11–15]

11. Ἐπεφάνη γὰρ ἡ χάρις τοῦ θεοῦ ἡ σωτήριος πᾶσιν ἀνθρώποις.

11. For the salvific grace of God has shone on all men.

12. Παιδεύσουσα ἡμᾶς, ἵνα ἀρνησάμενοι τὴν ἀσέβειαν καὶ τὰς κοσμικὰς ἐπιθυμίας, σωφρόνως, καὶ δικαίως, καὶ εὐσεβῶς ζήσωμεν ἐν τῷ νῦν αἰῶνι.

12. Teaching us to live soberly and justly and piously in the present age, impiety having been rejected along with worldly desires.

13. Προσδεχόμενοι τὴν μακαρίαν ἐλπίδα, καὶ ἐπιφάνειαν τῆς δόξης τοῦ μεγάλου θεοῦ, καὶ σωτήρος ἡμῶν Ἰεσοῦ Χριστοῦ.

13. Awaiting that blessed hope and the appearing of the great glory of our God and Savior Jesus Christ.

14. Ὅς ἔδωκεν ἑαυτὸν ὑπὲρ ὑμῶν, ἵνα λυτρώσηται ἡμᾶς ἀπὸ πάσης ἀνομίας, καὶ καθαρίσῃ ἑαυτῷ λαὸν περιούσιον ζηλοτὴν καλῶν ἔργων.

14. Who gave himself for us that he might redeem us from all iniquity, and purify for himself a peculiar people, one that follows good works.

15. Ταῦτα λάλει, καὶ παρακάλει, καὶ ἔλεγχε μέτα πάσης ἐπιταγῆς. μήδεις σου περιφρονείτω.

15. Say these things and exhort and reprove with all zeal for instructing. Let no one look down on you.

Notes from text.[193]

Analysis and Explanation of the Second Part

Lest it should seem surprising to anyone why the Apostle would require so many virtues, and so splendid, from various kinds of men,

---

[193] Balduin's text has *praecipiendi studio* (zeal for instructing), which he uses everywhere in this commentary, but the Vulgate has *imperio* (authority).

not even excepting slaves, now in the second part of the chapter he adds his reason for this, and by it declares at the same time that excellent article of the coming of the Messiah: "For the salutary grace of God has appeared," he says, "to all men" (v. 11). We no longer dwell in darkness, he wants to say, that one should with impunity carry out the works of darkness. At one time, this was generally done among the nations, but the time of grace has illumined all men, of whatsoever station they may be. It is therefore right that all men live in a manner worthy of their calling, worthy of that light, worthy of the Gospel. "The grace of God" is what he calls the Good News about Christ, insofar as it has already been revealed in the New Testament, when "the rising from on high visited us" [Luke 1:78], the Son of God having been sent into the flesh, who rendered God propitious to us and procured the remission of sins. Thus it is called "salutary grace." In the Greek that is χάρις σωτήριος, in place of which word some have read σωτήρος, which is why in the Vulgate version it is "the grace of God the Savior; but it is "salutary," because it imparts salvation, which is not to be hoped for outside of that grace of God. At one time this grace was hidden under the types and shadows of the Old Testament, but now it has appeared, ἐπιφάνη, illumined, and suddenly, as it were, has shown brilliantly out of the darkness, partly through the incarnation of the Son of God, partly through the preaching of the Gospel, which is why Christ Himself is also called the light of the world (John 8:12), and the Word preached about Christ is called "a lamp for our feet" (Ps. 119:105). But now it has appeared to all men, because no one has been passed over in the counsel of God, but God gave His Son for all, and also commanded it to be announced to all in the Word, which is why He is called in other places "the Savior of all men" (1 Tim. 4:10) and "the true light, that illumines every man coming into this world" (John 1:9). The fruit of this revealed grace is our learning and instruction, for it is said to educate us. In the Greek it is παιδεύουσα, shaping us as if we were simple children, for to παιδεύειν is to instruct ignorant children in letters and conduct. And the Apostle uses this term appropriately, because in divine matters we are all infants and children, who need a pedagogue, for which reason the whole of Christian training is not at all unfittingly called pedagogy. In this passage, it is attributed in particular to the Gospel, which shapes those who are simpler: in part directly, or in those matters that pertain properly to the teaching of the Gospel, since it has to do with grace and the will of God, which He has revealed to us in Christ; and in part indirectly, or in those matters that have regard properly to the Law, which latter kind of learning Paul deals with here. "For that grace of God teaches us to live soberly and justly and piously in this world, rejecting impiety and worldly desires" (v. 12). First it removes from the heart of the Christian man those things that are harmful, then it puts in salutary things. He reduces the harmful things to two headings, by which the condition of all the unregenerate is expressed. The first one is ἀσέβεια, impiety, and the second is ἀδικία, injustice. The one transgresses against God, and embraces all false or superstitious kinds of worship, idolatry, hypocrisy, impurity of life, despair or mistrust, etc. The other is brought against the neighbor, and embraces in its orbit all vices against the Second Table, which Paul describes with the single term of "worldly desires," and takes that to mean not only perverse lusts, but also all the "things that are placed under the prince of this world. And because they are of the world, because they pass away with the vapor of this world," according to Jerome,[194] all the things with which a man can harm himself and his neighbor are worldly. St. John calls them "the lust of the flesh, the lust of the eyes, and the pride of life; for these are not from the Father, but from the world" (1 John 2:16). All these things, therefore, should be rejected by all those who have been made sharers of that salutary grace, that is, who have embraced the teaching of the Gospel; for it is not the instructress of crimes, but the one who drives them out. Now, he uses the language of "rejecting" which denotes not a simple laying aside, but full renunciation, hatred, and detestation, in such a way that the things that were pleasing beforehand are now displeasing. For as many times as we deny ourselves, Jerome says, treading down our former vices each time, we cease to be what we were and begin to be what we were not before. But without a doubt, the Apostle is referring to that renun-

---

194 Jerome, *Commentary on the Epistle to Titus*, 2:12 (PL 26.586 CD).

ciation of the Catechumens in Baptism, by which they give notice to the Devil and all his pomps and all his works, which the Godparents now do for infants who are to be baptized. Augustine mentioned this custom in sermons 116, 163, 215, *de tempore*,[195] and Dionysius greatly commends it in the *Ecclesiastical Hierarchy*, in the last chapter.[196] And so, vices having been set aside, the Apostle then sets up worthy virtues. He wants us to live (1) soberly, σοφρόνως, (2) justly, δικαίως, (3) piously, εὐσεβῶς. These three things are the rule of our whole life. Sobriety brings it to pass that we do not harm ourselves, for passion is moderated, lest we should exceed the limits of moderation either in food or drink, or in sexual love, wrath, hate, or even in judgment of ourselves, for moderation in all things is profitable for men. Justice brings it about that we do not trouble our neighbor, but render to him what is his, deserving well of all, just as we would desire others to deserve well of us. Piety brings it about that we do nothing against God, either by strange kinds of worship or profane morals. All our life ought to be distinguished by these virtues, as long as we are in this world, for here there must be struggling and sojourning, and in the other world follows rest and the crown, toward which we eagerly strive. So the goal of this our zeal is added: "Awaiting the blessed hope," Paul says, "and the coming of the glory of our great God and Savior Jesus Christ" (v. 13). That is, we renounce vices and put effort into virtue for this reason: in order that our Savior, whom we hold in expectation until then, might find us entirely prepared at that last and glorious coming of His. The goal of our faith, then, and of all our piety, is eternal life, which having been prepared for the pious, indeed from eternity, will be bequeathed and fully possessed at the certain, final coming of Christ. In the meantime, we must long for that hope, because "as long as we are in the body, we are sojourning away from the Lord, for we walk by faith and not by sight" (2 Cor. 5:6[–7]). Now the hope is called "eternal life"

---

195 The *De tempore* sermons of St. Augustine are those that address a specific day of the liturgical calendar. Converting Balduin's citations to modern numeration (Migne's), the sermons mentioned here are respectively no. 267 (PL 39:2242), no. 168 (PL 39:2070), and no. 265 (PL 39:2237).

196 Pseudo-Dionysius the Areopagite, *Ecclesiastical Hierarchy* 7.2.11.

by metonymy, for the thing hoped-for, and it is a blessed hope indeed, because all the tribulations of this world will be banished there, with all sins. And finally that hope is blessed, it is excellent without a doubt, a hope than which there is none greater, which was promised by God and predicted by the prophets, by which hope also the faithful in the world at every time have steadfastly borne the most bitter things. To this hope he adds "the coming of the glory of our great God," either by transposition of the parts, for that coming precedes the hoped-for eternal life, or by way of ἑρμενείαν (interpretation), doubtless because all the hope of the faithful should be fixed on that glorious coming of the Son of God. In Greek it is ἐπιφάνεια (epiphany, manifestation), a term that among the Greek writers signifies the appearance of a deity, by whatever means it comes to pass. Thus in Diodorus Siculus, book 1, an ἐπιφάνεια is attributed to Isis because she showed signs of her presence,[197] and they called the feast days that they instituted in memory of appearances of this sort τὰ ἐπιφάνεια (the Epiphanies). It is thus also in 2 Maccabees chapter 3, verse 24. Τὸ ἐπιφάνειαν ποιεῖν (to make an epiphany) is to give evidence of one's presence. When this term is used concerning Christ, it is understood in two senses, because His coming is two-fold: one of humility, the other of glory.

The former is named the ἐπιφάνεια ἐνσάρκου σωτῆρος (epiphany of the incarnate Savior) by Eusebius in the beginning of his *History*,[198] and again ἔνσαρκος, οἰκονομία (incarnate, the economy) by Suidas[199] in the entry for the word ἐπιφάνεια. It is about this coming of Christ that our Paul writes in verse 11, ἐπεφάνη ἡ τοῦ θεοῦ χάρις (the grace of God has appeared), *etc.*, and in 2 Timothy 1:10. Hence they once called the day of Christ's Nativity, on which the memory of the former coming is celebrated in the church, ἐπιφάνεια (Epiphany), as appears in Epiphanius, book 3, towards the end,[200] in book 3 of Eusebius's *Life of*

---

197 Namely through miracles of healing. *Bibliotheca historica* 1.25.3–4.

198 *History of the Church* 1.5.1.

199 The *Souda* is a 10th century Byzantine encyclopedia, long attributed (probably in error) to an author named Suidas.

200 *Panarion* 3.22.6.

Constantine,[201] and in Isidore, book 3, letter 110.[202] They called it θεοφάνειαν (the Theophany), because at that time God appeared in the flesh. Concerning this matter, see Casaubon, *Exercises Against Baronius* 2, p. 138ff.[203] The latter coming is named ἐπιφάνεια τῆς δόξης (the epiphany of glory) by our Paul (v. 12). He mentions the same coming in 2 Timothy 4:1, and in 2 Thessalonians 2:8, where he adds ἐπιφάνειαν καὶ παρουσίαν (epiphany and *Parousia*). Now, he names it "the coming of glory" by way of a Hebraism, that is, "the glorious coming of our great God and Savior Jesus Christ" which all hangs together by apposition, so that Christ Himself, as He is coming with glory for the Judgment, is called "the great God, and our Savior." He is the great God because He is God not only by office, but by Nature and power, the Creator of the whole universe and the Judge of all flesh, and our Savior because by His merit He has acquired salvation for us and announced it in the Gospel. Therefore the former epithet pertains to His Nature or Person, and the latter to His office. So this is a clear testimony against the Arians, who corrupt it in the way we shall hear in the questions. But there is added an outstanding description of this Person whose coming the Apostle has described: "who gave Himself for us that He might redeem us from all iniquity, and purify for Himself an acceptable people, one that follows good works" (v. 14). These things pertain to the priestly office of Christ, which consists in our redemption from sins, accomplished through His death. Paul called His death a "handing-over of Himself for us," as in Ephesians 5:25, "Christ loved the Church and handed Himself over for her." The death of Christ is a δῶσις, then, or a *traditio* (a handing-over), because He was destroyed not by natural death, but having been surrendered to the hands of His

---

201 The site of Christ's birth is mentioned in book 3, chapter 43, but there is no mention of the name "epiphany," at least in modern editions.

202 Isidore of Seville (c. 560–636), Spanish bishop and encyclopedist, wrote *The Etymologies*. Isidore explains Epiphany in *Etymologies* 6.18.6–8.

203 Isaac Casaubon (1559–1614), a French Huguenot who was a renowned classical scholar and philologist, relocated to England in 1610, joined the Anglican Church, and was commissioned to refute the *Ecclesiastical Annals from Christ's birth to 1198* of Cardinal Baronius (d. 1607). He died in the early stages of this project.

enemies. It was a handing-over of Himself, because it was not a coercive but a voluntary death, which He arrived at not at the pleasure of His enemies, but when and where it had seemed right to Himself. Also it is a precious death, because He did not offer something foreign, but His own body on the cross, about which Hebrews 9:12 says, "He entered once into the holy places, not through the blood of goats and calves, but through His own blood," *etc*. Finally, this handing-over was done for us, because the salutary death that he endured in our place, so that we would not have to die as we had deserved, was not owed by Him, but by us. Paul deals expressly with this in 2 Corinthians 5:14–15 and Romans 4:25. The goal of Christ's death is twofold: first, liberation from iniquity. In Greek the word is λυτρώσεται, which is a forensic word and signifies redeeming something that had been sold or seized, which is why λύτρον and ἀντίλυτρον mean the price of a redeemed captive, and λύτρωσις means redemption, and a λυτρώτης is a liberator or redeemer. These terms are used of Christ everywhere in Scripture, in the New Testament: Luke 1:68, 2:38, and 24:21; 1 Peter 1:18, Hebrews 9:12, Acts 7:35, *etc*. Now, our misery is indicated, because we have by nature been handed over "under sin" (Rom. 7:14), and hence are captives of Satan; but Christ has paid the λύτρον in our place: "not gold or silver, but His precious blood" (1 Pet. 1:18[–19]). From this comes our redemption from all iniquity, both that in which we were born, and that by which we have daily defiled ourselves, and here is the primary goal of the handing-over, or death, of Christ. The other goal is our renewal, for this was the reason Christ handed Himself over for us: "that He might purify for Himself an acceptable people, one that follows good works" [v. 14]. He calls it an "acceptable people," λαὸν περιούσιον. The Syriac translates חדתא, new,[204] but it is περιούσιον, or something that we have among our goods or pay, and elsewhere it is called personal property, for περὶ is sometimes like *circum* (around), and οὐσία is substance or resources, so περιούσιον means "what is around our goods and resources," or "that which is choice and precious among our goods," and

---

204 Balduin is indeed referencing the Syriac Peshitta here, which says "a new people."

because of that, dear and acceptable to us beyond other things, as are rings, gems, large pearls and the like, amulets hanging from the neck down below the breast, for περὶ sometimes denotes prominence. Hence it has happened that some change Paul's words to "a peculiar people, and His own," as Aquila has it, and others to "ἐξαίρετον, chosen and choice," as Symmachus has it.[205] Either interpretation fits with Paul's meaning and can be connected to it, for Christ by His obedience has made such a people, that is God's personal property, that cleaves to God and serves Him, and on account of that is chosen, choice beyond all other men, and is especially dear to God. Thus the Greek word corresponds to the Hebrew סגלה, which is used of the People of God in Exodus 19:5, Deuteronomy 7:6, 14:2, and 26:18. In these passages the Septuagint has the word περιούσιον. The same Hebrew word is found in Psalm 135:4, and the Greeks rendered it περιουσιασμὸν (private possession). By nature, therefore, we were not the kind of personal possession that is chosen and especially dear, but were rather a people cast aside, impure and unacceptable to God; but Christ, by His death, has made out of men such a personal possession of God, after He "cleansed their consciences from dead works" by His blood [Heb. 9:14]. Because of this, Christians have now been redeemed from sins by the death of their Savior, like a most splendid treasure in the eyes of God, because they are no longer wallowing in the impure mire of sins, but are followers of good works. In the Greek they are called ζηλωταὶ, zealous imitators, who pursue virtues not perfunctorily, but with great zeal and exertion, and in this way contend among themselves so that no one might snatch the palm of piety away from them.[206] This, then, was that glorious reason of the Apostle, why he wanted men of every station, excepting not even the lowest, each to carry out his own business in his own

---

205 Aquila (fl. A.D. 130) and Symmachus (fl. late 2nd c. A.D.) were ancient translators whose Greek translations of the Old Testament were used by the church Fathers alongside the Septuagint for reference purposes. Balduin here means that some "change Paul's words" to make them conform to one of the other's rendering of the OT passages Paul is quoting, and which Balduin is about to mention.

206 "The palm" (*palma*) is the palm branch or wreath awarded to the victor in a contest.

place as befits Christians: clearly that Christ has been manifested to all men in the flesh for this purpose, that all men, having been freed from their impurity, might serve God with a pure heart and thus be transported to the joys of eternal life at the next coming of Christ. Therefore at the end of the chapter he instructs that these things be diligently inculcated: "Speak these things," he says, "and exhort, and reprove with all authority. Let no one look down on you" (v. 15). Note here the progression of the words. First he says, "speak," which pertains to simple teaching, then "exhort," which adds weight to the teaching, because the things that should be known are also driven home, and one is admonished to store them deep in the mind. Third, "reprove," obviously those who were not going to attend to the teaching. Now he adds, "reprove them with all authority," that is, do not handle Word-despisers of this sort with a gentle arm, but use your power, and employ a certain sharpness in the rebuking. "Let no one look down on you," μηδείς σοῦ περιφρονείτω, "let no one look down on you or make you out to be worthless, a thing set beneath himself." Which indeed was not in Titus's power, for who can prevent it happening, that he might perhaps be despised by someone? Yet he wants Titus to resist his despisers, lest he should be shaken by their unjust judgments, and become more hesitant in the duty of refutation. He wrote something similar to Timothy: "Let no one καταφρονείσται your youth" (1 Tim. 4:12), but to Titus he writes, "Let no one περιφρονείτω you." Jerome noted a certain distinction here: to καταφρονεῖν is to have contempt for another; to περιφρονεῖν is to consider oneself better than another. Thus he warns Timothy not to present himself as the kind of man who could justly be contemned by someone, but Titus not to live in such a way, by acting hesitantly, that one of those who are in the church might think himself to be better.

Titus 2

Questions from this Part of the Chapter

Question 1

Is the universality of grace and of Christ's merit rightly proven by the Apostle's words, "The salutary grace of God has appeared to all men" (v. 11)?

Answer: Although the words that exclude no man from this grace are sufficiently clear, as Jerome writes on this passage, "We are all together called to the Kingdom of God; we all must be reconciled to our Father after the offense."[207] Still, there is no lack of men who restrict these words to some particularity. For thus Calvin writes on this passage: "He does not mean individual men, but denotes rather classes, or different kinds of life." Beza renders the word πᾶσιν (to all) as *quibusvis* (to whomever, plural) and adds in the Larger Annotations,[208] "This particle, in this passage and very many others, is not universal, but indefinite, by ignorance of which distinction the spirit of error has introduced great and most dangerous debates into the church, which have been renewed in our time." He writes similarly on the passage 1 Timothy 2:1[ff.]. Piscator, who translates the Apostle's words thus, "*Es ist erschienen die heilsame Gnade Gottes allen Menschen*" ("The salutary mercy of God has appeared to all men"), follows these interpretations. The great mass of the Calvinists say that these universal statements are talking about kinds of individuals, not about individuals from kinds, because according to their opinion, the grace of God revealed in Christ pertains to all men of whatsoever sex, condition, nation, age, class, or rank they might be, but not to each individual or person. This is what they express more clearly elsewhere, when they restrict the grace of God and the merit of Christ only to the Elect, as Zanchius[209] does in

---

207 PL 26.586B.C..

208 That is, the expanded version of the annotations to his edition of the Greek New Testament (1565), which also included his own translation, from which this rendering of πᾶσιν comes.

209 Jerome Zanchius (Girolamo Zanchi, 1516–90), Italian Calvinist theologian.

Miscellanies, p. 297.[210] He calls Christ "the Advocate of the Elect only, and indeed of all those, even the holiest," and Bucanus[211] writes, in *Institutes*, locus 36, question 23, "If you consider the plan and eternal purpose of God and the will of the Mediator, Christ died for the Elect only." Pareus also, in the *Irenicum*, p. 241, calls it "the dogma of Christ, the dogma of the Apostles, and the dogma of all the Fathers," that Christ our Lord did not suffer and die for the redemption of all men; but Beza writes in Response 2 to the Acts of the Colloquy of Mömpelgard, that there has never been a time, nor is there, nor will there be, at which God desired, desires, or is going to desire to have mercy on every single man, and therefore that the damned are not saved because God, by an eternal but just decree, for reasons known only to Himself, created, ordained, and destined them to eternal damnation. This horrible dogma is refuted everywhere in Scripture, when it speaks of the will and grace of God, the merit of Christ, and the preaching of the Gospel universally, in such a way that it excludes no one from the intention of God on this account: for instance, Isaiah 52:10, and compare with this Luke 1:51 and 2:30; Zechariah 3:8–9, John 3:17, 1 John 4:10, John 6:33 and 51, John 1:9–12 and 4–7, 1 John 1:9, 1 John 2:2, Romans 11:32, 1 Corinthians 8:11. Also when God is said to call even those who do not wish to come: Proverbs 1:24, Isaiah 65:2, Isaiah 66:4, Jeremiah 7:13, to all of which we add at length the passage of our Apostle, "The salutary grace of God has appeared to all men," *etc*. Here we judge that the passage does not have that Calvinist restriction to kinds of individuals: (1) from the text, for that "salutary grace of God has appeared" to those whom God wants to "live soberly, justly, and piously, impiety having been rejected along with worldly desires," as is clear from verses 11 and 12. But God wants every single man to live in this way, something no one will have denied unless he is impious. Therefore, that grace of God has shone on all those whom He also wants to be liberated from all iniquity,

---

210 Probably the *Miscellaneorum libri tres*, a collection of Zanchi's various "Miscellanies" published at Neustadt in 1582.

211 William (Gulielmus) Bucanus (d. 1603) was a French-Swiss Calvinist theologian who published a systematic theology (*Institutiones theologicae*) the year before his death.

without which grace that very liberation could not happen. But God also wants all those to be liberated who are perishing because of their iniquity, as He says in Ezekiel 18:32. "Why will you die, O House of Israel? Because I do not desire the death of the one who is dying, says the Lord. Return, and live." (2) from the use of the universal particles *omnis* (all), *totus* (whole), and *similium* (alike). We are not ignorant that those particles sometimes admit of restriction, but then only when the restriction is either added expressly, as in that John 3:17 passage, "all who believe in Him have eternal life" (3:16), where the universality has been pronounced to be of believers, what Ambrose calls the fullness of the People of God; or when the very nature and condition of the thing with which the passage is dealing proves that the universality is not simple and absolute, as when "all Judaea" is said to have "gone out to John" (Matt. 3:5), where infants and the sick were exempted, at a minimum. Ambrose[212] has this distinction in book 1 of *On the Call of All Nations*, chapter [9].[213] "Sometimes," he says, "all the earth is named for part of the earth, and the whole world for part of the world, and all men for a part of men, yet for the most part, Scripture quickly reveals the difference between these things, so that the reader's understanding is transferred from the name of universality to the part that should be understood." For the fact that mention was made a little earlier of different stations and times of life, as of old men, old women, slaves, *etc.*, cannot restrict that universality to particular classes of men, or as the adversaries say, to kinds of individuals, unless it should be shown to be contrary to the nature and condition of God's grace that it should shine upon all men, something that we are convinced can never be shown. For why would it not shine on certain men, since by nature all men are darkness (Eph. 5:8), and God is no προσωπολήπτης (respecter of persons, [Acts 10:34]), who would exclude certain men from His grace, although all were unworthy of it. He has rather "confined all men under sin, that He might have mercy on all" ([Gal. 3:22;] Rom.

---

212 This book was actually written by Prosper of Aquitaine (c. 390–c. 455), not Ambrose of Milan.

213 *On the Call of All Nations* 1.142–43.

11:32), and as broadly as iniquity spread itself, so broadly does grace also have dominion. Hence Chrysostom writes in Homily 4 on chapter 2 of Hebrews, "'By the grace of God, the gift of the one man Jesus Christ abounded to many, just as by the grace of God he tasted death for all,' not only for the faithful, but for the whole world, and He did indeed die for all; and so what if all do not believe? He completed what was His."[214] Augustine writes thus in Tractate 12 on John: "As much as lies with the physician, he comes to cure the sick man. The man who does not want to heed the physician's instructions kills himself."[215] We conclude from this that the physician has come even on account of those who do not want to heed a physician's instructions, as Anselm writes on this passage: "We all are called to the Kingdom of God. We all, after the offense, must be reconciled to our Father."[216] This is the common opinion of the better Fathers. We do not deny that elsewhere both Augustine (in *Enchiridion* chapter 103) and Fulgentius (in his *Book on the Incarnation*,[217] chapter 21) make use of this distinction between kinds of individuals and individuals from kinds, and especially Augustine. He writes about the Apostolic text 1 Timothy 2:2[ff.], "We should understand 'all men' as 'every kind,' divided up by every difference."[218] But in the consequent will of God, people from every nation, tongue, status, age, and province have indeed come to this [knowledge], by which God actually saves believers or damns unbelievers. But if it is defined according to the antecedent will of God, in what way God might desire all to be saved, although each and every individual will not actually be saved, because all and each one do not make use of those means of salvation that have been offered to each individual and to all—more about that elsewhere.

---

214 Chrysostom is quoting and commenting on Heb. 2:9.
215 *Tractates on the Gospel of John* 12.12, commenting on John 3:17.
216 From Anselm of Canterbury's Commentary on Titus.
217 *Book to Scarila on the Incarnation*, by Fulgentius of Ruspe.
218 *Enchiridion*, chapter 103.

Question 2

If "the salutary grace of God has appeared to all men" and to each individual, who might bring it to pass that it is salutary to all men and to each individual? For many perish.

Answer: The fault is not in the grace of God itself, but in men, who are either unwilling to embrace that offered grace, as the Pharisees once were, and other Jews, concerning whom Christ said, "How many times I have wanted to gather you together, but you were not willing" (Matt. 23:37); or do not use it rightly, as all Epicurean and secure men, who confess that they know God, but deny Him by their works (Tit. 1:16), concerning whom Paul writes that "they receive the grace of God in vain" (2 Cor. 6:1); or they are not content with grace, but want to add something of their own, concerning whom Paul writes, "You have been emptied of Christ, you who are justified by the Law; you have fallen from grace" (Gal. 5:4). Therefore one must distinguish between the potential efficacy of grace, and the actual.

The potential efficacy is that by which the grace of God, having been offered to all, is salutary in itself, and able to work salvation in all, in the way Christ is said to be "the light illumining every man coming into this world" (John 1:9). The actual is that which works salvation in believers in actuality, which actuality is obstructed in many by means of unbelief and impenitence. For just as the light of the sun has the power of illumining all things that are under the horizon, and yet does not illumine those that dwell in subterranean places, or close their eyes, or take cover, so also the light of grace has the power of working salvation in all, but in those who resist this working, it accomplishes nothing. Hence it happens that in Scripture the grace of God and merit of Christ is referred indeed to those to whom it imparts salvation in actuality, that is, to believers, as when "the righteousness of God" is said to be "through the faith of Christ unto all and upon all those who believe" (Rom. 3:22), that Christ is said to have died "to gather together the children of God, who were scattered" (John 11:52), that He is said to have redeemed His own (Isa. 63:4), and sayings that are like these, which do not take away universal grace, but show its actual efficacy in the elect. "For it is characteristic of the faithful servant to think of the benefits of his Lord, which have been given to all, as if they had been tendered specifically to him. For example, from the Apostle: 'Who loved me and gave Himself for me'" [Gal. 2:20]. Chrysostom says this in book 2 of *On Compunction of the Heart*.[219]

Question 3

Is the divine nature of Christ rightly proven from the fact that Paul calls it "the coming of the glory of our great God and Savior Jesus Christ"?

Answer: Most rightly, for Christ is not only called "our Savior" in v. 13, which is an epithet of the true God (Isa. 43:3) because in Him alone is our salvation (Hos. 13:9), but also "God." And lest anyone should think it is the name of an office or an honor when he is called by the epithet, "great God," which belongs to the true and natural God alone, whose name is great (Jos. 7:9, 1 Sam. 12:22, 2 Chron. 6:32, Jer. 10:6, Mal. 1:11, 2:11, *etc.*). Hence the Fathers triumphed against the Arians with a single saying. "Where is the serpent Arius?" exclaims Jerome in his commentary; "Where is the snake Eunomius? The great God is said to be 'Jesus Christ our Savior'; not 'the Firstborn of all Creation,' not 'the Word and Wisdom of God', but 'Jesus' and 'Christ,' which are the names of the assumed man."[220] See also Chrysostom and Theophylact

---

219 *On Compunction* 2.6 (*PG* 47.420).

220 Jerome, *Commentary on Titus*, *PL* 26.586D–587A. Jerome's point may be that the Arians can argue that "Firstborn of all Creation" (Col. 1:15) and "Word and Wisdom of God" (John 1:1–14 and 1 Cor. 1:24) are titles that apply to Christ simply as to a demigod, but "Jesus Christ" clearly applies to Christ as to a *man*. A demigod might be called "a great god" on his own rights, but a man would not be, unless Christ is literally man and God at the same time. And if He is, His humanity can explain the degree to which He is less than the Father, and this can no longer be used as evidence of His demigod status. Note: the term "assumed man," (as opposed to "assumed human nature") came to be associated with the Nestorian heresy soon after Jerome's death, since it is language that lends itself to a two-person Christology. In fact, Jerome qualifies the term in his next sentence: "But we do not say that Jesus Christ is one, and the Word another, as a new heresy falsely claims, but that He is the same both before the ages and after the ages, both before the world and after Mary." Balduin does not include this qualification or introduce one of his own. At the time, Lutherans understood "assumed man" to mean the assumed human nature.

on this passage, and Athanasius in his Letter to Adolphus[221] against the Arians and concerning the common essence of the Father and the Son; but even so, there has been no shortage of those who distort this clear passage by tearing asunder things that should be taken together. For by "great God" they understand the Father, whom no one denied is the true and natural God, but they called Christ the Savior, and the author of those commentaries that are read in *The Works of Ambrose* volume one tore this text apart by this method. But someone denies somewhere that those commentaries are Ambrose's, and somewhere else the same man laments that many forged and false things have been inserted into the commentaries.[222] Therefore it is in vain that Erasmus uses the authority of Ambrose in his *Annotations on the New Testament*. Of course he does not dare deny the divine nature in Christ, but he does contend that it cannot be proven from this Apostolic text, and so he mocks Chrysostom, Theophylact, and Jerome because from this passage they exulted against the Arians as if they were victors, although it is uncertain. The more recent Arians tear this text apart in the same way, and refer "great God" to the Father, and "Savior" to Christ. For so they write in the *Racovian Catechism*,[223] page 39: "The Apostle is not talking about Christ." But that this interpretation is violent, and accordingly false, we prove by these arguments: (1) the copulative does not tear apart, but conjoins "God and Savior" in an undivided unit, just as it was said above without the copula: τοῦ σωτῆρος ἡμῶν θεοῦ (of

---

221 That is, Adelphius (Letter 60).

222 This is quite a vague citation, but correct at least in the first point, as the commentaries in question were not by Ambrose, but rather the author who modern scholars call Ambrosiaster. On this verse Ambrosiaster writes, "He says that this is the blessed hope of believers, who await the coming of the glory of the great God, which he holds to be revealed when Christ is the Judge, in whom the power and glory of God the Father will be seen: that they might attain the reward of their faith" (*PL* 17.530A). The opinion of Balduin's unnamed source "that many forged and false things have been inserted into the commentaries" may have resulted not only from disagreements with Ambrosiaster, but also from the fact that some pseudo-Ambrosian manuscripts included commentaries by another author whom modern scholars have identified as the proto-Nestorian commentator Theodore of Mopsuestia (c. 350–428).

223 The *Racovian Catechism* was written by Fausto Sozzini (1539–1604), founder of the Socinian heresy, and posthumously published at Raków, Poland.

God our Savior, v. 10). Thus Peter joins the righteousness of God and of our Savior Jesus Christ without rupture in 2 Peter 1:1. Thus Ephesians 5:5 says, "in the kingdom of God and of Christ," that is, in the kingdom of that Christ who is also God. (2) In the same way, "God and Father" are not torn asunder by the copula, but conjoined in one Person in 2 Corinthians [1:3], Ephesians 1:3, and 1 Thessalonians 1[:3]. Therefore, although the occasional copulative does distinguish different things, as in 1 Timothy 5:21 and 6:13, it still does not follow that it does here too, with Titus 2[:13], because examples to the contrary are not lacking. So an inference might be made from particular instances. Enjedinus[224] has brought up contrary examples in which the copulative disjoins "God and Christ," as in 1 Timothy 5:21 and 6:13. The argument proceeded entirely from particular instances, and it cannot be inferred from it that the reason for the copulative is the same in this passage too. For an obvious reason for differentiation is added by the cited passages.

In the first passage, Paul delivers a charge "in the presence of God and the Lord Jesus Christ and the elect angels," distinguishing God and the Lord by their Persons, and both from the angels, as the Creator from the creatures. In the second passage, "God" is distinguished from "Christ" who suffered "under Pontius Pilate," and this is from His human nature. This kind of difference cannot be conceded between "great God" and "Savior," because Paul is dealing with the one whose coming is described, something that indeed fits a single person. Therefore the examples cited to the contrary are ἀπροσδιόνυσα (irrelevant). Enjedinus brings up the passage of Luke 16:29, "They have Moses and the Prophets," where there is only one article,[225] but I answer: Moses and

---

224 Georgius Enjedinus (d. 1597), was a Socinian who held the position of Superintendent of Churches in Claudiopolis, Transylvania (modern-day Cluj-Napoca, Romania). The reference is probably to his posthumously published *Explanations of Passages of the Old and New Testaments from Which the Dogma of the Trinity is Customarily Established*. (Source: Johann Cloppenburch, *Socinianism's Little Compendium Refuted* [Franeker, Holland, 1652], p. 21.)

225 Meaning that the Greek text has only one article for the two nouns. Enjedinus is replying to an argument Balduin has not explained, namely that since τοῦ is the only article in the disputed phrase (τοῦ μεγάλου θεοῦ, καὶ σωτῆρος—of *the* great God and Savior), it should be construed with both θεοῦ and σωτῆρος as one person with two titles. Enjedinus points out that the clause ἔχουσι Μωϋσέα

the Prophets are not considered there as different sources, but as one, because they present a single testimony to the truth. He brings up the passage of Acts 3:3, where Peter and John are conjoined without any article at all,[226] but we suggest concerning those passages where the Holy Spirit does use articles, that where He uses an article, He is talking about only one person, and where He uses two, it is because the utterance also concerns two people. Paul has dealt with someone's gracious coming in verse 11; he is dealing with the glorious coming of the same person in verse 13. But that gracious coming was of the Son, not of the Father. Therefore, Paul is dealing with that God whose glorious appearing and coming we await, and to be sure, that is not God the Father, but the Son, for He will appear in majesty and glory (Matt. 25:31), and His action will be that of the Last Judgment, with respect to which the Father has given judgment to Him (John 5:22). Nor is an ἐπιφάνεια (epiphany, appearing) attributed to God the Father anywhere else in Scripture, but always to the Son. Therefore the Son is that great God of whom our Paul speaks.

The *Racovian Catechism* states against this last argument, on page 80, that Paul does not say that we await the coming of the great God, but of the *glory* of the great God—the Father's glory, that is, which is going to appear at the coming of the Son for judgment—because Christ is going to come in the glory of God His Father, *etc*. But they err, not knowing the custom of Pauline Scripture, where this Hebraism is frequently encountered: for "the coming of glory" is said for "the glorious coming" of the great God. And thus we conclude in this passage. In this text, the one whose glorious coming is treated *is* that great God; but it is the glorious coming of the Son that is treated here, not of the Father. Therefore the Son is that great God. But if you should refer that glory especially to the Father, that which will be manifested at that coming of the Son, nothing is offensive to us, for the Son has

---

καὶ τοὺς προφήτας (they have Moses and *the* prophets) also has just one article (τοὺς).

226 ὅς ἰδὼν Πέτρον καὶ Ἰωάννην μέλλοντας εἰσιέναι εἰς τὸ ἱερὸν ἠρώτα ἐλεημοσύνην λαβεῖν (who, seeing Peter and John about to go into the temple, asked to have alms).

the same glory with the Father, and thus the Father's glory, in which the Son is going to appear (Matt. 16:27, Mark 8:38), is called the glory of the Son, for He will appear in His glory (Matt. 25:31). For that is the glory that He had with the Father before the foundation of the world (John 17:5). But outside of the True and Natural God, there was nothing there. So this Apostolic testimony concerning the True and Natural Deity of Christ remains firm and unshaken.

Question 4

Can it be firmly proven from v. 14 that the death of Christ is satisfactory and meritorious?

Answer: The Photinians[227] deny this part of Christian doctrine in every way, and Socinus[228] especially has directed his books *On the Savior*[229] against it, but since the fortress of our salvation is founded on this doctrine, it belongs to us to support it with the soundest arguments, such as occur everywhere in Scripture, especially Psalm 69:5, Isaiah 53:10, Romans 5:8, 2 Corinthians 5:14–15, Hebrews 2:14, John 11:50, 1 Peter 3:18, Galatians 1:4, Hebrews 10:12. Our passage also pertains to this, and we reckon it to be in this category, among the *loci classici*,[230] because it demonstrates that satisfaction of Christ's death by means of several reasons. [1] The Apostle says that He handed Himself over, into death that is, which phrase he uses also in Ephesians 5:2 and 25, and Galatians 1:4 and 2:20. This handing-over denotes the voluntary passion and death of Christ, to which His love for the human race drew Him. Therefore He died, not when His enemies wished it, but when it pleased Him—something that is not said of those whose death is in-

---

227 Followers of Photinus of Sirmium (d. 376), who denied the pre-existence of Christ. Balduin means modern-day Photinians, such as the Socinians.

228 Fausto Sozzini (1539–1604), or Socinus, denied the Trinity (and hence the deity of Christ) and the immortality of the soul. The Socinians followed his teachings.

229 *On Jesus Christ the Savior* (1578).

230 In general, a *locus classicus* is a standard passage from some authoritative work, used to demonstrate something. In Lutheran theology in particular, it is a passage of Holy Scripture that establishes some doctrine as a dogma that the church must teach (a *sedes*).

deed an example of faith and a testimony to their teaching. It is said of them that "another must gird them, and lead them where they do not wish" (John 21:18). (2) It is said that He handed Himself over *for us*, that is, in our place, going to meet the death that we had deserved. This is the very one of whom it is written elsewhere that he died for all, that by means of him dying in this way, all might at the same time have died (2 Cor. 5:14). This is the description of an alien death, or of one that has been taken upon oneself in the place of others. And because our sins had to be expiated through this death, He is thus said to have died for our sins (1 Pet. 3:18), and to have given Himself for our sins (Gal. 1:4), and to have offered Himself as a sacrifice for sins (Heb. 10:12). This is nothing other than to make satisfaction for sins, or to expiate sins by death, in the same way as sacrifices were once offered for the atonement of the soul. That is, they atoned for the soul (Lev. 17:11), and profited towards expiation (Lev. 1:4). Now, that expiation happened by means of satisfaction, because by the ordination of God, the blood of the cow was shed in order that the blood of the man might be spared. This is why the sacrifice was called "an odor of peace to Jehovah" (Lev. 1), because Jehovah was now sweetly coming to rest, since He saw this satisfaction being made according to that means that He had prescribed for His justice. Now all these things were Typical,[231] "for it was impossible that the blood of bulls and of goats should take away sins" [Heb. 10:4], but the blood of Christ, foreshadowed by it, is truly superior to it. The Epistle to the Hebrews elaborates on this subject at length (10:5ff.). (3) Christ thus handed Himself over for us in order that He might redeem us from all iniquity, which redemption was accomplished when the price of His blood was paid, according to Peter (1 Pet. 1:18[–19]). "For without blood, no remission of sins may happen" (Heb. 9:22). This is why Christ is said to give His soul as a λύτρον, or price of redemption, for many (Matt. 20:28), and why Paul says that He has been "put forward as a propitiation through faith in His blood" (Rom. 3:25). (4) By handing Himself over, Christ has purified a people for Himself, as long as He has "purged our consciences from dead works," by His interven-

---

231 Meaning that they were types, OT pictures prefiguring a NT reality.

ing blood and death, "to serve the living God," according to the Apostle (Heb. 9:14). Thus the blood of Jesus Christ, the Son of God, is said to purify us from all sins (1 John 1:7). Nor was there any other means of this our purification than the blood of Christ. For that reason, redemption is attributed to the blood of Christ (Eph. 1:7), and pacification, or reconciliation (Col. 1:20), and we are said to have been made near through the blood of Christ and by His testaments (Eph. 2[:12–]13). These are the firm foundations of our redemption and of Christ's satisfaction, which can satisfy the consciences of the pious. But the Photinians, as long as they have once declared war on the merit of Christ, seek out various ways by which they dare, if not to evade this truth, at least to shake it. First, when Christ is said either to have died or to have been handed over for our sins, they by no means agree that this is the same thing as to have made satisfaction for our sins, but say that He died "because of, or on the occasion of our sins,"[232] as Socinus says in *On the Savior* part 2, chapter 7, and as he explains more clearly in chapter 8, they think that "the statement 'Christ has died *pro nobis* (for us)' means nothing more than that He has disregarded His own life in order that He might grace us with the greatest benefits."[233] So gloss *pro* (for) not as *vicem* (instead of) or *locum alterius* (in place of another), but only as *commodum et utilitatem* (for the advantage and profit of), just like we are commanded in 1 John 3:16 "that we also lay down our life for the brethren," although nobody dies in the place of another, to make satisfaction for him. He says, then, that Christ was handed over because of us, because He was willing to die in order that we might embrace and pursue eternal salvation, which He Himself had brought us from heaven. Socinus says those things. R[esponse]. The argumentation of Socinus proceeds entirely from particular instances, in this way: in certain passages of Scripture, *pro* (for) is the same as *causa* (because of) or *commodi alicujus gratia* (for the sake of someone's advantage), and

---

232 Quoted from p. 110 of the 1594 reprint, with the exception that Balduin has changed *iniquitatis* ("of iniquity") to *peccatorum* ("of sins").

233 Ibid., p. 111. The argument from 1 John 3:16 appears on the same page, but Balduin paraphrases that, and summarizes from a number of passages the comments about how to gloss *pro*.

not *vice* (instead of) or *loco* (in place of); therefore in this text of Paul, too, "Christ has been handed over *pro nobis* (for us)" has the same sense. Who does not see that these are careless speculations? There are other sayings of Scripture where the particle *pro*, or ὑπὲρ, is the same as *vice* or *loco alterius*, for instance: Exodus 7:1,[234] Proverbs 11:8,[235] Numbers 25:13[236] (*cf.* v. 11; 2 Cor. 5:15, Phil. 1:29). And thence it is established that in our text also, that preposition should be understood this way, because this is the reason Christ was handed over for us: that He might redeem us from iniquity. Certainly, we had all been obliged to perish in bondage to iniquity. Christ, then, was handed over for us or in our place for this reason: that we might not perish. For a λύτρωσις (ransoming) is the kind of redemption that is accomplished by the payment of a price for someone else. Hence in other passages when it is dealing with this redemption of ours, Scripture uses the preposition ἀντὶ (Matt. 20:28 and Mark 10:45, where what our Paul says, ὑπὲρ ἡμῶν [for us], is expressed by means of ἀντὶ πολλῶν [in place of many]). Now, the preposition ἀντὶ denotes not only some *commodum* (advantage), but substitution or *vicem alterius* (instead of another), as is established from a comparison of the passages Matthew 5:38, Luke 11:11, John 1:16, Romans 12:17, 1 Thessalonians 5:15, and 1 Peter 3:9. Furthermore, when Caiaphas prophesied about this very merit of Christ's death—unknowingly, yes, but still by God's inspiration—he explains clearly what it would mean to die *pro alio* (for another), namely in such a way that

---

[234] It is not clear why Balduin includes this verse ("And the Lord said to Moses, 'See, I have made you like God to Pharaoh, and your brother Aaron shall be your prophet.'"), because in the Vulgate, the LXX, and the Hebrew there is no *pro* equivalent (e.g., "See, I have made you *in place of* God").

[235] Vulgate: *Justus de angustia liberatus est et tradetur impius* pro eo ("The righteous has been delivered from distress, and the wicked will be handed over for him"). The LXX has the same idea, but not with ὑπέρ: ἀντ' αὐτοῦ (in place of him). This clarifying phrase does not appear in the Hebrew.

[236] It is not clear why Balduin includes this verse, either. The Vulgate does not have the prepositional phrase, saying just that Eleazar *expiavit scelus filiorum Israhel* ("expiated the crime of the children of Israel"). The LXX has περί, not ὑπέρ: ἐξιλάσατο περὶ τῶν υἱῶν Ισραηλ ("made atonement for/about the children of Israel"). The Hebrew says he *wayekapper 'al-bene yisra'el* ("made atonement on/ about the children of Israel").

others, who otherwise would by law have to die, might not die. "It is expedient," he says, "that one man should die *pro populo* (for the people), and the whole nation should not die" (John 11:50). What else is this than to say that it is expedient that one man should die *vice* (instead of), *loco atque nomine* (in the place and name) of the whole people? Therefore, an utterly great *commodum* (advantage) redounds to us from the death of Christ, not only that He might bring us rational souls to subdue death, as Socinus wants, but that we might not be constrained to taste death, but preserved for eternal righteousness and life. Next the adversaries concede that Christ did hand Himself over for us in such a way that He redeemed us from all iniquity, but that "to redeem," as Socinus says in part 2 of *On the Savior*, chapter 1, "means nothing else than to free and to appropriate for oneself, even should the paying of an actual price not occur,"[237] in the same way as God redeemed the people from Egypt (Ex. 15:13, Deut. 7:8), and as Moses was the λυτρωτής (redeemer) of the people without the means of a price (Acts 7:35). "Nor is it read in the Epistle to Titus 2:13," or anywhere else, "ever, that Christ has redeemed us from the judgment or justice of God through which we sinners deserved to be condemned,"[238] but only from all iniquity. Thus he speaks metaphorically of our "redemption," which does not fit in all the details if properly so-called, because the one who would receive the price is missing (under the beginning of chapter 2).[239] In chapter 2 he writes that our redemption can be considered in two ways: either in that we are delivered and freed from sin itself in this life, where we certainly *have* been made followers of good works, or in that sins have not been imputed to us (that is, having been delivered from eternal death, we are given eternal life). He writes that both redemptions are accomplished by the means of Christ's death, but not in such a way that Christ's death was some kind of price or merit. He says that the former redemption is thus because the hope of eternal life has been given to us, which we receive by means of the faith communicated in

---

237 Quoted from p. 70 of the 1594 reprint.

238 Ibid., p. 72.

239 The preceding paraphrases Socinus's conclusion at the bottom of Ibid., p. 76.

the words of Christ Himself, which faith is born in us through the resurrection of Christ, which the death preceded.[240] Therefore we excel at obedience to God with an eager mind, and in the process are freed from servitude to sin. He says it is about this that our Paul says that "Christ gave Himself for us that he might redeem us from all iniquity, and purify for Himself a peculiar people, one that follows good works." He says that the latter redemption has been accomplished by the means of the death of Christ in this way, that freedom from eternal death and a firm hope of life eternal are born in us from nowhere else than from the resurrection of Christ, which the death preceded. This is nearly the sum of that verbose Socinian discourse on our redemption as accomplished through the death of Christ, which it seems a good idea to examine here in a few words, because it pertains to the text of our Apostle, whom he abuses. First, the claim that the word "redeeming" sometimes simply means "liberation," with no redemption price serving as the means, we freely concede, especially in those passages that are cited by Socinus, where God, though Moses, dealt with an inferior, from whose power He was able to wrest His people by right, without any price. But the inference would be badly made from that to the business of our justification, where Christ the Redeemer treats in our place with God, the Judge of all flesh, that he might release captives under sin from death and the devil, which could not be done without the means of paying a price, because God is just, and He could not release those captives without a λύτρον (redemption price). Thus Christ is said to have repaid it, "what he did not steal" (Ps. 69[:4]). And so from-the-particular-to-the-universal is not allowed as a legitimate consequence. Second, our Redemption is not metaphorical, although it is spiritual, for all the things that are required for actual redemption come together here: (1) the captive human race, (2) Christ the Redeemer, (3) a λύτρον,

---

240 Marginal note: "Ostorodus has similar things in *Instit.*, ch. 37, § 8." The reference is to Christoph Ostorodt, *Unterrichtung von den vornemsten Hauptpuncten der christlichen Religion, in welcher begriffen ist fast die gantze Confession oder Bekentnis der Gemeinen im Königreich Polen, Grossfürstenthumb Littawen und anderen zu der Kron Polen gehörenden Landschaff*ten (Racovia: Sebastian Sternacki, 1604).

or price of redemption: the life, or blood, of Christ. (4) God, to whom, as to a just judge, the λύτρον is rendered for the captive who is to be released. For it is not the case, as we might here imagine with Socinus, that this price has been paid to the Devil; for he the minister or executioner of God, without whose consent it is not possible to release any of the captives; but in order that God's consent might come, first there had to be satisfaction of His justice, which made it so that it was not possible to release anyone except by the price being paid. Third, it is false that Scripture never says that Christ has redeemed us from the judgment, justice, or wrath of God. For what is this, that Isaiah writes, "The discipline of our peace is upon Him" (Is. 53:5)? That is, He bore the punishments owed by us, in order that we might be exempt from them in the judgment of God. So writes Paul, clearly: "Having been justified by His blood, much more will we now be saved from wrath through Him" (Rom. 5:9). "Christ redeemed us from the curse of the Law, as He was made a curse for us" (Gal. 3:13). (This passage so crosses Socinus's eyes, that he couldn't respond any other way than to claim that Paul had been "playing around with the word 'curse,'" p. 73.)[241] And again: "Jesus freed us from the wrath to come" (1 Thess. 1:10). Scripture has both, then: both that Christ has redeemed us from all iniquity, and from the wrath of God and the curse of the Law—that is, as is commonly said, from sins and from the penalties of sins. Fourth, it is false that our redemption has been accomplished without the means of a price. For we are expressly said to have been redeemed at a great price (1 Cor. 6:20), and this very purchase (which word Scripture uses of our salvation in 2 Peter 2:1 and Rev. 5:9) presupposes an actual price, and Christ is said to have reconciled and redeemed us to the Father through His own blood (Rom. 3:25, Eph. 1:7, Col. 1:14), which is like the actual price of the payment of "the blood of goats" in Hebrews 9:12, and is contrasted to corruptible gold and silver in 1 Peter 1:18. Hence on this

---

241 Socinus does indeed say this on p. 73 of the 1594 reprint edition, so this must be the same edition Balduin had access to. What Socinus says exactly is, "*Amauit enim Paulus, vt in aliis fæpe folet, in Execrationis verbo argutus effe.*" ("For Paul loved, as he is accustomed to do frequently in other places, to play around with the word 'curse.' ")

fourth point, the doctrine of Socinus and his allies concerning redemption as accomplished by the means of Christ's death seems exceedingly weak. For this was not the securing of our faith alone, so that *we* might be able to be sure of the promises of God. For the Patriarchs also had that certainty, Abraham especially, even though Christ had not yet died at that point in time. Of course we do not deny that the death of Christ puts a vigorous signature on the love of God to us, and the truth of the divine promises, but on that account alone, there would have been no need at all for the death of Christ. It follows, therefore, that the true and primary reason for Christ's death was satisfaction for our sins, the propitiation of God, and the removal of divine wrath from us. Then secondarily, the new obedience follows, and amendment of life, in those who by true faith embrace that death of Christ as having been accomplished also for themselves. Our Paul conjoins both reasons for His death when he says that "Christ handed Himself over for us (1) that He might redeem us from all iniquity, and (2) that He might make a peculiar people, following after good works." At times Scripture speaks of only one or the other, separately. Colossians 1[:14] says of the primary, "In Christ we have redemption through His blood, that is, remission," but Hebrews 9:14 says of the secondary, "Christ has purified our conscience from our works, to serve the living God," *etc.*

Question [5]

Can it be that the office of the Law is attributed to the Gospel when Paul writes in verses 11–12 that the salutary grace of God teaches us to live soberly, piously and justly, impiety having been rejected"?

Answer: The Gospel is concerned with grace, the Law with works; this distinction of Law and Gospel needs to remain inviolate. But these two foundations of Christian doctrine are so considered in their own proper use, when any direct teaching deals with a man, for then the Law knows nothing of grace or Christ, and the Gospel nothing about good works or sins. Only indirectly, and as it were *per accidens*,[242] does

---

242 This means "by accident," but not in the modern sense of a blunder or an unforeseen consequence. It means, rather, "by means of an Accident, as opposed

the [Law] perform the office of the Gospel. The office of the Gospel is to point out Christ and to lead to Him. This the Law does indirectly, when it convinces a man of his imperfection and shows him that it is vain to seek salvation in the Law, at which opportunity it sends the man back to Christ, who is the fulfilling of the Law, even though in itself it is ignorant of Christ. For this reason, the Law is called "a pedagogue leading to Christ" (Gal. 3:24). The office of the Law is to prohibit vices, to exhort to works worthy of the Gospel, and in a single word, to teach the new obedience that is necessary for the reborn as the salutary fruit of faith. This the Gospel does indirectly, to wit, when it shows a man the immense love of God toward us, and the merit of Christ, consideration of which spurs the pious to love God and obey His commands, all impiety and malice having been rejected. And this is why the Gospel could acceptably be called a pedagogue leading to the study of the Law in this text from our Paul, where it is said to παιδεύειν, to teach us how to order life rightly: because as a result of the consideration of grace, it sends us back to the works of the Law, which we owe to God as gratitude for the so many and so great benefits provided for us in His Son.

Question [6]

Did Paul confer authority on his Titus? "Reprove," he says, "with all authority" (v. 15). Why then does Peter prohibit that for the other ministers of the church? "Not domineering," he says, "among the clergy" (1 Pet. 5:3).

Answer: The authority allowed by Paul is one thing, the dominion prohibited by Peter, another. The one rendered *imperium* (authority, command) is ἐπιταγή; the one rendered *dominium* (possession, lordship) is κυρία. *Imperium* lays on the ministers of the church authority and dignity in teaching and exhorting, lest because of the liberty of the hearers, they should leave unmentioned the things that should be done, or should be avoided; so that instead they might sternly give commands (for an ἐπιταγή is properly a command, as above in Titus

---

to an Essence," *i.e.,* as a side-effect resulting from some non-essential detail.

1:3, and in Romans 16:26, and it is opposed to τῇ συγγνώμῃ, a concession, in 1 Corinthians 7:6), and make it known that they will prepare ecclesiastical punishment for the unwilling, and strike fear into them. For in order that the Word might begin to be heard with joy, it is necessary that it be heard with reverence and some fear on the part of those who are taught. Thus we read that Christ taught with authority, not like the scribes (Matt. 7:29), because He was speaking not for popular applause, but for the benefit of the hearers, reproving even the especially learned men of this age. Paul also used this *imperium* on the Corinthians: "Which do you want?" he says, "Should I come to you with a rod, or with charity?" (1 Cor. 4:21). He calls "a rod" that just investigation into the bad ones, and that reprimand and excommunication by which care is taken for the salvation of the hearers, and their life is spared. For it is not the rod of the executioner, but of the father, that all ministers of the Word should use on their hearers like spiritual fathers, if they become rebellious and disobedient, just as they can also treat them agreeably when they are compliant. By this ἐπιταγῇ, Paul commends a rod of this sort to his Titus, on account of the duller dispositions and depraved morals of the Cretans, whom it was necessary to restrain with harsher laws. In this sense Chrysostom also, in Homily 33 on the Acts of the Apostles, called "*imperium*" the law of the Apostolic Synod, which they prescribed for Gentiles who had been converted to the faith: "See," he says, "a brief letter, having neither dialectics nor syllogisms, but *imperium*."[243] But *dominium* denotes external power and coercive force of the kind that the Pope and the Roman Bishops assume for themselves over the clergy. This, St. Peter prohibits, for the ministers of the churches are not tyrants, but fathers; nor did Christ allow His disciples such *dominium*, because it is owed to political lords. "The princes of the nations," He says, "lord it over them, and it will not be so among you" (Matt. 20:25[-26]). In that passage He uses the same Greek word that appears in St. Peter, κατακυριεύουσιν, which means "to exercise an external power over others," something that has not been

---

243 Chrysostom is commenting here on Acts 15:28–29. The word Balduin renders *imperium* is ἐπίταγμα (*PG* 60.242).

allowed to the ministers of the church. For they have not been sent to dominate (1 Cor. 3:10, 2 Cor. 5:20).

Question [7]

The Apostle writes to Titus, "Let no one look down on you" (v. 15). Why then does he write elsewhere, "that we might present ourselves as ministers of God, etc., through glory and ignominy, through bad repute and good repute," etc. (2 Cor. 6:[4,] 8)?

Answer: A distinction must be made here between contempt for the person and for the office. Persons can easily be despised by the enemies of the ministry, who not infrequently consider the servants of God to be a joke, since they are neither powerful in the world, nor do they live for the world's pleasure, but the world has been crucified to them (Gal. 6:14). Christ Himself was despised in this way by the Pharisees, since from earliest youth He was held to be the son of a carpenter (Matt. 13[:55]). He predicted the hatred of the world for His disciples also (John 15:19), and Paul writes of the Apostles in this way: "I think that God has displayed us Apostles as the last of men, like those destined for death, since we have been made a spectacle to the world," *etc.* (1 Cor. 4:9). Contempt of this kind must be patiently borne, nor must a reply be made to all the jests or insults of bad men, for "the disciple is not above the teacher, nor the slave above his master," and "If they have called the *paterfamilias* Beelzebub, how much more the members of his household?" (Matt. 10:24–25). But the office is divine, the embassy in which they are busy for the sake of Christ (2 Cor. 5:20), and contempt of it redounds upon Christ Himself (Luke 10:16). They must be borne, then, those who refuse to listen to the ministers of the Word, who are themselves averse to their ministry, and also lead others away; but they must be sternly rebuked, as Paul has also admonished above, because Christ Himself is despised in them.[244] Therefore, Christ was the most patient sufferer of injuries at other times, yet refused to bear the abuse of the Jews not so much against His person as directly

---

244 That is, in the ministers of the Word. When these critics despise the ministers, they thereby despise Christ.

against His office (John 8:50ff.). Paul too seriously defends the authority of his office against his despisers, the Pseudo-apostles (2 Cor. 10:9 and the whole 11th chapter). Second, a distinction must be made between the contempt of the hearers and of those outside. If some outside the assembly of the hearers, who have not been committed to the guardianship[245] of the ministers, should think of them less favorably, it can be borne as long as it does not come to pass with scandal for the church, since it happens that there is no just claim against them, the way Paul bore the fact that the Athenian Philosophers were calling him a σπερμολόγον (babbler) and a proclaimer of demons (Acts 17:18). But when the hearers committed to his guardianship spurn his admonitions or teaching as though they were much too distinguished to learn the truth from such a man, as sometimes happens, and those who are strong in the world because of wealth, power, and authority submit themselves most reluctantly to ecclesiastical discipline and instruction, that is when this contempt must by all means *not* be borne, because this would be done with scorn for the ministry, and to the detriment of their hearers. And here our Apostle's dictum has its place: "Let no one look down on you," let no one judge himself to be superior in this respect, as the Greek word signifies. For all citizens of the church—of whatsoever order or dignity they may also be—should be subjected to the ministry, because they are all sinners who have need either of instruction, or exhortation, or rebuke, or consolation, all of which things the ministers of the church provide through the Word that has been commended to them. They also should be heeded by all "as the ministers of Christ and the stewards of the mysteries of God" (1 Cor. 4:1). If any do not want to listen, they should not be winked at, but should be authoritatively reproved, as our Apostle admonishes, that they might understand that the authority of the ministry exceeds all the power of the world. To this end Bernard famously writes to Pope Eugene, in book 4 of *On Consideration*,[246] "Where power has been joined to malice, something beyond man must be claimed for you; your

---

245 *Fidei*, or "faith".
246 Addressed to Pope Eugene III, c. 1150.

countenance should be upon those who are doing evil. Let the one who does not respect man, who does not fear the sword, fear the spirit of your wrath. Let the one who has despised your admonition, fear your prayer. Whomever you are angry with, let him consider that *God* is angry with him, not a man; whoever will not listen to you, let him be terrified that God *will* listen, and will be against him."[247] Ambrose used such παρρησία (freedom of speech) against the Emperor Valentinian when he was demanding that the basilicas be handed over to him.[248] "Do not burden yourself, O Emperor," he said, "so that you think you have some imperial jurisdiction in matters that are divine. Do not exalt yourself, but if you wish to be emperor much longer, be subject to God. It is written, 'What things are God's, to God; what things are Caesar's, to Caesar.' Palaces pertain to the imperial power, churches to the priest; jurisdiction has been committed to you over public walls, not sacred ones, *etc.*" And to the Emperor Theodosius he wrote, book 5, [249] letter 29, "Nothing is so popular in kings, and so attractive, as to love liberty even in those who have been subjected to them by obedience. Indeed, this is the difference between good and bad princes, that the good ones love liberty, the wicked ones servitude. For a priest, nothing is so dangerous in the sight of God, so disgraceful in the sight of men, as not to declare freely what he thinks."[250] Hosius, Bishop of Cordoba responded to the Emperor Constantine in this way: "Desist, I ask, O Emperor, lest you mix yourself up with ecclesiastical affairs, nor command us in this kind of thing, but rather learn from us yourself. God has committed the empire to you, but to us He has entrusted the things of the church."[251] In accord with the admonition of our Apostle, none of these men permitted themselves to be looked down on, even by the

---

247 *On Consideration* 4.7.

248 See note 172 above.

249 "Book 5" must refer to a contemporary collection of the works of St. Ambrose. The cited letter is Letter 40 in modern numeration.

250 Ambrose, Letter 40.2. In this letter, he urges Theodosius to rescind his order that a synagogue, allegedly burned at the instigation of a Bishop, be rebuilt at that Bishop's expense.

251 Hosius was addressing Emperor Constantius II, not Constantine.

highest heads of the Empire. But on the other side, it is reckoned as a fault to Basil Camaterus[252] that, in order to acquire the Patriarchate of Constantinople, he bound himself to the Emperor Andronicus by a written agreement, shameful and unworthy of a Bishop, that he would carry out everything that pleased the Emperor, and assiduously avoid the things that displeased him, as is written in Camerarius,[253] part 3, *Operar. succisiv.*, chapter 6. Others think that by this precept, "Let no one look down on you," Paul means this, that rebukes should be made in such a way that no one has an opportunity to despise them, something that may be accomplished when they are made prudently, and one lives piously and leads others by a good example. If this is not done, admonitions and rebukes are spurned by the hearers.

Theological Aphorisms from this Part of the Chapter

1. Only the grace of God brings salvation to men, not the Law, not sacrifices, not anything else. Therefore the grace of God is called salutary (v. 11), and everywhere in Scripture is opposed to works (Rom. 11:6, Eph. 2:8–9, 2 Tim. 1:9). And nothing could be found in man by which God might be moved to restore our nature. Out of grace, then, He had mercy on us, giving us His Son, that He might satisfy divine justice, and in His Son the remission of sins, life, and eternal salvation. This is God's highest benefit, preached everywhere in Scripture, especially John 3:16, Acts 3:26. 4:12, 10:43, Rom. 3:24, 1 John 4:10.

2. That salutary grace of God, which is elsewhere called mercy and the will of God concerning our salvation, having indeed been decreed by God from eternity, was nevertheless hidden from men, and would have been of no use if it had not become known to them. Therefore it appeared in time, first through the incarnation of the Son of God, then

---

252 Basil II Kamateros, Patriarch of Constantinople (1183–86) during the short reign of Byzantine Emperor Andronikos I Komnenos (1183–85).

253 Philippe Camerarius, *operae horarum subcisivarum, sive meditationes historicae* (Frankfurt am Main: Peter Kopf, 1601).

through the preaching of the Gospel in all the world, which is why that incarnation of Christ was named the ἐπιφάνεια (epiphany) in ancient times, and the Gospel was called "the mystery quiet and hidden for eternal times, but now made clear through the writings of the Prophets" (Rom. 16:[25–]26).

3. The benefit of our salvation is universal, for it is said in v. 11 that that salutary grace of God has appeared to all men. For no one was passed over in the counsel of God, who "enclosed all under sin that He might have mercy on all" (Rom. 11[:32]). He also gave His Son to all (John 3:16), and "This is the will of God, that all might be saved and come to the knowledge of the truth" (1 Tim. 2:4). Also, "Christ died for all" (2 Cor. 5:15), for which reason He is called "the Savior of all men" in 1 Timothy 4:10. And so no one has been excluded from this grace, and it has been set forth equally to all, but not all actually come to enjoy it, because they drive that grace away from themselves by their unbelief and obstinate malice. Hence it happens that Scripture sometimes speaks particularly, saying, for example, that Christ died for "many" (Isa. 53:12, Matt. 20:28), or for "the children of God who had been dispersed and must be gathered" (John 11:52), not as if He died for them only, but because they also savingly enjoy the salutary grace that has been offered us through Christ. Thus is he called "the Savior of all men, but especially of the faithful" (1 Tim. 4:10).

4. Exhortation to true piety should be sought not only from the Law, but also from the doctrine of grace, as Paul shows in v. 12. The former should be done principally and directly, because the Law teaches the rule of living; the latter indirectly, because the doctrine of grace shows us the fatherly will of God, and the immense mercy by which He has procured our salvation, for which benefit we therefore, out of gratitude, owe Him everything that is ours, and should accordingly arrange our whole life in such a way as not to be declared unworthy of so much grace. He has loved us, and we should love Him in return. He gave His Son for us, and we should give and consecrate our heart to Him. He has pardoned us all our offenses, and we should pardon our enemies. This is true gratitude for that grace, which otherwise could not be repaid with all the world's treasures.

5. There are two chief springs, as it were, of our corruption: impiety and wickedness (v. 12). One of these is committed against God, the other against our neighbor, and we have rejected both in Baptism, and we should also reject both by daily penitence, and in all things show ourselves to be the kind of people who sin neither against God, nor against the neighbor, nor against ourselves. That is why Paul commands us to live soberly in respect to ourselves, justly in respect to others, and piously in respect to God.[254]

"Constantly ponder these three adverbs within yourself;
Let these three be the fixed rules of your life."[255]

But we are not able to pursue these virtues unless we have bewailed the command because of our prior life, which had been contaminated by sins. From this comes that saying of Gregory, *Moralia* 33, chapter 6,[256] "Except one withdraw from himself to Him who is above himself, he does not draw near; nor can he attain what is beyond himself, if he has not known to sacrifice what is."

6. Our salvation, having certainly been decreed from eternity, was also acquired long ago through the Son, but in this life it is not yet possessed, so what we await is called a "blessed hope" (v. 13). We are also said in Romans 8:24 to be saved by hope. This fact can soothe all the miseries of this present age, for we strive for our fatherland through many dangers, and as Scripture says, "through many tribulations we enter into the kingdom of heaven" (Acts 14:22).[257] Here there is need of patience, "that doing the Lord's will, we might obtain the promise" (Heb. 10:36). But this delay should not be grievous to us, because that hope is blessed and sure, and those who have gone before us as saints,

---

254 This application of the three adverbs to ourselves, others, and God comes from the interlinear gloss for Titus 2:12.

255 These lines are separately indented in the text, clearly meant as a poetic couplet. I have found it quoted in a number of other 17th century books, sometimes with "holy" (*sanctam*) instead of "fixed" (*certam*), but always anonymously.

256 The citation is to Gregory the Great's *Morals in Job*, chapter 33 (of Job), ch. 6. However, the quotation does not appear there, but in his *Homilies on the Gospels* 32.2 (*PL* 75.1234A).

257 The verse says "through many dangers we *must* enter into the kingdom of *God*."

of whom the Apostle has recounted an extensive list in Hebrews 11, have received it. Concerning this hope St. Bernard says in Sermon 9 on that Psalm "He who dwells, *etc.*,"[258] "This is the whole reason of my expectation: whatever must be done, whatever must be borne, whatever must be desired, You are my hope, O Lord. This is my one hope, because of all Your promises; you are my hope, O Lord. Some hope in other things: here, perhaps, in a knowledge of letters, here in the wisdom of the world; that one in nobility, that one in dignity. For Your sake 'I have suffered the loss of all things, and reckon them as dung' [Phil. 3:8], since You are my hope, O Lord. Let him who wishes hope in the uncertainty of riches, but I hope not even for the very necessities of life, unless they are from You. If rewards are promised me, I will hope that they are to be obtained through You. Brothers, know this: to live is from faith."

7. The final coming of Christ is the coming of glory (v. 13), or the glorious coming, because that great God will come with majesty and glory, with many thousands of angels, unto the judgment of all flesh, "to render to each one as he has done in his body" [cf. Matt. 16:27; 2 Cor. 5:10] without respect of persons. Then the impious shall see Him whom they have pierced [*cf.* Zech 12:10], whom they have blasphemed, whom they have persecuted [*cf.* Acts 9:14]. It will be glorious, therefore, for the Elect, who will then lift up their heads because their redemption will draw nigh (Luke 21:28), and they will appear with Christ in glory, judging the world (1 Cor. 6:2), and "will always be with the Lord" (1 Thess. 4:17). But it will be dreadful for the impious; it will be the day of wrath and judgment, for that great God will come and "will bring to light the hidden things of darkness, and will reveal the councils of hearts" (1 Cor. 4:5). Then let us so live in this age that the hope of the age to come might cheer us. Here let us patiently bear dishonor, that when the Lord comes we might enter joyful into glory.

8. Christ our Savior is the great God (v. 13). He is great (1) with respect to His nature, which is above all things, for it created all things and is before all things, (2) with respect to His power, since He alone

---

258 Psalm 91, which begins "He who dwells in the shelter of the Most High...."

is powerful (1 Tim. 6:15). He is the Lord of all, whom the powers of the Angels also serve; "heaven is His throne and earth the footstool of His feet" [Isa. 66:1], "God high-exalted forever" [Daniel 3:52, Apocrypha];[259] (3) with respect to His incarnation, for clearly, "great is the mystery of piety, that God was manifested in the flesh" (1 Tim. 3:16), whence also that Son of Mary is called great (Luke 1:32); (4) with respect to his office, because He is the Savior and Redeemer of our race—there can be no greater work than it—for which no human or angel would have sufficed; but it was for that reason necessary that our Savior be God, because the works of the Devil had to be destroyed and his palace torn down, for which deed one was required who was stronger than the Devil. So let us honor Christ, because He is our Savior. Let us adore Him, because He is God. Let us fear His majesty, because He is great, whom none of the world's power surpasses, at whose name every knee bows (Phil. 2:10), who is glorious and "blessed above all things forever" (Rom. 9:5).

9. The death of Christ was voluntary, because He gave Himself, and meritorious, because He gave Himself for us (v. 14). These two conclusions follow upon each other, for if it had not been voluntary, it also could not have been meritorious, since a compelled worship cannot please God. There is also a distinction between these two things, the death of Christ and the death of the martyrs, who did not turn themselves over to the hands of their enemies, but have often been led by them, in great number, "where they would not," as Christ says of Peter in John 21:18. And much less was their death meritorious, because "a brother does not redeem a brother" (Ps. 49[:7]). Therefore let us magnify the death of Christ, "who has redeemed us from a vain way of life, not by silver or gold, but by His precious blood" (1 Pet. 1[:18]), that we hand our whole selves over to Him, and serve Him in His kingdom. For as Tertullian says in his book *On Flight in Persecution*, "Since the God of might has purchased man from earth—nay from hell—into heaven, who is it that devalues and stains His merchandise, acquired

---

259 *Deus superexaltatus in secula*, from "The Song of the Three Children." Daniel chapter 3 ends at v. 30 in Bibles that lack the Apocrypha.

at so great a price?"²⁶⁰ Let us remember that we are servants, because we have been created, and we are accepted as those who have been redeemed, *etc.*²⁶¹

10. Christians are God's private possession (vv. 1, 14), which as a title was once divinely bestowed on the Israelites (Ex. 19:5). For there was "no other nation so great that it had gods near to them" (Deut. 4:7). Today this title suits Christians, who have been chosen out of all people, whom God "has cleansed from dead works through the blood of His Son" [Heb. 9:14] "that they might follow good works" [Tit. 2:14]. For this reason they are said elsewhere to have been "created in Christ Jesus for good works, that they might walk in them" (Eph. 2:10). This title, then, reminds us of our office, that we might abstain from the world's uncleanness, having been cleansed from these things through Christ; for the private possession of God is pure. And it is usual for us to be in adversities, for we are accustomed to direct a private possession more diligently than the rest of our property, and to beware lest any loss should be suffered, and so also does God have special care for His own. Thus it is said that He has "engraved them into His hands" (Isa. 49:16), out of which no one will snatch them (John 10:28). The consolation in Isaiah 43:1ff. pertains to this.

11. The reproving office in the ministry should not be performed perfunctorily, but with all authority (v. 15) that is, seriously and diligently, without any respect of persons. For although gentleness of speech is commended to ministers elsewhere (2 Tim. 2:24), it does not always find a place with the hearers. Thus it must be tempered with severity, that the Word of the Lord might make it to the heart and the hearers might feel its power. For this reason God Himself commands the Prophet, "Cry out and do not cease" (Isa. 58:1). Elsewhere, Paul wants to ἐπιστομίζειν the adversaries, or to shut their mouth (Tit. 1:11). Christ also wanted His disciples to have not only peace, but also salt

---

260 Chapter 12 (*PL* 2.115A).

261 This etc. suggests that Balduin is still quoting Tertullian, but the last sentence is a loose paraphrase at best. Tertullian does talk here about how we have been redeemed, but not about how we have been created.

(Mark 9:50). For as Theophylact writes on that passage, "Just as salt preserves meat, and does not allow worms to breed, so also the speech of a learned man, if it be vigorous and sharp, constraining carnal men, does not allow the unquiet worm [Mark 9:48] to be generated in them." This is the zeal for God that Paul had in 2 Corinthians 13:2, and that the Son of God commands the angel of the church of Laodicea, who was neither cold nor hot (Rev. 3:16), to put on. By this zeal Polycarp attacked Marcion in Irenaeus, *Against Heresies*, Book 1, chapter 3,[262] and Irenaeus the Valentinians in Book 1, chapter 5,[263] and Jerome Jovinian. The examples of Christ, the Prophets, and the Apostles have been noted, so I pass over these men who are worthy of mention. Therefore they should not be heeded who view that righteous zeal of the doctors of the church as abuse, and who—even in this time and place—use this same label, so that they malign them as loudmouths and railers. In this manner the vehemence of Luther too is criticized, by which he attacked the Roman Babylon, even though it was foretold that Babylon was going to be cast violently into the depths (Rev. 18:21). Also what Aristotle said in book 4 of the *Ethics*, chapter 11,[264] should be generally noted: "The man who has a just reason to be angry, and who is angry with those with whom it is just for a good man to be angry, and who is angry in due measure and duration, his anger deserves praise."

12. It is in the interests of the church that the ministers of the Word should not be despised. Paul therefore closes the chapter in this way: "Let no one look down on you." For one who has been despised in his person usually tolerates contempt of his office along with himself. A minister of the church, then, should teach in such a way that nothing blameworthy presents itself, and also live in such a way that he might not himself be found guilty of those vices that he is beholden to rebuke in others. And he should carry out the correction of other men at the

---

262 Actually book 3: "And Polycarp himself replied to Marcion, who met him on one occasion, and said, 'Do you know me?' 'I do know you, the first-born of Satan'" (*Against Heresies* 3.3.4).

263 All throughout book 1, actually.

264 In modern editions of Aristotle's *Nicomachean Ethics*, the correct citation is book 4, chapter 5.

right time, for untimely speech—even if it is the best speech—causes harm by its insolence; and insolence, if it does not know how to wait for an opportunity, destroys itself by its own baseness in the mind of the hearer," as Gregory says in the second part of his *Pastorale*, chapter 4.[265]

---

265 Gregory the Great, *Pastoral Care* 2.4.

Chapter 3

Argument and Division of the Chapter

The Apostle continues with his admonitions, which he began in the preceding chapter, and in the same way as he previously wrote to Timothy, what one should teach men of different classes. So now he sets forth the things that ought to be made known to all men in general, in order that they might adorn the teaching of the Gospel. Taking this opportunity, he digresses into a brief treatment of the article of the justification of the sinner in the sight of God, comparing the state of men before and after conversion, that he might more easily obtain from the justified works worthy of them. Also he exhorts Titus himself to avoid in his ministry heretics, and the foolishness of useless questions. And so, having appended certain private salutations and pieces of business, he brings this Epistle to a close. There are two parts to the chapter.

In the first, down to verse 9, are contained general precepts for all Christians.

In the second, from verse 9 to the end, are certain special precepts concerning Titus's office and certain of Paul's associates.

The First Part of the Text [Titus 3:1–8]

Ὑπομίμνησκε αὐτοὺς ἀρχαῖς καὶ ἐξουσίαις ὑποτάσσεσθαι, πειθαρχεῖν, πρὸς πᾶν ἔργον ἀγαθὸν ἑτοίμους εἶναι.	1. Admonish them to be subject to dominions and powers, to be obedient to the magistrates, to be prepared for every good work,
Μηδένα βλασφημεῖν, ἀμάχους εἶναι, ἐπιεικεῖς, πᾶσαν ἐνδεικνυμένους πραότητα πρὸς πάντας ἀνθρώπους.	2. to speak evilly of no one, not to be quarrelsome but polite, showing all gentleness to all men.

Ἦμεν γὰρ ποτε καὶ ἡμεῖς ἀνόητοι ἀπειθεῖς πλανώμενοι, δουλεύοντες ἐπιθυμίαις καὶ ἡδοναῖς ποικίλαις, ἐν κακίᾳ καὶ φθόνῳ διάγοντες, στυγητοὶ μισοῦντες ἀλλήλους.

Ὅτε δὲ ἡ χρηστότης καὶ ἡ φιλανθρωπία ἐπεφάνη τοῦ σωτῆρος ἡμῶν Θεοῦ.

Οὐκ ἐξ ἔργων τῶν ἐν δικαιοσύνῃ, ὧν ἐποιήσαμεν ἡμεῖς, ἀλλὰ κατὰ τὸν αὐτοῦ ἔλεον ἔσωσεν ἡμᾶς, διὰ λουτροῦ παλιγγενεσίας καὶ ἀνακαινώσεως πνεύματος ἁγίου.

Οὗ ἐξέχεεν ἐφ' ἡμᾶς πλουσίως, διὰ Ἰησοῦ Χριστοῦ τοῦ σωτῆρος ἡμῶν.

Ἵνα δικαιωθέντες τῇ ἐκείνου χάριτι, κληρονόμοι γινώμεθα κατ' ἐλπίδα ζωῆς αἰωνίου.

Πιστὸς ὁ λόγος, καὶ περὶ τούτων βούλομαί σε διαβεβαιοῦσθαι, ἵνα φροντίζωσι καλῶν ἔργων προΐστασθαι οἱ πεπιστευκότες τῷ θεῷ, ταυτά ἐστι τὰ καλὰ καὶ ὠφέλιμα τοῖς ἀνθρώποις.

Notes in text.[266]

3. For at one time, we too were fools, disobedient, erring, enslaved to various desires and lusts, passing our time in malice and envy, hateful, and pursuing hatred in return.

4. But afterwards appeared the goodness and love of God our Savior towards men.

5. Not out of works that we have done, works that comport with righteousness, but according to His mercy He saved us, through the bath of regeneration and of the renewal of the Holy Spirit,

6. Whom He poured out upon us richly through Jesus Christ our Savior,

7. so that having been justified by His grace, we might be made heirs according to the hope of eternal life.

8. It is a sure saying. And I want you to confirm them in regard to these things, that those who have believed in God might be careful to excel in good works, for these are honorable and useful to men.

---

[266] Verse 2 (English): Or "to curse" (*male dicant*).

Analysis and Explanation of the First Part

There are three general precepts in the first part. The first is that obedience must be rendered to the magistrate: "Admonish them to be subject to dominions and powers," to obey what is said, "to be prepared for every good work" (v. 1). This precept is frequently inculcated by Christ and the Apostles. Christ says, "Render to Caesar what things are Caesar's" (Matt. 22:21). The Apostle Paul says, "Let every soul be subject to the higher powers" (Rom. 13:1), and in this passage, "Admonish them to be subject to the powers." St. Peter says, "Be subject to every human creation for God's sake, *etc.*" (1 Pet. 2:13). The reason for this precept is twofold: (1) because at the beginning of the church, that is, at the time of Christ and the Apostles, there was a rumor that the teaching of the Gospel abolishes states and secular powers, and introduces licentious living, especially because they heard the Apostles teaching that "We must obey God rather than men" [Acts 5:29]. Clement of Alexandria may be read concerning this rumor, in book 4 of the *Stromateis*, and Augustine in his 31st Sermon on Psalm 118. (2) because in those times the sect of the seditious [followers] of Judas of Galilee and Theudas, of whom mention is made in Acts 5, was still active. They did not want a Christian to submit to a Gentile magistrate, saying that no one should be called "Lord" except God alone, and that those who brought tithes to the Temple should not render tribute to Caesar. This sect was so strong that it troubled the Pharisees also, who referred this question to the Lord, whether it is allowable to give tribute to Caesar (Matt. 22:17). Concerning these seditious men, see Josephus, *Antiquities*, Book 18, chapter 1. They were so strong that they could in no way be brought to call Caesar "Lord," for which reason also, when their leader was Eleazar, they did not allow themselves to be enrolled and counted in the census by Cyrenius, the governor of Syria, lest they should seem to be subjected to Caesar, as the same Josephus recounts in Book 7 of the *Jewish Wars*, chapters 28 and 29.[267] Therefore, since the Apostles were Jews,

---

267 Josephus mentions this occurrence in 7.8.1, which is the 29th section in Book 7, but he is talking about something that happened when Eleazar's ancestor Judas

and Christ also taken for a Galilaean, they spoke quite frequently about the subjection that Christians owed to the political magistrate, lest they should be thought to be tied to the sect of the Galilaeans. And Jerome has this reason for the Apostolic precept in his Commentary on this passage. So Paul wants Titus to give admonitions—in the Greek that is ὑπομίμνῃσκε, suggest and recall to their memory—because the license that exempts the mind of man from all restraints of the laws is pleasing to the flesh, and easily stifles the obedience that is owed to one's superiors. Therefore he should suggest to them that they should remember that it is right that they be subject to dominions and powers—in the Greek they are called ἀρχαὶ καὶ ἐξουσίαι, where the abstract is put for the concrete, as in Romans 13:1, Ephesians 3:10 and 6:12, Colossians 1:16, 2:10 and 15, *etc.* Now the Apostle wanted to use abstract language for this reason: that in this obedience, respect might be given not so much to the personage who carries out the magistracy, as to his office, which he has from God, and the obedience might become readier. That is why St. Peter commands them to be subject for God's sake (1 Pet. 2:13). Now, he expresses the obedience of the subjects by means of two terms, seeing as he wants them to ὑποτάσσεσθαι (be subject) and to πειθαρχεῖν (obey). The former term is general and signifies subjection, but even the subjection by which private persons submit themselves to one another for the sake of moderation, as in Ephesians 5:21, "ὑποταζόμενοι ἀλλήλοις ἐν φόβῳ θεοῦ" ("submitting to one another in the fear of God"). The latter term signifies the obedience owed τοῖς ἄρχουσι, or to superiors, to the magistrate and princes. He restricts this obedience to a certain kind of work, namely what is honorable, pious, and pleasing to God; thus he adds, "prepared for every good work." He indicates two things here. One of them pertains to the form of obedience: it should be free, not coerced, for he wants us to be *prepared*. The other pertains to the matter, for he wants us to be prepared *for every good work*. Indeed, it is not permissible to prepare for impious works, but God must be obeyed rather than the magistrate when the One forbids, and the

---

was leading them, not when Eleazar was. Later in 7.10.1, Josephus tells how captured Zealots could not be induced even by tortures to call Caesar "Lord."

other commands the same thing. The second precept (v. 2) is that no one should be cut apart by reproaches: "To blaspheme[268] no one," the Apostle says; that is, "Admonish them to blaspheme no one." Βλασφημεῖν means in general "to disparage" and "to detract from someone's reputation," or even "to curse," for the word comes Ἀπὸ τοῦ βλάπτειν τὴν φημήν, from fame being damaged, and it is ordinarily applied to God or to religion, when something is cursed, against which the Law considers it sin [to speak] (Lev. 24:15). Sometimes it is also used concerning disparagement of the ministers of the Word, as in Romans 3:8 and 1 Corinthians 4:13, for whoever curses them, sins against God Himself. In this passage, it is applied in the most general sense to all creatures, who should not be cursed. In the same way, the Angel Michael did not want to curse even the Devil himself as he disputed concerning the body of Moses, as appears in the Epistle of Jude, verse 9, because it was not fitting that a curse[269] should proceed through the mouth of an angel. Such is Jerome's opinion on this passage. But one especially should not curse the magistrate, to whom some specifically restrict this precept. For it is written in the Law, "You shall not curse the prince of your people" (Ex. 22:28). The third precept is "Not to be someone who has to be quarreled with, but one who should bear injuries with gentleness; not to be litigious," the Apostle says, "but moderate, showing all gentleness to every man" (v. 2). He repeats the same precept in Romans chapter 12, verses 17–18: "repaying no man evil for evil; having peace with all men, if it can be done." So he wants contentions to be entirely absent from Christians, to whom he proposes gentleness, which pardons a neighbor his injuries and puts up with evil and unpleasant things. This gentleness ought to show itself to everyone, even to the pugnacious and the peevish, whom one should overcome with mildness, for anyone can boast of his gentleness as long as he lives among

---

268 Balduin is now using the Vulgate rendering, which uses the borrowed Latin form of the Greek verb instead of translating it, as he has done above.

269 Here and throughout, the words "curse" and "cursing" are used to translate various forms of *maledico* and *maledictio*, which mean broadly "evil speaking; malediction," a word broader than the modern English concept of a specific set of "curse words."

agreeable and upright people, friends of peace, but to be able to bear with the contentious, lest we should be implicated in their quarrels, is the mark of the man who is gentle and patient in injuries. And this is what "to show gentleness toward all men" means: not only to claim great patience with the mouth, while no one is harming us yet, but also to declare it against the wicked—what it is—by means of the thing itself, when we do not fight with curses. But even when we are walking according to our Law, we "bless those who curse" us, something that Christ also wanted (Luke 6:28). These were general precepts. Now he adds a most important reason from the comparison of our status before and after conversion has been sought. Because we have been reborn from God, the old man having truly been put to death, because we have been redeemed and justified through Christ, it is entirely right that we should earnestly devote ourselves to genuine piety, and keep all the works of the old man far away from us. But first he describes the condition of men who have not yet been converted, so far as they might be considered in their nature. He says, "For we were also once foolish, unbelieving, erring, serving various desires and lusts, acting in malice and envy, hateful, and hating each other" (v. 3). These words have the appearance of anticipation. For the Christians would have been able to say, "How many men with whom we must live are coarse, quarrelsome, and wicked, excepting not even the magistrate," who was a pagan in those days, harsh and peevish enough. "How then is it right for us to be gentle? How can we avoid quarrels?" Paul answers that they should not begin quarrels, but should remember their former condition, when they had not yet been converted, which was no better than those whom they should patiently bear until they too might be led to the bosom of the church, toward which state they might be able to advance them by their mildness and gentleness. Now Paul includes himself: "*We* were once," describing his condition before he was converted, which was no better than other men, even though he had been of great authority among the Pharisees. But he depicts the nature of corrupt man, as pertains to the understanding as much as to the will. To the understanding pertains what he says, "We were [1] foolish," ἀνόητοι, corrupted with respect to the mind, or mad, understanding nothing about

Titus 3

divine matters, (2) "unbelieving," ἀπειθεῖς, unpersuadable, whom the truth can in no way persuade; elsewhere they are called υἱοὶ τῆς ἀπειθείας (sons of disobedience, Eph. 2:2), (3) "erring," πλανώμενοι, led around by many and vagrant errors. To the will pertains what he says, (1) "We were serving various desires and lusts," something that has reference to the internal motions of the mind, for depraved desires occupy the heart, and they are said to serve them who indulge and relax the reins so that they delight the heart and court destruction, so the unregenerate are called slaves of sin (Rom. 6:16). (2) "Acting in malice and envy, hateful and hating each other," these things have reference to external acts. For when depraved desires break out, malice must come to pass, and when this is combined with προαιρέσει (purpose) and seeks the neighbor's harm, its distinguishing feature is envy, which is sad on account of others' happiness. The fruit of this is that such malicious men both hate others, whom they ought to have loved, and make themselves worthy of hatred. This is a description of corrupted nature, which has been healed by God, concerning which things Paul says, "But when the goodness and kindness of God our Savior appeared, not from works of righteousness that we have done, but according to His mercy He saved us, through the bath of regeneration and the renewal of the Holy Spirit" (v. 4–5). This is an outstanding passage, which deals summarily with the whole business of our salvation. God the Father is the Efficient Cause, for He is called "God our Savior," as in 1 Timothy 1:1 and 1 Samuel 14:39, Isaiah 45:15, Hosea 13:4, and everywhere in the Scripture of the Old Testament, where even our temporal salvation is said to be received from God the Father; now here, the eternal salvation of our souls is ascribed to Him. For our salvation is from Him, who was the first of all to be concerned about it, because among the creatures, no one was giving thought to it. Bernard refers these words to Christ, in whose humanity, or advent into the flesh, that goodness of God shined forth. "Before He had appeared," he says, "His power was apparent in the creation of things, and His wisdom in their governance, but the goodness of His mercy now appeared to the greatest degree in His humanity," *Sermon 1 on the Lord's birth*, and again, "Before His humanity had appeared, His goodness was hidden, since it existed also beforehand, for 'The mercy of the Lord is even from everlasting' [Ps. 102:17a]," *Sermon 1 on the Epiphany*. All of these things are indeed true, but do not pertain to Paul's meaning, for he is not dealing with Christ's human nature here, but with the φιλανθρωπία (kindliness) of God. He is speaking not of Christ but of God the Father, concerning whom he says a little while later that He has poured out the Holy Spirit upon us through Christ (v. 6). The προκαταρκτικὴ (predisposing) cause that impelled God to save us is expressed in these three terms here: goodness, kindness, and mercy. He calls the goodness that he writes has appeared χρηστότητα (goodness). For God was by nature the *best*, and has remained such eternally, even as all men pass away; but He was such within Himself, and thus His goodness was hidden, as it were. But that we too might be certain of it, He willed to share it with us, and to bring it out into the open light by that splendid work of redemption and of our salvation. By this word is also indicated in God a ready desire for our salvation, who in none of His other works was more eager. For "all goodness makes haste, and it is characteristic of one who acts freely, to act quickly," says Seneca[270] in book 2, *On Benefits*, chapter 5. He calls the kindness φιλανθρωπίαν (philanthropy, love for mankind), which Jerome translates "clemency," for that love of God is immense and ineffable, which moved Him to take thought for our restoration—the severity of His justice having been relaxed, according to which all of us had to perish—and to assign us, who were worthy of eternal death, to eternal salvation. From here on, he expresses these two things by means of the one word "mercy," which presupposes the miseries of men, into which they have fallen on account of sin; for we are accustomed to pity the miserable. Now, these causes of our salvation having been laid down, he removes all our works, not only the ones that are done by the unregenerate, but also the works of the righteous. "Not from works of righteousness," he says, "that we have done, but according to His mercy," *etc*. In the business of our salvation, then, these things are opposites: the mercy or grace of God, and our works, even though no good work could be done in us otherwise, without the

---

270 Seneca the Younger, *De beneficiis*.

grace of God. The Instrumental Cause, for God's part, is baptism, which is, as it were, the first door to salvation, or as the ancients called it, the first gate of grace.

It is called "the bath of regeneration and of renewal in the Holy Spirit." It is a *bath* because in baptism, by Christ's institution, we are sprinkled with water that is sacramentally united with the blood of Christ, and thus we are cleansed in the conscience from dead works (Heb. 9:14). For it pleased the eternal God to offer and apply to us through baptism as much as through the Word, the death of His Son for the remission of sins. It is the bath *of regeneration* because there we are reborn as children of God (John 3:5), *and of renewal* because the righteousness and holiness lost through Adam's Fall is restored in the baptized, not by the power of the water in itself, but "in the Holy Spirit," who has been joined with this water, and who is poured out upon the baptized in this holy action.

For the Holy Spirit is given to them, He who kindles faith, generates new motions, and makes them prepared for every good work. Now he uses the term "poured out" of the Holy Spirit, using the prophetic phrasing of Isaiah 44:3, Joel 2:28, and Zechariah 12:10, on account of the abundance and sweetness of the Holy Spirit's gifts in the reborn. For He works in them faith and the knowledge of the true God, an understanding of divine mysteries. He teaches them to pray and kindles an ardor for prayers. He gives holy desires, lavishes patience in adversities, confirms and seals the promises of grace within us, increases and preserves the hope of eternal life, *etc.* So the Apostle set up baptism as the ordinary instrument of our salvation, whence Christ says, "Unless a man shall have been reborn from water and the Spirit, he will not be able to enter the kingdom of heaven" (John 3[:5]). The Meritorious Cause of our salvation is Christ, for "God poured out the Holy Spirit upon us through Christ Jesus our Savior" (v. 6). Apart from Christ, God could neither have pitied us, nor regenerated us, nor given the Holy Spirit, because there had to be someone who could quench God's wrath, aroused by our sins—something no one but Christ could do. This is why He said to the disciples, "Unless I depart to the Father, the Holy Spirit will not come to you, but if I do depart, I will send Him to you" (John 16:7). This was accomplished not only when He visibly poured the Holy Spirit out upon the Apostles, after His ascension into heaven, but also happens daily in baptism,[271] where we put on Christ and are filled again with His Spirit, as it is written: "Since you are sons, God has sent the Spirit of His Son into our hearts, crying 'Abba, Father'" (Gal. 4:6). Now where Christ is, there also is faith, without which Christ is of no benefit to us; and so the Instrumental Cause, for our part, is included at the same time.[272] Finally, the Final Cause is expressed in verse 7: "that having been justified by His grace, we might be made heirs according to hope." Three things are conjoined here as synonyms: (1) the salvation from which He saved us, verse 5 above; (2) Justification; (3) the inheritance of eternal life. First among these terms is Justification, which is nothing else than absolution from sins and the donation of Christ's righteousness. Next is salvation, which we obtain even in this life, but not yet by full possession, "for we are saved by hope" (Rom. 8:24) and we do not yet "walk by sight, but by faith" (2 Cor. 5:7). And in this text of ours, we are said "to be made heirs according to the hope of eternal life." "For we are children of God already, but what we will be has not yet appeared" (1 John 3:2). "Now if we are sons, we are heirs" (Rom. 8:17). But full possession of this inheritance is the final complement of this benefaction that is so great, and it follows at length, in the other age, when "God will be all in all" [1 Cor. 15:28], "and we will always be with the Lord" [1 Thess. 4:17]. All these things, therefore, are removed from our works and ascribed to the grace and mercy of God, and from this passage we are able to put together what the grace of God *is* to the Apostle Paul in the article of Justification—namely, not a free gift of God *in us*, or a disposition (*habitus*) of righteousness

---

271 Balduin seems to be speaking here not of new baptisms, though doubtless they were being performed every day, but rather of the daily remembrance of our past baptism, as per Luther in the Small Catechism: "What does such baptizing with water indicate? It indicates that the old Adam in us should by daily contrition and repentance be drowned and die with all sins and evil desires, and that a new man should daily emerge and arise to live before God in righteousness and purity forever."

272 At the same time as the Meritorious Cause, that is.

poured freely into us, as the Esauites[273] explain it, but the very mercy of God, the φιλανθρωπία (philanthropy, love of mankind) and free favor by which He embraced the human race in Christ, for these four terms, goodness, φιλανθρωπία, mercy, and grace, are conjoined in this text as synonyms, as that singular cause that moved God to embrace the human race after the Fall. This, then, is a description of our status after conversion: full of righteousness, life, and salvation. But because this salvation is hidden under the cloud and gloom of so many of this world's calamities, he therefore asserts the truth of this teaching with great vehemence: "It is a faithful saying," he says, "and I want to confirm you concerning these things, that those who believe God might be careful to excel in good works. These are good and useful for men" (v. 8). He calls it a πιστὸν λόγον (faithful word), about which it would not be right to doubt, just as in 1 Timothy 1:15, "a faithful saying, and most worthy of all acceptance," and Apocalypse (Revelation) 21:5, the words of God are called "faithful," and "the promises made to David" are called "holy and faithful" in Acts 13:34. The Greek word πίστος (faithful) corresponds to the Hebrew באמר or נוס, which the Prophets use when they set forth an oracle of God as worthy of all faith, as in "*Neum adonai*," that is, "The Lord says," or rather "the most-true saying of the Lord," for the learned judge that this word, where it is found, should be explained not so much as a verb, but as a noun, as with Isaiah 1:24, "Therefore says (*Neum*) the Lord," *etc.* So they translate, "Therefore a certain saying of the Lord *Iehova* ...," and they consider this word to be assigned, in the Scriptures, only to God and to men who are divinely inspired. Opposed to this word among the Hebrews is כזב, "false" in Jeremiah 15:18: "You will be to me as false waters, not faithful." Now it can be observed that this term πιστὸς λόγος is used by Paul several times, yet in such a way that in the other places the affirmation precedes the things affirmed, as in 1 Timothy 1:15, 1 Timothy 3:1, and 2 Timothy 2:11. But in our text it comes afterwards, for the

---

273 *Esauitae*, meaning "those who have sold their birthright, like Esau," that birthright being the pure promise of the gospel. The term was derogatory, referring often to the Jesuits (*Jesuitae*).

Apostle writes that what he had said about the hope of eternal life is certain and indubitable. And he orders Titus to confirm, or inculcate, this in his hearers, that they might not become sluggish in the way of good works, but might press on vigorously, knowing for certain that an abundant recompense has been prepared in heaven for their labors and calamities. In this way, they will judge that their faith is life, and will be able to serve their neighbor usefully.

Questions from this Part of the Chapter

Question 1

In verse 2, the Apostle wants us "to blaspheme no one." Has all blasphemy and cursing been prohibited, then?

Answer: In his commentary, Jerome understands the Apostle's words in the most general way. "Blaspheme no one," he says, "is not taken simply, for he does not say, 'blaspheme no man,' but absolutely 'no one.' Not an angel, not any creature of God. Indeed, all things that have been made by God are very good."[274] Indeed, these things are most true, but because we find in Scripture that both God and man have cursed others, the matter must be handled with distinctions. Blasphemy or cursing, in general, is some kind of disparagement or injury of the reputation, which is both why it has that name in Greek, and why it is applied either to God, or to religion, or to the Word of God, or to men, or to angels, or to other creatures. Sometimes it is used lawfully and without sin by God and men, but other times it is unlawfully used by men. The lawful cursing is that which arises from righteous indignation and the punishment of those to whom punishment is applicable, and it never fails to have its effect. Thus God cursed the earth on account of fallen man (Gen. 3:17), which curse is nothing else than the privation of spontaneous fertility and the invocation of unfruitfulness upon the hardest labor of man. He repeated a curse of this kind on ac-

---

274 Jerome, *Commentary on Titus*, PL 26.591CD.

count of the extreme malice of His people (Ps. 107:34). He appointed the fruitful land to bloodshed on account of the malice of those who lived in it. Also Isaiah 24:6, "On account of these things, a curse will devour the land"—specifically on account of adultery. Jeremiah 23:10, "Because the land is full of adultery, the land has mourned in the face of the curse, and the fields have become deserts," etc. In general, God curses all transgressors of the Law (Deut. 27:15ff). But although God sharpens the Sword of punishment with the oil of His mercy, He thereupon tempers this curse also with a blessing, which is why the earth is said to be full of God's mercy (Ps. 33:5). Therefore the ministers of the Word, because they are God's ambassadors, can also lawfully curse the wicked—especially the Prophets and Apostles, whose curses are frequently predictions and omens, which of course desire nothing evil, but also portend nothing good, if the impious persist in their malice. Concerning them Augustine writes in book 5, Against Faustus the Manichee, chapter 22, "Curses, when they are spoken from prophecy, are not from the bad desire of one who is invoking evil, but from the prescient spirit of one who is making an announcement." Thus David said from the Prophetic Spirit, Psalm 6[:10], "Let all my enemies blush and be violently confounded," etc. Peter cursed Simon Magus: "Let your money go with you into perdition" (Acts 8:20). Paul curses all generally who do not love Jesus Christ (1 Cor. 16:22). And this curse is from righteous zeal against the enemies of God. Other ministers too, if by reason of their office they say something very harsh against the wicked, are cursing lawfully. Their curse is not so much an invocation of evil as a just announcement of the penalties; not that the sinners might perish, but that they might be corrected, having been frightened. Parents can even curse their children, as Noah cursed Ham and his son from his paternal power (Gen. 9:25), and the righteous curses of parents against their unworthy children are not usually fruitless. "A father's blessing makes firm the houses of his children, but a mother's curse razes the foundations" (Sirach 3[:9]). An unlawful curse is one that is brought against God or creatures either from impiety, or from impatience, or from wrath, or even from perverse custom. They curse from impiety who utter anything abusive against God, and this can be done three ways: (1) when something is attributed to God that does not fit Him, as when He is said to be the cause of sin, or when He is imagined to be corporeal and mortal, as the Gentiles gossip about their gods. (2) When something that is owed to God is denied, as when His providence, justice, mercy, omnipotence, or truth is denied. To this also pertains the security of the impious, who live day to day, and say in their heart, "There is no God" (Ps. 14:1), by whose impiety the name of God is blasphemed among the Gentiles (Isa. 52:5, Rom. 2:24). They deny God by their deeds, as if He neither saw their works, nor could punish them. (3) When something that is a proper trait of God alone is attributed to a creature—as it is to scrutinize the heart, to know future things, to adore or to call upon in need, and similar things, which are not attributed to creatures without blasphemy. Next, they curse God from impiety who speak against His Word, calling it into doubt or denying it, either in whole or in part, either willingly or out of fear or seduction; who care for no religion, who do not want to acknowledge the truth made known in the Word, who behave insolently to the ministers of the Word and persecute them, even if it is done under the supposition and from the pretext of a singular zeal and of the worship of God. And this is properly the sin of blasphemy, that which is brought against the Word and true religion; and it is divided by Christ Himself into blasphemy against the Son and blasphemy against the Holy Spirit (Matt. 12:32). It is called blasphemy against the Son when someone rejects the teaching of the Gospel concerning Christ when it has not yet been rightly understood, or attacks it—even with hostility—and blasphemes, either ignorant or not yet convicted of the truth in his conscience, the way Paul was a blasphemer before his conversion (1 Tim. 1[:13]), and the way many in the time of Christ who were offended by the lowliness of His person and way of life, either did not attach themselves to Christ, or separated themselves from Him. To this class pertain also those who, driven by the experience of torments, blaspheme acknowledged truth, such as those were whom Paul compelled to blaspheme when he was still the ravager of the churches (Acts 26:11). It is blasphemy against the Holy Spirit when someone is not ignorant of the teaching of the Gospel, but although he has been convicted of its certainty through the Holy Spirit, denies, rejects, attacks and blasphemes; and it is by far the greatest sin, which Christ says is unforgivable, on account of the adherent hardening that makes it so that sinners of this kind do not want to return, and because they attack the Gospel of Christ with hostility, and by that very act reject the means of remission, and expel all the grace of God. Christ expressly calls this sin blasphemy (Matt. 12:31, Mark 3:28, Luke 12:10), and Heb. 10:29 says that such people greatly ἐνυβρίζειν (mock) "the Spirit of grace" with an insult, or treat Him with contempt. Next, they curse God out of impiety who blaspheme His works,[275] like those who teach that some men have been made for damnation, who find something lacking in the creatures, although God has made all things very good (Gen. 1:31); who slander the governance of all things, the temper of the weather, the arrangement or kinds of life among men; who call into doubt the care of the human race and of all things, although the marvelous wisdom of God shines forth in all these things; finally, who conclude from the punishments with which God afflicts men by His righteous judgment, that He hates them—as the Babylonians were concluding from the captivity of the Israelite people, and were profaning this holy name of God itself, saying, "That is the People of God, and they have gone out from His land." So the Lord promises liberation, in order that His great name, which had been profaned among the Gentiles, might be sanctified (Ezek. 36:21–23). From that impiety also flow things evilly said against parents, teachers, magistrates, and any of the ministers of God, in whom God Himself is blasphemed, in whose place they are acting. Thus Paul writes that he himself is being blasphemed by the Pseudo-apostles, who are accusing him as if he was teaching us to do evil that good might result (Rom. 3:8).

To this also pertain the hearers' perverse judgments about their teachers, which have the semblance of a curse, concerning which Paul deals in 1 Corinthians 4:3. Now this is a great sin, concerning which

---

275 A note begins here in the left margin: "Requirements of sin against the Holy Spirit: (1) in doctrine, (2) in the doctrine of the gospel, (3) knowledge of the doctrine, (4) rejection of the same, (5) the will rejects, (6) hostile attacking and cursing."

the Lord says in Leviticus 20:9, "He who curses father or mother shall die the death." Then also, a curse may be made out of impatience, when someone who is wearied by evils utters violent reproaches against himself or his ancestors, the way Job cursed the day on which he was born (Job 3[:3]), and Jeremiah (20:14[–15]) cursed not only the day of his birth, but even the one who announced it; the way many even now, broken by toils and hardships, desire things of which they afterwards repent. For curses of this kind pertain to the infirmity of the flesh, which of course does not please God, but He patiently tolerates it, and lavishly bestows the strength to overcome. Many curse out of wrath, who invoke the wounds of Christ, the sacraments, and other things against their neighbor, polluting themselves with a double sin, for (1) they are blaspheming Christ Himself, (2) they want to bend to destruction for others the thing by which their salvation has been acquired, a crime more grave than any other. To this pertain all those imprecations that tend to the ruin of one's neighbor, who is betrayed, to the extent that he is in these impious curses, to be taken into the power of the Devil. These kinds of curses almost always spring from angry men, in whom the wrath is a brief fury, for which reason we must learn to govern both our emotions (*affectus*) and our tongue, "for the wrath of man does not produce things that are right in the sight of God" (Jas. 1[:20]). "Where the sinner's state of mind (*affectus*) is unknown, there can be no just reason for cursing," Origen says, *Homily 15 on Numbers*. But a man cannot know another man's state of mind (*affectus*), nor whether he has been cursed by God. "How, then, may I curse one whom the Lord has not cursed?" (Num. 23:8). Yet often such a thing is done by habit, even from childhood, the kind of curses that are usual for many men, who for that reason eventually become desensitized themselves. Now, although this is also a great sin, it still attains pardon, because it has been joined with penitence and the earnest desire to abstain in the future. Finally, it can happen that curses are directed at irrational creatures, or even the devil himself. In this kind too, emotion (*affectus*) must be moderated and the tongue governed, for every creature of God is good in itself, even if it becomes harmful to us on account of malice that comes from elsewhere and has been added to it. "It is useless to curse a creature that does not exist, and vicious if it does exist," Gregory says, book 4 of *Morals*, chapter 3.[276] From this, Thomas writes, Question 76 of the Second Part, Article 2,[277] "To curse irrational things is the sin of blasphemy, insofar as they are creatures of God; but to curse them as considered according to themselves, is useless and vain, and consequently unlawful." Christ cursed the fig tree (Matt. 21:19), David the mountains of Gilboa (2 Sam. 1:21), Job the time or day of his birth (Job 3[:3]), but none of these examples should be imitated. For Christ cursed the fig tree not as a creature of God, but by way of a parable to signify Judah being cast aside through Christ. For as Bede writes on Mark chapter 11, in the same way the Lord said many things in parables, so He was also accustomed to do many things in parables.[278] See also: Augustine, book 2 of *Questions on the Gospels*, chapter 68,[279] and *Sermon 74, De Tempore*; Gregory, book 8, Letter 42. Others say that the fig tree was so cursed because it was the tree of the transgression, the leaves of which they used to cover the body of the first-formed woman.[280] This is the opinion of Athanasius, Question 22,[281] and of Isidore of Pelusium, book 1, Letter 51 to Theopompus.[282] But this should not be imitated by us. David cursed the mountains

---

276 Gregory the Great, *Morals in Job* 4.2 (*PL* 75.634C). Balduin is citing chapter 2 of Gregory's book 4, which is commenting on chapter 3 of Job. He has also reversed the halves of the sentence.

277 Thomas Aquinas, *Summa Theologica* II-II. Q76. A2.

278 Bede on Mark 11:13 in the Ordinary Gloss: "As He speaks through parables, so He acts." ("*Sicut per parabolas loquitur, ita facit*," a much leaner version of Balduin's *Quomodo Dominus multa in parabolis dicebat, ita & multa in parabolis facere solebat*).

279 Chapter 51 by today's numeration.

280 In other words, Adam and Eve used fig leaves to clothe the nakedness of Eve, which according to one traditional interpretation of Gen. 3 was the occasion of the first sin. This opinion also assumes that the tree of the knowledge of good and evil was a fig tree, Adam and Eve grabbing the foliage that was nearest and handiest when "their eyes were opened."

281 A short work of Athanasius survives called *Questions on the Gospels*, but Question 22 concerns the reconciliation of Matthew and Mark on the crowing of the cock when Peter denied Jesus.

282 Isidore of Pelusium, d. 450, an Egyptian anchorite who wrote many letters to contemporaries (see *Patrologia Graeca*, vol. 78).

of Gilboa, Job the day of his birth, and both out of great grief, which David had on account of Saul and Jonathan having been slain on those mountains, and Job on account of his calamities and domestic evils. It seemed to him as though he had been born to them. But both men sinned, and so these examples should not draw us to imitation, for one must use God's creatures with thanksgiving, and if anything happens with them that could harm us, it must be borne patiently, for all the guilt is ours, not the creatures'. We repay both the time and all the negative things in time with our sins. "The creation has been subjected to vanity, not willingly, but on account of the one who subjected it" (Rom. 8:20) and the one who subjected it is God, who since He was going to punish man, allowed creation, which had been made for man's use, to be harmful. So it is not lawful to curse even the Devil, which they do who (1) having been caught in some malice, assign all the blame to the Devil, by whom they supposedly were seduced. But "when the impious man curses the Devil, he curses his own soul" (Sir. 21:30), no doubt because he is an imitator of the Devil. (2) They curse the Devil who execrate him on account of the malice that he performs in the world. But although he is in every way deserving of execration, and his works especially are accursed, still the pious man, as much as is in him, will hold his tongue, lest he should utter some curse. In this way even "Michael the Archangel, when contending with the Devil about the body of Moses, did not dare to produce a judgment of blasphemy, but said, 'The Lord rebuke you,'" as the Epistle of Jude testifies in verse 9. This was done for this reason, that a curse ought not to have come through an angel's mouth, as Jerome writes on our text. That is so, and it does not befit the Christian children of God to curse others. From this it is understood in what way it has been prohibited by our Paul to blaspheme[283] anyone.

Question 2

How could Paul be "foolish, unbelieving, erring, acting in malice and envy," as he writes in verse 3, though elsewhere he reports that he had

---

283 That is, revile.

been "educated according to the truth of the fathers' Law" and had "lived without blame according to the righteousness that is in the Law" (Acts 22:3, Phil. 3:6)?

Answer: Jerome proposes this question in his commentary, where he refers those words to the person of Paul alone, and answers that before the advent and passion of the Savior, the Jews had some partial righteousness, as Simeon and Anna were discovered in the temple, but after the passion, when they had cried out "Crucify, we have no king but Caesar, let his blood be upon us and our children," *etc.*, the Kingdom of God was taken away from them and from this time, the one who does not believe in Christ has been a fool, wandering about, unbelieving, serving various lusts, and so Paul was a fool too, because he had zeal without knowledge, persecuting the Church and taking letters against those who were absent, and devastating the disciples of Christ everywhere, from which fact his malice and envy could not have been greater; for he did not want to be saved, and for the rest, those who could be saved, he envied, hated the Christians, and deserved hatred from all.[284] By this sentence, Jerome solves this question. But although we do not need to refer these words only to Paul, still we can in no way exclude him from the number of those whom he describes there, because the natural corruption of all men is here described in general. And so a distinction must be made between the natural and spiritual powers of man: the former have to do with matters pertaining to this life, the latter with the business of our salvation. Insofar as civil and natural matters are concerned, something of the image of God still remains to man, since there is a kind of spark of concreated light in the mind, by which he perceives the arts and sciences, devises many things ingeniously, and arrives at apt conclusions through discursive reason, distinguishes honorable things from disgraceful ones, is zealous for justice, establishes laudable rules of custom, the laws and statutes of the Republic, and dictates rewards for those who observe the laws and penalties for those who transgress them. In all these things, men have

---

284 Jerome, *Commentary on Titus*, 3:3 (*PL* 26.593AB).

not naturally been considered ἀνόητοι (irrational), but Paul attributed σοφίαν (wisdom) to them (1 Cor. 1:21), and Sirach says, "Everyone is wise in his own art" (Sir. 38:35). Luther also writes of them in chapter 2 of Galatians, "There are natural things unimpaired in man, but which natural things? That man," he says, "although sunk in impiety and a slave of the Devil, has reason, will, and free choice, and the power of building a house and of carrying out a magistracy, of steering a ship, and of performing other offices that have been subjected to man. These things have not been taken away from man, nor indeed have begetting, the state, or the economy been removed by these sayings, but confirmed."[285] Thus far, Luther. But God wanted to confer these gifts upon the unfaithful: (1) that they should understand that there is some God from whom all good things proceed, (2) on account of the public good, that they should live peacefully and piously among themselves, (3) that if they should not use these things rightly, they should be ἀναπολόγητοι (without excuse). Thus Paul learned good doctrines also before his conversion, and having been taught, went forth and followed the Law of Moses, and ordered his life according to it; but all these things accomplished nothing towards salvation, and nothing towards a perfect knowledge of the mysteries of God. For those natural powers are very weak and imperfect in those who have not been reborn, nor are actions performed by them, clearly, without all the help of God, who as the First and Universal Beginning, by means of the operations of nature and voluntary actions,[286] preserves the things themselves, moves their actions, and disposes the means and finally the outcome by His divine ordination. This is why even the Gentiles have sought wisdom from God, and the success of their counsels and actions, and Solomon too sought political prudence (1 Kings 3), and it cannot be denied that even eminent artists have been inspired by a special kind of divine breath for devising and adorning

---

285 Comment on Gal. 2:20, cf. *AE* 26:174.

286 Meaning the voluntary actions of created wills, which here are paired with "the operations of nature" so that created means are divided into involuntary and voluntary, but both are used by the over-ruling will of God.

works of art, something that is expressly written of Bezaleel and Aholiab in Exodus 31:2 and 35[:34], and of the workmen in general, in Isaiah 54:16. Whence God also compares Himself to a workman, and men to the saw that is pulled by the workman (Is. 10:15). Also the outcome and the success of counsels and actions are not in our power, but are governed by God. If He does not furnish sound counsels and bring them to pass, what is written in Psalm 35:6 happens: "Let their way be shadowed and slippery," that is, let them err in their counsels, and let them lack the desired successes. Sometimes God also punishes the impiety of men by that blindness of the natural intellect, so that they go disgracefully astray even in obvious matters of sense, about which Paul writes: "Although they knew God, they did not glorify Him as God, or give thanks, but they became weak in their thoughts, and their foolish heart was darkened. For while saying that they were wise, they were made fools" (Rom. 1:21–22). Therefore, although some wisdom in natural and civil matters is attributed to those who have not been reborn, they are nevertheless also foolish and evil in this respect, that they are weak and do not use things rightly unless God has ruled the man and has given success, just as Paul had been eager for righteousness and endowed with zeal, but the zeal was not according to knowledge [Rom. 10:2], and the righteousness was Pharisaical; he dared to oppose it to the righteousness of God, and so it profited him nothing, as he confesses himself in Philippians 3:7. And then in spiritual matters, to be sure, both Paul and all other men before conversion are constrained to confess their foolishness and malice. For all men, by nature, "walk in vanity, having their intellect obscured by the shadows of their sense, alienated from the life of God through the ignorance that is in them on account of the blindness of their heart" (Eph. 4:17–18). Thus the world is said not to have known God through its wisdom (1 Cor. 1:21), and Paul himself says that he was through ignorance a blasphemer and persecutor of Christ and the Church (1 Tim. 1:13). Nor is it known to them who is a true worshiper of God, and although they may be able to distinguish honorable things from disgraceful ones, still they have no readiness for performing the honorable ones, because "the sense and thought of the human heart are prone to evil from youth" (Gen. 8:21).

But especially if they should begin to do something good, that spiritual arrogance immediately appears, because they trust in themselves and scorn others, as is said of the Pharisees in Luke 18[:9]. It cannot be denied: Paul too, before his conversion, was not entirely immune to this hazard. Hence he numbers himself deservedly with those foolish and bad men, so that the goodness and φιλανθρωπία of God, which he would later preach, might be that much plainer, even in himself. It is well known, also from the first chapter of the previous letter to Timothy, what he did.

Question 3

Was Paul agitated by the pricking of the lusts (libidinum), since he reckons himself with those who once were given to various desires and lusts (voluptatibus) (v. 3)?

Answer: Jerome thinks it is legitimate to say this about Paul before his conversion. "For could he have had any virtues," he says, "without the virtue of God, of Jesus Christ, or could he have quenched the burning fire of lusts when he was not the temple of God?"[287] Some attribute libidinous ardor of this kind to him even after his conversion, and come to this understanding through the pricking of his flesh of which he complains in 2 Corinthians 12:7.[288] Lyra agrees with this opinion in his notes on this passage, and Jerome in *Letter 22* to Eustochium, about the guarding of virginity,[289] and Gregory in book 8 of the *Moralia*, chapter 20. Bellarmine writes, in book 2 of *de monach.*, chapter 30, "The Apostle was tempted by great and daily prickings of the flesh, and

---

287 *PL* 26.593AB.

288 That is, the "thorn in the flesh." The Vulgate has *stimulus*, which is the word Balduin uses here and also in the question.

289 Jerome quotes the verse about the "thorn in the flesh" in section 31 of this letter, but does not apply it in this way. In section 5, however, he writes that Paul, "by reason of the pricks (*aculeos*) of the flesh and the allurements of vice keeps under his body and brings it into subjection, lest when he has preached to others he may himself be a castaway (1 Cor. 9:27); and yet, for all that, sees another law in his members warring against the law of his mind, and bringing him into captivity to the law of sin (Rom. 7:23)." Jerome, Letter 22 to Eustochium, NPNF² 6:24, 36.

yet he did not marry a wife." Cornelius à Lapide follows him on that passage, and others of the Papists.

Others add that Thecla,[290] a woman most devoted to Paul, incited the flames of perverse desire in him while she was following him. But the claim is not plausible, that the Apostle Paul was excited to lusts after his conversion, because he was surrounded everywhere, as it were, with labors, vigils, and dangers, so that there could scarcely be space for filthy thoughts of this kind, which do not seek lodging except in a spoiled and idle soul. Therefore certain of the most ancient Fathers [have understood] this σκόλοπα (stake, thorn) or pricking in Paul's flesh not with reference to temptations to lust, but either with reference to some pain of the body, as Augustine on Psalm 130, Nicetas,[291] and Oration 30 of Nazianzen,[292] *etc.*, or with reference to Paul's persecutions and adversities in general, as Chrysostom, Theophylact, and Theodoret, whom Erasmus follows. Even some of the Papists conclude that it is clearly absurd to claim that Paul felt the prickings of lust. "What is more absurd," writes Benedict Justinian on 2 Corinthians 12, "than to think that the Apostle, already an old man, is burning so greatly with the ardor of lust? What is alleged concerning Thecla is utterly mythological, not only because Jerome, the describer of the Ecclesiastical writers,[293] in his entry on Luke, ascribes the travels of Paul and Thecla to a certain Presbyter in Asia, whom he calls a σπουδαστήν (partisan) of St. Paul, and confirms this with Tertullian's testimony, and takes it as a book that is accordingly less trustworthy, but also because Gelasius, in [*Corpus Iuris Canonici,*] distinction 15, ch. *sancta Rom.*,[294]

---

290 A reference to the apocryphal 2nd century work *The Acts of Paul and Thecla*.

291 Niketas Choniates (c. 1155–1217) was a Byzantine official who wrote a history of the Byzantine Empire from 1118 to 1207.

292 Oration 30 is the fourth theological oration of Gregory of Nazianzus (there are five), devoted along with oration 29 to proving the Son's divinity against the Arians. It is not clear which passage Balduin means.

293 This is an expansion of Balduin's abbreviation "*Eccles.*," based on the fact that he is referencing Jerome's work *On Illustrious Men*, the purpose of which (according to Jerome's introduction) was "to give a systematic account of ecclesiastical writers" (*ecclesiasticos Scriptores in ordinem digeram*).

294 The *Gelasian decretum*, traditionally attributed to Pope Gelasius I (d. 496), but

mentions this book as listed in some places under the name of Paul, and condemns it among the Apocryphal writings. Furthermore, the authors of this fable write that Thecla had already been espoused to a certain Thamirus, but was shaken by an oration of Paul's that he held at Iconium concerning virginity, so that she vowed celibacy against the will of her parents and spouse, and followed Paul, and was consecrated by this same holy veil, and received the power to teach and to baptize, and to veil virgins and consecrate them to a vow of perpetual celibacy, as is well known from the legend of Thecla and Tertullian's book *On Baptism*. How then do they pretend that Paul was tempted to lusts by her? This extends to Paul's life before his conversion. There are those who do not want him to have been exposed to temptations of this kind even at that time, and this for the reason that he embraced the sect of the Pharisees, who as Epiphanius writes, *On Heresies* 16, were zealous for chastity and modesty to a wonderful degree. On this matter see Justinian[295] in his introduction to the Pauline Epistles, disputation 3, chapter 3. Whatever the case may be, in our text he joins himself to those who were at one time "enslaved to various desires and lusts." Where there is no need for us to restrict those desires specifically to the flames of lusts, it is enough that Paul confesses that he also, according to the common lot of men, was subject to perverse desires, which are like the fruits of original sin, and signs of extreme corruption. So they are found sometimes even in the reborn, concerning which St. Paul laments in Romans 7:22ff. It is not amazing, then, if they have found a place in the soul of one who is not yet reborn.

Question 4

Since the Apostle writes in verse 5 that God "saves us through the bath of regeneration and of renewal in the Holy Spirit," is it rightly inferred from this that baptism works regeneration?

Answer: The confession of our churches is that baptism "works the

---

actually of later composition, defined the Canon of Scripture for the Medieval Western Church.

295 That is, Benedict Justinian.

remission of sins, frees from death and devil, and gives eternal blessedness to those who believe,"[296] and it is proven in our Catechism by this text of our Apostle, where baptism is called "the bath of regeneration and of renewal in the Holy Spirit." By these words, the Instrumental Cause of our regeneration is expressed, which God uses especially with those who are first entering the church, that is baptism. For just as the Word is preached to adults, that incorruptible seed through which we are reborn, (1 Pet. 1:23), so baptism is that water of salvation through which we are washed and reborn in infancy, and added to the assembly of the children of God, as it is written, "Unless one has been reborn of water and the Spirit, he will not enter the Kingdom of Heaven" (John 3:5). Now, this extraordinary power is attributed to the baptism of water, not in itself, as if the water had that strength, but in the Holy Spirit. That is, as our Paul says, on account of the Holy Spirit having been added, who sanctifies the water of baptism, sets it apart from common water, and makes it the ordinary means of our regeneration, as in Ephesians 5:26. Paul writes that God has "cleansed His church by the bath of water in the Word," that is, on account of the Word of command and promise having been added. For baptism is not simply water, but water combined with a divine command and sealed with the Word of God. "Without the Word of God, this water is simply water, and no baptism, but once the Word of God has been added, it must become a baptism; that is, a salutary water of grace and life."[297] Hence it is called "the bath of regeneration and of renewal" not by metonymy, but instrumentally, just as the Gospel is called "the power of God unto salvation for all who believe" (Rom. 1:16). Against this truth arise on one side the Photinians,[298] on the other side the Calvinists. The Photinians deny that Paul is dealing with baptism in this passage, since he makes no mention of baptism; but they say that he calls regeneration

---

296 Balduin quotes here from Luther's *Small Catechism*, the answer to the question, "What benefits does Baptism give?"

297 This sentence is quoted from the Small Catechism's answer to the question, "How can water do such great things?"

298 I.e., the Socinians.

itself a bath, because in Scripture the cleansing of souls that happens by means of the Word may be figuratively called a bath (Eph. 5:26, Heb. 10:22), and they say that our Paul himself declares what he understands by "the bath of regeneration," that is, "the renewal of the Holy Spirit," for they say that the particle "and" (*et*) can mean as much as "that is" (*hoc est*). See the *Racovian Catechism*, Latin version, chapter 4, vers. 197; Smalcius[299] against Franzius[300] part 1, disputation 10, page 312 and part 2, disputation 8, p. 422; Socinus, *On the Baptism of Water*, chapter 3, page 59. Smalcius writes about our passage, "It should be reckoned an idolatrous thing to take baptism as the bath of regeneration, especially if this is understood of pedobaptism, which would be a childish bath." Socinus writes that the bath of regeneration is nothing else than true penitence through the preaching of the Gospel, through which we are made new men, and can be born again. Those are their words, which are all most false and on the side of wickedness. For although Paul does not have the term "baptism" itself in this passage, yet he does have the definition itself when he names it "bath," a term that in Scripture is assigned to Baptism, which is properly speaking a kind of washing, and is expressly opposed to washing filth off the body, as a washing of the conscience (1 Pet. 3:21). Therefore it is said to be the bath of our regeneration, which Christ openly declares is accomplished from water (John 3:5). So we do not deny that our regeneration is accomplished through the Word also, but it would have to be proven that this should be understood from this passage. For Scripture teaches a two-fold regeneration. Let one be done through baptism, of which Christ speaks in John 3:5, which regeneration, along with the administration of baptism, He expressly says is from the preaching of the Word; and so He commends two distinct parts of His gift[301] in

---

299 Valentinus Smalcius, German Socinian who emigrated to Racow, Poland, and translated the New Testament into Polish (*Racovian New Testament*, 1606) and the *Racovian Catechism* into German.

300 *Refutation of the Theses of Wolfgang Franzius*, which Franzius (a Wittenberg professor) had proposed for disputations in the years 1609–1611.

301 *Muneris* (*munus*) is the word translated "gift" here. Throughout the rest of his commentary, Balduin uses this word in the sense of an "office," especially the

Matthew 18:19. Let the other be done through the Word, of which Peter speaks in 1 Peter 1:23; and this is nothing other than the turning of a man to God through penitence, which is sometimes metaphorically called "washing" or "purification," as when the Lord exhorts in Isaiah 1:16, "Be washed, be clean, remove the evil of your thoughts from my eyes." But nowhere is either the Word or man's penitence called "the bath of regeneration." For when God is said, in the passage cited from Ephesians 5, to have cleansed His church "through the bath of water in the Word," it is not done either from the preached Word or from penitence, for even infants are part of the church, and they cannot hear the Word, nor do they need penitence (which is for adults); but it is from baptism, which is in the Word, that is, according to the Word of command and of promise; but the "bath of regeneration" is done *by* God. In the other passage, from Hebrews 10, nothing is said except that we must approach God baptized and cleansed from our sins; but we must be cleansed "with pure water" in baptism, and sprinkled with the blood of Christ, by which our consciences are cleansed (Heb. 9:14). But the claim that "regeneration" in our text is the same thing as "renewal," in such a way that "and" could mean the same thing as "that is," is utterly empty, and is said without any reasoning.

Indeed, two fruits of this salutary bath are proposed: one is regeneration, which consists in the washing from sins and the putting-on of Christ, "for however many of you have been baptized in Christ, you have put on Christ" (Gal. 3:27). The other is renewal, which follows those who have been baptized, and is brought about by the Holy Spirit in the reborn through daily penitence. The former is perfect, making children of God out of those who by nature are children of wrath [Eph. 2:3]; the latter is imperfect, because the flesh always lusts against the Spirit (Gal. 5:17). Because of this, the inner man needs to be "renewed from day to day" [2 Cor. 4:16], something that is not said of regeneration. And it is not idolatrous in the least to call baptism the bath of regeneration, for we do not attribute that power of regenerating to the water of baptism in itself, nor do we depend on the work having been

---

Office of the Ministry.

worked (*in opere operato*), but we put this down to the Holy Spirit, who is pleased through this external means to work so excellent a gift of regeneration in our hearts. The Calvinists do indeed call baptism "the bath of regeneration," but in such a way that the work of the thing signified, that is, of the blood and the Holy Spirit, is attributed to the external act through sacramental metonymy, as Beza says in the Colloquy of Mömpelgard.[302] He has the Photinians as allies in this respect, for they set up this rule in the *Racovian Catechism*: "When something that pertains directly to salvation is ascribed in the Scriptures of the New Testament to an external act or ceremony, it may not, by any rationale, be done by that thing as if that external ceremony has the power, but it must be done by that thing in the sense that it is a kind of shadow—no more—of the thing that does pertain directly to salvation."[303] I have written more about this rule in the *Examination* of that Catechism, chapter 5, page 350, Latin edition. I add only a few things here. The opinion of the Adversaries is contrary to the nature of the Sacraments of the New Testament, for signs and shadows have no place there, so neither do metonymies. Christ ordained the water of baptism not to signify the grace or benefit of regeneration, but to confer it, because He uses this salutary means ordinarily when He works regeneration in us, just as He works faith in adults through the hearing of the Word. Nor does it follow from our teaching—something with which the adversaries especially reproach us—that the work of God and the work of the creatures are confused, for one and the same operation is not attributed in the same way to God and to the baptism of water, but to God alone as the Efficient Cause, and to the baptism of water as the Instrumental Cause. Thus the work of our salvation is attributed to God and to the ministers of the church, who are also said to save both

---

302 Jakob Andreae and Theodore Beza, *Lutheranism vs. Calvinism: The Classic Debate at the Colloquy of Montbéliard 1586*, trans. C. J. Armstrong (St. Louis: Concordia Publishing House, 2017), 501–79.

303 See *The Racovian Catechism, with Notes and Illustrations; Translated from the Latin. To Which Is Prefixed a Sketch of the History of Unitarianism in Poland and the Adjacent Countries.*, trans. Thomas Rees (London: Longman, Hurst, Rees, Orme, and Brown, 1818), 261–62.

themselves and their hearers through the Word (1 Tim. 4:16). But God does this efficiently, and the ministers ministerially, in the same way as both God and food are said to feed a man, but the one as Efficient Cause, and the other as Instrumental Cause.

Question 5

God is said to pour out the Holy Spirit upon us (v. 6). Does this not detract somewhat from the Holy Spirit's Person, which cannot be poured out?

Answer: The Photinians deny that the Holy Spirit is a Person subsisting by Himself, because He is said to be poured out, which does not befit a person. See the *Racovian Catechism*, Latin version, page 213. But the saying is metaphorical, and is used not rarely in Scripture, even of other persons and things that subsist by themselves. Thus it is frequently said, when someone discloses to another all the desires, sorrows, and anguishes of his heart, that he pours out his soul, as it says in 1 Samuel 1:15, "I have poured out my soul in the sight of the Lord," and Psalm 42[:4], "I have poured out my soul within me," and the afflicted are commanded in Psalm 62[:8] to pour out their hearts before the Lord. Even men themselves are said to be poured out, as when David says, "I have been poured out like water" (Ps. 22[:14]). The love of God, also, which is not really distinct from God Himself, is said to be poured out in our hearts (Rom. 5:5). In the same way, God is said to pour out both wrath and indignation (Ps. 79:6, Ezek. 30:15, 36:18), which in God are not emotions. All these things are said metaphorically, either on account of dispersion, or on account of vehemence, or on account of abundance, or on account of the sweetness of the thing about which it is written. In the same way, the Holy Spirit is frequently said in Scripture to be poured out upon men (Joel 2:28–29, Zech. 12:10, Acts 2:17, 18, 33; 10:45, etc.) in consideration of His gifts, which are both the sweetest things, and are shared with the faithful, as they say, πιόνι μέτρῳ (in plenteous measure), or as our Apostle says, "richly." For this reason, the gift of the Holy Spirit is elsewhere compared to "waters poured out on one who is thirsting, and streams poured out upon dry land" (Is. 44:3). Therefore, it is not an outpouring properly-so-called, by which the

Substance of the Holy Spirit might be somewhat diminished, but He is metaphorically said to be poured out when the gifts of the Holy Spirit are bountifully conferred on the pious, something that takes nothing away from the Holy Spirit's Person, as is clear from the examples cited.

Question 6

When Paul writes, "God saved us according to His mercy through the bath of regeneration and of renewal," etc. (v. 5), is it rightly inferred from this that inhering formal righteousness is the cause of our justification?

Answer: Bellarmine does indeed infer thus from this passage in book 2 of *On Justification*, chapter 3, where he calls the first regeneration and renewal itself "justification." Then he attempts to prove by three arguments from this text that this justification is done formally through some inhering gift. (1) Because the nature of regeneration would demand this, since it could not be understood as if someone were regenerated without any change of his, through only the goodwill of God existing in God Himself, *etc.* (2) Because the Holy Spirit is said to have been poured out into us; but the poured-out Spirit, he says, is a Formal Cause, through which nothing is more rightly understood than His primary gift, which is charity, which is therefore also said to be "poured abroad (*diffusa*) in our hearts" [Rom. 5:5]. (3) Because we ourselves confess that through the Holy Spirit there is some inhering renewal within us, although we deny that it is properly righteousness, or that we are justified simply by means of that, *etc.* In order that we might respond to all these things, we say first that regeneration and renewal are not very appropriately called "justification itself," for although we do not deny that renewal is in the justified, we nevertheless do not make it the cause of justification, because these two things are not from the same and equal condition. For regeneration properly-so-called consists in the remission of sins, the imputation of righteousness, and the translation of men from the kingdom of Satan into the kingdom of God, but renewal is the devotion of the new obedience, by which man, already having been adopted into the kingdom of God, is devoted to God had to His commandments.

Regeneration is perfect, nor can it be increased or diminished, just as natural generation does not admit of greater and lesser. But renovation can grow and diminish in us, for the devotion of piety is not always equal in a man. That is why we are commanded daily "to be renewed in the spirit of our mind" (Eph. 4:23), and to perfect our sanctification (2 Cor. 4:16). Regeneration comes before; renewal follows in man, for no one can offer works pleasing to God unless he has been born of God, since God delights in the works of His Son, not of strangers. Hence it follows that regeneration and renewal do not jointly constitute our justification, but this consists in regeneration alone, or the remission of sins and the adoption of the children of God. Nor does our Paul, when he writes that we are saved through the bath of regeneration and of renewal, make them two parts of justification, but the two-fold effect of baptism, following upon each other.[304] For a person first becomes a son of God in baptism, and then he does good works, which are worthy of God's children. Next, Bellarmine's arguments that one attains what one has first worked for are fallacies τῆς ἑτεροζητήσεως (of heterozetesis),[305] for none of us denies that some change happens in the regenerate, for the Holy Spirit kindles in them the light of knowledge and of faith, gives grace to work well, mortifies the flesh, and engenders new affections in the heart, whence comes renewal. But it is asked: Is that renewal the formal cause of our regeneration? That is what we cannot concede at all, nor is it plain from our text, but rather contrary to it. For God is said to pour out the Holy Spirit into us, who is doubtless not poured out into an impure vessel, but one that has been purified and washed, that is, into a man who has been reconciled with God; and so this is a consequence of regeneration, and yet not separated from it. The next argument begs the question, for where is it proven that the Holy Spirit in this text is the same thing

---

304 By "follow upon (*insequuntur*) each other," he probably means "logically imply each other," since he has just said, "Regeneration comes before; renewal follows (*sequitur*) in man," and is about to repeat that sequence.

305 This is the logical fallacy of *ignoratio elenchi* ("ignorance of proof"), *i.e.,*, answering a different argument than one's opponent has actually made, and making out that one has thereby answered his argument.

as charity? By this rationale, the Holy Spirit would not be the Efficient Cause, but the effect of justification or of faith, because faith is said to work through charity (Gal. 5:6). But we know that the Holy Spirit is the Efficient Cause of our justification, who leads us through the Word to the acknowledgement of sins, instructs us concerning the grace of God and the merit of His Son, grants faith, and lavishes the power to live well. Hence the old writers compare Christ to a physician in the work of our salvation, but the Holy Spirit to a pharmacist. For Christ provides us the medicine against sin through His obedience, but the Holy Spirit prepares and applies it through Word and sacrament. This fact concerns the passage Romans 5:5. It is clearly cited ἀπροσδιονύσως (irrelevantly). For that "charity poured abroad in our hearts" is not put there passively, as if it were that charity by which God is loved by us, but should be understood actively, of that charity by which God loves us, as the first epistle of St. John interprets it in chapter 4, verse 10. For our charity is far feebler and fainter than something that could have the term *diffusio* (pouring abroad) attributed to it. But the Holy Spirit Himself cannot be said to be that charity, because the charity is said to be poured abroad *through* the Holy Spirit, no doubt by Him impressing that love of God upon us. This is the way Benedict Pererius[306] understands this passage of Paul to the Romans in disputation 2 on Romans chapter 5. He says, "Whether we read 'poured abroad' or 'poured out,' nothing else is signified by this word except that God's charity has been declared openly and evidently through many and various gifts of the Holy Spirit, which He has poured out upon us: that is, conferred generously, copiously, and abundantly."[307] The third argument is of no moment, for the sense in which we confess a renewal inhering within us is doubtless the sense in which we say that it is not as a part but as a fruit of our justification. For it is false, what Bellarmine writes, that

---

306 The Spanish Jesuit Benedictus Pererius (Benedict Pereira), who wrote commentaries on Genesis, Exodus, Daniel, the Gospel of John, Romans (published 1603), and Revelation.

307 Benedict Pereira, *Second Volume of Selected Disputations on Holy Scripture, Containing Eighty-Eight Disputations on the Epistle of Blessed* (beati) *Paul to the Romans* (Ingolstadt: 1603), p. 564.

Paul says that we are justified through regeneration and renewal, but he teaches that we are regenerated and renewed through baptism, "so that having been justified, we might be made heirs of eternal life." Here he established baptism as the means of our justification for God's part, but a two-fold fruit of baptism: regeneration, in which our justification formally consists, and renewal, which is an effect for the justified. But it is clearly established from the text that renewal is not part of justification, for Paul opposes the mercy, goodness, and φιλανθρωπίαν (philanthropy, love of mankind) of God to the works of righteousness in which renewal consists (vv. 4–5). This passage of our Paul, then does nothing for inhering righteousness as the Formal Cause of justification.

Theological Aphorisms from this Part of the Chapter

1. Obedience is owed to the magistrate as to the ordinance of God. Who resists the magistrate, resists Him (Rom. 13:2). But obedience up to the altars; that is, in matters that are not contrary to piety. Our Paul, therefore, wants subjects to obey their princes in such a way that they are prepared for every good work (v. 1), and the Apostles were not willing to obey princes and the Jerusalem Pontiffs when they prohibited the preaching of the Gospel, because "It is necessary to obey God rather than men" (Acts 5:29). And Tertullian says in *ad Scapulam*,[308] "We are devoted to the Emperor in the way that is lawful for us and expedient for him." And Jerome writes on this text, "If it is good, what the Emperor and the ruler commands, submit to the will of the one who is commanding; but if it is bad, give him the reply from the Acts of the Apostles: 'It is necessary to obey God rather than men.'" We understand this very thing also concerning slaves with their masters and concerning wives with their husbands, and concerning children with their parents, that they ought to be subject to masters, husbands, and parents only in those things that do not come against

---

308 *Letter to Scapula* (A.D. 212), written to the Proconsul of Asia to protest his recently-begun persecution of Christians.

the commandments of God."[309]

2. Blasphemies and curses should be far from Christians. Thus they should be admonished to blaspheme no one (v. 2). Blasphemy against God is prohibited by the Second Commandment, and when it is either about God or about His Word and divine matters, we are thinking and speaking evilly. Such is the blasphemy of Sennacherib (Is. 36:18ff.) and of Nicanor (2 Macc. 15:5), or when we curse the wounds of Christ, the sacraments and like things that serve our salvation, and others to destruction. A certain man suffered capital punishment in the wilderness on account of this kind of blasphemy, from the Lord's commandment (Lev. 24[:10]ff.). But cursing or slanderous talk is brought against the Eighth Commandment, and is abuse done to one's neighbor, and the higher he is than us, the graver a sin is committed. This is why God made a prohibition in species, "Do not curse the prince of your people" (Ex. 22:28), and Christ commanded in genus, "Bless those who curse" (Luke 6:28).

3. Concord and gentleness are frequently commended in Scripture, two virtues that our Paul also has conjoined, so long as he wants Christians not to be quarrelsome, but to show gentleness to all men (v. 2). Thus in other places he wants us to keep peace with all, as much as rests on us, and if it can be done (Rom. 12:18). For we do not live among perfected men, but infirm, who can both offend us and be offended by us; where there is always need of mutual giving, not always of strict law, but one must deal with his neighbor fairly and well. "Blessed are the meek," the Savior says, "because they will possess the earth" (Matt. 5:5). And the Apostle Paul's advice is, "Be kind to one another, merciful, giving to each other as Christ also has given to you" (Eph. 4:32).

4. Blindness of mind in divine matters, rebellion of the will, an inclination to malice, depraved concupiscence, mutual hatreds, which flare up sometimes even among the reborn, are from the corrupted nature of man, and a manifest judgment how greatly the sin of origin has infected us. This natural condition of ours should certainly not be extenuated, which they do, who attribute it to nature—in divine mys-

---

309 PL 26.591B.

teries, of course—and those who want to contribute something of their own also to conversion. For what would the senseless understand? What would the malicious do? How would they love, who are blazing with hatreds and envy? For this reason, the Apostle Paul so frequently reminded the Gentiles to whom he wrote of their former state (Eph. 2:1ff., 1 Cor. 6:11, Gal. 4:8, *etc.*), that they might know themselves aright, lament their lapse, receive the leading of the Holy Spirit, and especially, know the greatness of God's love toward us in the work of redemption, from which one departs to the extent that nature is extolled. So however many of those vicious affections we observe in our flesh, envy, wrath, hatred, and other depraved desires, let us rebuke them, always thinking on this: we were like that, yes, but since we have been born of God, this life demands other manners. Paul, therefore, commands the reborn to beware "lest sin should reign in their mortal body, so that they should obey its lusts" (Rom. 6:12).

5. Salvation and our righteousness is purely free, because, first, it is simply removed from our works of righteousness (v. 5); that is, even from the works of the reborn. By this statement is plugged up that crack of the Papists, by which they otherwise try to slip away when someone presents to them the things that have been said: "We conclude that a man is justified by faith, not from works of the Law" (Rom. 3:28); "By grace you have been saved through faith, and this is not from you; it is the gift of God, not from works" (Eph. 2:8[–9]). They say that these dictums rule out righteousness and salvation by works performed from free will alone, or by the works of those who are not reborn; but in our text, even the works of the righteous are excluded from the work of our redemption. "For here there is no distinction" (Rom. 3[:22]). Next, our salvation, having been entirely received, is reckoned to "the goodness and φιλανθρωπία of God our Savior" (v. 4), likewise to "the mercy of God" (v. 5). For truly great and worthy of acceptance is the goodness of God to us, and His love, He who, in order that He might spare a slave,[310]

---

310 Balduin is about to go into a quotation of Rom. 8:32, but this juxtaposition of slave and son, along with the exclamatory character of the sentence, may have been suggested to him by the Proclamation or Proper Preface of the Easter Vigil, which in one place runs, "O inestimable love! That You might redeem a slave,

"did not spare His Son, but gave Him for all" [Rom. 8:32]. Christ Himself preached this in John 3:16, and St. John marvels at it in 1 John 3[:1] ff. This φιλανθρωπία of God admonishes us that in the same way as He is φιλάνθρωπος (loving mankind), so also we should be φιλόθεοι (loving God), and just as He promotes our salvation, so also we should promote His honor, renouncing all depraved desires and serving Him in His kingdom, which is not the least goal of our redemption that has been wrought through Christ. Luke 1:74–75 speaks of it.

6. Baptism is the salutary and ordinary means by which righteousness and our salvation is procured. For in it "those who were by nature children of wrath, are reborn as children of God, washed from their sins by the blood of Christ, and presented with the Holy Spirit, who awakens new affections in us, and renders us fit for the service of God. Thus it is called by Paul "the bath of regeneration and renewal in the Holy Spirit" (v. 5), and by the Prophet Zechariah, "The open fountain of the Lord for David and the inhabitants of Jerusalem, for the washing-away of sins" (Zech 13:1). St. Peter compares it with the Flood, "in which eight souls were saved through water" in the ark of Noah, "as we also are saved through baptism, which is not the putting-off of the flesh's dirt, but the inquiry of a good conscience to God through the resurrection of Jesus Christ" (1 Pet. 3:21). So the fruit of baptism is regeneration, with which faith is connected, υἱοθεσία (adoption as a son), grace, righteousness, and the inheritance of eternal life; and renewal, which includes the renunciation of Satan, the putting-off of the original impurity in which we have been born, and obedience to the divine commandments. They all receive this fruit, who do not erect a barrier to the Holy Spirit, who works these things in the baptized. Therefore all baptized infants and faithful adults are regenerated according to that dictum, "As many of you who have been baptized, have put on Christ" (Gal. 3:27). But hypocrites are not regenerated, because they block the working of the Holy Spirit with their warfare, and the benefit of regeneration, which does not exist without faith,

---

You handed over Your Son!" (*O inæstimábilis diléctio caritátis: ut servum redímeres, Fílium tradidísti!*).

cannot stand with unfaithfulness and hypocrisy. But let the baptized remember that baptism is of no profit to them unless they take care to live piously, for baptism is a bath not only of regeneration, but also of renewal; and one who lives as an enemy of God cannot be called a son of God. This is why Augustine called baptism "the sacrament of new life and of eternal salvation, which many possess not to eternal life, but to eternal punishment, since they do not make good use of so great a good."[311]

7. God's magnificent gift is the gift of the Holy Spirit, which in baptism is bountifully given to all who are regenerated. Thus it is said to be "poured out upon us," and indeed "poured out richly" (v. 6), because great is the abundance of the Holy Spirit's gifts. The Spirit is commonly said to be sevenfold in His office, not as if there were only seven gifts of the Holy Spirit, but because the number seven is the number of perfection, for there are various gifts of the Holy Spirit, and also various effects of the same. He is called "the Spirit of wisdom and of understanding, the Spirit of counsel and of might, the Spirit of knowledge and of piety, the Spirit of the fear of the Lord" (Is. 11:2). For all wisdom is from Him; thus Bezaleel, that brilliant artisan, is said to be filled with the Spirit of God, with wisdom and understanding and knowledge in every work, etc. (Ex. 31:2). All sound counsel is from Him, and the uprightness of our life, whence David asks, "Let Your good Spirit lead me in the right path" (Ps. 143:10). All our strength is from Him, "for God has not given us a spirit of fear, but of power" (2 Tim. 1:7). True piety is from Him, and the fear of the Lord, "for they are children of God, who are led by the Spirit of God" (Rom. 8:14). He is called "the Spirit of grace and of prayers" (Zech. 12:10), because He seals the grace of God in our hearts (Rom. 8:16). From this, those who believe are said to be "sealed with the Holy Spirit of promise, who is the down payment of our inheritance unto the redemption of acquisition, to the praise of His glory" (Eph. 1:13[–14]). Without the Holy Spirit, we cannot call Christ "Lord" (1 Cor. 12:3). He teaches us to pray, and "helps our infirmity, for we do not know what to pray, ourselves; but the Spirit

---

[311] *Against Cresconius, the Donatist Grammarian* 2.13(16).

Himself asks on our behalf, with indescribable groans" (Rom. 8:26). And besides this, He is our teacher and comforter (*paracletus*, John 14:26). All these things make it so that He is said to be poured out upon us. Let us then acknowledge the riches of the Lord's mercy toward us, and let us gladly receive the governance of the Holy Spirit, taking care in all ways "not to grieve the Holy Spirit within us, by whom we have been sealed for the day of redemption" (Eph. 4:30).

8. The gift of the Holy Spirit that has been received is something that must be acquired by our Lord Jesus Christ, for the Holy Spirit is said to be poured out upon Him (v. 6). This is why He said to the disciples, "Unless I go away to the Father, the Comforter (*Paracletus*) will not come to you, but when I go away, I will send Him to you" (John 16:7). This was not fulfilled only once, by that visible outpouring upon the Apostles, but is fulfilled daily when men are regenerated—that which is the extraordinary fruit of the passion and death of Christ, in which He first purged our hearts from dead works by His blood, through faith, so that the Holy Spirit might find a place there, who "does not enter a wicked heart or a body yielded to sin" (Wis. 1:4) in any other way. So let us magnify the merit of Christ for this reason also, and give Him thanks on this account, that without the guidance of the Holy Spirit, this was done with regard to us.[312]

9. The testimony of the three Persons of the Deity should be noted (v. 6). For God the Father is the One who has poured out the Holy Spirit upon us, through Jesus Christ. This is Jerome's observation. So all three Persons of the Most Holy Trinity meet in the work of our redemption and sanctification. God the Father works, the Son earns, the Holy Spirit seals and confirms salvation in us; and so we are righteous and holy through God, and are obliged for this reason to gratitude to the whole Trinity for these devoted services.

10. Although good works do not enter the article of our justification, for He did not save us by works, they are nevertheless the fruits

---

[312] That is, let us thank Christ that when we did not have the guidance of the Spirit within us, nor could attract Him to us, Christ performed the acquisition of the Spirit on our behalf (*siquidem sine ductu Spiritus S. actum esset de nobis*).

of righteousness, with which those who have been justified through faith are necessarily occupied. Paul thus wants the faithful to "be careful to excel in good works" (v. 8); that is, to "walk in newness of life" [Rom. 6:4] so as to offer an example to others, and invite them by [the believers'] virtue. For one should live well, not so much for himself as for others, who are moved by examples more than by precepts and exhortations. Thus both Christ and the Apostles compare the saints to lights that illumine others by their brightness, and remove from detractors the opportunity for making false accusations (Matt. 5:16, Phil. 2:15, 1 Pet. 2:12, *etc.*).

The Second Part of the Text [Titus 3:9–15]

Μωρὰς δὲ ζητήσεις, καὶ γενεαλογίας, καὶ ἔρεις, καὶ μάχας νομικὰς περιΐστασο. εἰσὶ γὰρ ἀνωφελεῖς καὶ μάταιοι.

9. But omit foolish questions and genealogies and contentions and legal disputes, for they are useless and superfluous.

Αἱρετικὸν ἄνθρωπον μετὰ μίαν καὶ δευτέραν νουθεσίαν παραιτοῦ.

10. After one and a second admonition, flee the man who is the author of factions.

Εἰδὼς ὅτι ἐξέστραπται ὁ τοιοῦτος καὶ ἁμαρτάνει ὢν αὐτοκατάκριτος.

11. Knowing that he who is of this sort has been overthrown and is sinning, having been condemned by himself.

Ὅταν πέμψω Ἀρτεμᾶν πρὸς σὲ Τυχικόν, σπούδασον ἐλθεῖν πρός με εἰς Νικόπολιν. ἐκεῖ γὰρ κέκρινα παραχειμάσαι.

12. But when I shall send Artemas to you, or Tychicus, make an effort to come to me at Nicopolis, for I have decided to winter there.

Ζηνᾶν τὸν νομικὸν καὶ Ἀπολλῶ σπουδαίως πρόπεμψον, ἵνα μηδὲν αὐτοῖς λείπῃ.

13. Let Zenas the lawyer and Apollos be brought carefully, that nothing may be lacking to them.

Μανθανέτωσαν δὲ καὶ οἱ ἡμέτεροι καλῶν ἔργων προΐστασθαι εἰς τὰς ἀναγκαίας χρείας, ἵνα μὴ ὦσιν ἄκαρποι.

Ἀσπάζονταί σε οἱ μετ' ἐμοῦ πάντες. ἄσπασαι τοὺς φιλοῦντας ἡμᾶς ἐν πίστει, ἡ χάρις μετὰ πάντων ὑμῶν. Ἀμήν.
Notes in text.[313]

14. And let our people learn to excel in good works, for necessary uses, that they may not be unfruitful.

15. All who are with me salute you. Salute those who love us in the faith. Grace be with you all. Amen.

Analysis and Explanation of the Second Part

Now follow certain special instructions, which partly concern Titus's office, and partly Paul's friends. The first instruction has to do with Titus's teaching, but negatively, for he warns him from what teaching one ought to abstain. He says, "But avoid foolish questions, and genealogies, and contentions, and disputes of the law, for they are useless and vain" (v. 9). We have a similar instruction above, in 1 Timothy 1:4 and 6:3-4. We gather from this repetition that not only the Gentiles, but also the Pseudo-Apostles pleased themselves greatly with this kind of teaching; but the Apostle wants Titus to be removed from these things, for the Apostolic teaching is not concerned with those follies, because it has loftier things that it treats, whence St. Peter also separates his teaching from those fables: "We have made known to you the power of our Lord Jesus Christ, not having followed cunning fables," he says, "but having been made eyewitnesses of His greatness" (2 Pet. 1:16). Now he calls "foolish questions" whatever is proposed beyond Scripture and without evident usefulness for the hearers. Such were the questions (1) of the Jews concerning the coming of the Messiah, about whom they did not know whence he was going to come

---

[313] Verse 10 (English): In this section of the original text (but not in the rest of the commentary below), Titus 3:10-11 have been combined as Titus 3:10, which puts the verse numbers off by one for the rest of the Scripture quotation. Verse numbers have been corrected here.

(John 7:27), or about the return of Elijah (Sir. 48:10), to which pertains what Jerome writes, that "the Jews seek God, hoping that they might be able to find Him without Christ,"[314] and to this pertain the questions about the great commandment (Matt. 22), or whether one ought to keep the Sabbath (Luke 14); (2) of the Heretics, such as questions about the Aeons of the Valentinians, and about the Earth, whether it existed and was made all at the same time (because one reads *in marq:* "the earth was void and empty"),[315] which, Tertullian writes, Hermogenes and his allies once asked foolishly (*Against Hermogenes*, chapter 27). Many questions of this kind are raised in the Papacy, as whether an angel is in a place by its essence or existence; whether a soul, by chewing the Eucharistic bread, chews the very body of the Lord; whether the crumbs left over after the consecration have the nature (*ratio*) of a sacrament; even whether the consecration happens if one little word should be omitted by the one who is consecrating, how the conversion of bread into body is done and wine into blood is done, and whether subsequently or instantly, *etc.* (3) The questions of the Poets, about the homeland of Homer, about the mother of Aeneas, about the name of the stepmother of Archemorus, about the age of Acestis, to which pertain also the useless subtleties and questions of the Philosophers in sacred matters, things that complicate more than they explain. (4) Of curious men who, not content with the simplicity of the faith, inquire scrupulously in the divine mysteries, how this might be done, something that Nicodemus and the Capernaites once did (John 3[:9] and 6[:52]); also what God did before the world was created, where paradise is, where Enoch and Elijah still live, *etc.* Concerning these things, see Augustine, Book 11 of the *Confessions*, chapter 30. Paul calls questions of this kind "foolish" because although they make a show of great wisdom, they are nevertheless the questions of foolish men, who when necessary things have been neglected, are excessively curious

---

314 PL 26.594B

315 A note in the margin here reads, "See Thomas, Part 3, Question 78, Articles 2 and 5; Bellarmine, Book 1 *On the Eucharist*, chapter 11; Lombard, Book 4, Distinction 13."

about less necessary things. He calls "genealogies" those enumerations of origins in which the Pharisees were especially superstitious, and by which they pretended to a certain precedence of erudition over the Gentiles. Their traces are visible in John 8:39, Romans 3:29, and Philippians 3:4. By this zeal for genealogies, they dared to pervert the very genealogy of Christ,[316] as Epiphanius reports, Heresy 49,[317] and required Gentiles who had been converted to the faith of Christ to thoroughly learn the orders of the genealogies, as Theodoret says on chapter one of the previous letter to Timothy. Jerome says on this passage that the Jews glory in genealogies for two reasons: (1) because "they boast that they have knowledge of the Law when they master the names of every single man, and their etymologies, which we do not know since they are foreign (that is, Hebrew), and many have been pronounced badly by us; and if by chance we have made a mistake in accent, in the length and brevity of a syllable, either stretching out the short ones or shortening the long ones, they are accustomed to mock us for our inexperience, especially in aspirated sounds and certain letters that must be pronounced with a scraping of the throat ..."[318] as when we say 'Rahel' and they 'Rachel'; we 'Hieriho,' and they 'Hiericho';[319] we 'Hebron,' and they 'Chebron,'"[320] *etc.* (2) Because they run through the names and generations "from the beginning, Adam, all the way to the end, Zerubbabel, with such good memory that you would think they were recounting their own name, and if by chance we, who either have learned other letters or ... have examined the written sense more than

---

316 A marginal noted here reads, "Herod destroyed the Jewish genealogies from the Temple, but since they had to be restored, they spread throughout all Judaea, Eusebius, Book 1 of the *History*, chapter 6." In modern editions, at least, the reference is actually to chapter 7 (*History of the Church* 1.7.13–14).

317 When all the heresies in the *Panarion* of Epiphanius are numbered sequentially, the correct number is 69, about the Arian heresy. Balduin is referring to paragraph 23 of that lengthy entry, about the abuse of the genealogy in Matthew 1 by various groups seeking to prove from it that Joseph was the true natural father of Jesus.

318 That is, a harsh guttural sound.

319 That is, Jericho.

320 *PL* 26.594D–595A.

the words, do not know them that way, they think that they are more learned in names having to be recorded and in the computation of years, and in grandsons and great-great-grandsons, and grandfathers, great-grandfathers, and great-great-grandfathers,"[321] *etc.* Paul wants his Titus, then, to be far from this zeal for genealogies, for they have no utility, and give birth to vain glory. "Contentions" refer to the thorny disputations of the dialecticians, often about things that are of trivial or no value, and when they are introduced into theological study, time is fruitlessly consumed and useless diligence exercised, which should rather have been applied to necessary things. Thus Jerome interprets: "Those who are occupied all day and night in this," he says, "in order that they might either ask a question or answer one, or give a proposition or receive and adopt, confirm and conclude one, they call certain litigants who dispute as pleases them, not by reason but by their tastes, 'contentious.'"[322] Next the Apostle calls "disputes of the Law" either the things that have to do with legal rites, as washings, sprinklings, foods, contact with unclean things, and the like, in which the Pharisees were continually occupied to the point of superstition; or the things that have to do with details that are contained in the Old Testament (which sometimes is generally named "the Law"), as "how many years Methuselah lived, in what year Solomon married a wife," where the four rivers of Paradise are today, "and many things of this kind, which are either discovered with difficulty, or even if we have discovered them with great study and labor, we have learned things that profit us nothing. These kinds of 'disputes of the Law' are frequently held not on account of desire for the truth, but on account of the boasting of glory, as long as we want to be considered learned among those who hear, or at least as we pursue filthy lucre from this idle talk,"[323] Jerome writes on this passage. Paul, therefore, gives the command to avoid all these things. In the Greek it is περίστασο, restrain, reject; for "to περιστάναι" is the same as "to surround" and "to stand in the way." Paul used this word

---

[321] *PL* 26.595C.
[322] *PL* 26.596A–B.
[323] *PL* 26.596B–C.

also in 2 Timothy 2:16, when he gave the command to avoid profane and vain talking. He indicates, then, that resistance should be offered to all these things, in order that we might keep them away from us, if by chance they should be introduced by others under the guise of singular erudition.

The second command concerns the enemies of sound teaching: "Avoid a heretical man," he says, "after one and another correction" (v. 10). According to the etymology of the word, a αἱρετικὸς is a follower who chooses something particular. A αἵρησις is a sect or a choice, for it has its name from choice, for which reason it is taken by Chrysostom even in a good sense, for the choice by which one was elected Bishop by the people. And a αἱρετικὸς, in Aristotle and others, is one who uses the faculty of choosing. But "heretic" is used chiefly of one who chooses some particular opinion, as among the Philosophers, those who were the "heretics" or followers of Zeno were called Stoics, those of Aristotle, Academics, and those of Epicurus, Epicureans.

In the church is it used of followers of false and new opinions. But because the crime of heresy is most serious, not just anyone who errs in doctrine should immediately be considered a heretic. For as Augustine says in the preface of his book *On Heresies*, "Not every error is a heresy, although no heresy that is regarded as a fault can be a heresy except by means of error."[324] But a heresy properly so-called is an opinion about matters of faith, chosen by human understanding, contrary to Sacred Scripture, destroying the foundation of the faith, taught publicly in the church, and defended obstinately. And a heretic is one who, within the bosom of the church, obstinately attacks some article in the foundation of the faith, gives birth to dissensions and causes of offense in the church, and contumaciously and maliciously perseveres in his opinion—none the less, however often he has been warned. And for this reason, he is defined as a heretic when the heresy has been confirmed in him and there is no hope of correction. But our Paul takes "heretic" ἐν πλάτει (broadly), as one who errs in doctrine and is separating himself from others by this very thing, where obstinacy has not yet set in, but can

---

324 St. Augustine, *One Book on Heresies, to Quodvultdeus*, Preface, 7.

Titus 3

eventually set in. Therefore, since men of this kind sometimes have business with the ministers of the church, the Apostle teaches how one ought to deal with them.

First, he wants him to be corrected. In the Greek text, he requires νουθεσίαν (admonition), a word that "signifies teaching and admonition without rebuke,"[325] for it is attributed to parents, who are commanded to educate their children ἐν νουθεσία κυρίου ("in the admonition of the Lord," Eph. 6:4) and to the faithful among themselves mutually (Rom. 15:14), and the word νουθετεῖν (to admonish) is attributed to brothers, and is opposed to hostile rebuke (2 Thess. 3:15). Before all things, then, the heretic must be admonished of his error, which must be demonstrated to him clearly from Scripture, and impressed on him that he might acknowledge it and lay it aside.

Then, if nothing is accomplished, the admonition must be repeated once and again, "so that every word might stand in the mouth of two or three witnesses" [Matt. 18:16], a reason that Jerome adds on this passage,[326] for this repeated admonition must be undertaken in the presence of others. But if he does not receive this either, he should be avoided or fled. In the Greek it is παραιτοῦ, reject him, and abstain from all association with him.

He adds a reason: "Knowing that he who is of this sort has been subverted and is delinquent, since he has been condemned by his own judgment" (v. 11). And when there is a precedent of obstinacy, and he is not willing to yield to demonstrated truth, and can make no objection that relates to the point, and yet does not stop contradicting, a sign is obtained of a mind "given over to a reprobate understanding" [Rom. 1:28], which accepts neither entreaties nor admonition. For such is the subverted man, that is, plainly hopeless and lost, in whom, though he needs to be recalled to the way, "effort and oil are lost."[327] He is even

---

325 This is an unattributed quotation from Jerome's commentary, with a little variation of wording: "νουθεσίαν, *quae vox doctrinam & admonitionem absque increpatione significat,*" as compared to Jerome's "νουθεσία *autem commonitionem magis et doctrinam absque increpatione significat*" (PL 26.597C).

326 PL 26.597CD.

327 "*Opera oleumque perditur,*" an expression from Plautus (*Poenulus* 1.2.122),

αὐτοκατάκριτος, condemned by himself, partly because he has been convicted of error in his conscience—though might he be afraid to confess it publicly?—and partly because of his own will he is separating himself from the gathering of the faithful, though as of yet he has been removed by no one. For as Cyprian writes in Letter 75, "It is obvious that they all have been condemned by themselves, and before the day of judgment have pronounced the sentence against themselves."[328] This was in accord with the Apostle's command.

The third command concerns Titus's coming to the Apostle: "But when I shall send Artemas or Tychicus to you, hurry to come to me at Nicopolis, for I have decided to winter there" (v. 12). Dorotheus writes in the Synopsis[329] that Artemas was Bishop of the Church of Lystra. Mention is made of him nowhere else. Tychicus, who came from Asia, was a disciple and companion of Paul (Acts 20:4), through whom he sent his Epistles to Rome, to the Ephesians, and to the Colossians (Eph. 6:21, Col. 4[:7]). Mention is made of him also in 2 Timothy 4:12. So he writes that he is going to send these two to Crete, in order that they might preside over the ministry in the meantime, because he had called Titus away to himself, to the city of Nicopolis in Macedonia, as the last words of this Epistle have it. Chrysostom calls it Nicopolis of Thrace, Jerome Nicopolis of Epirus.[330] Since Paul had decided to winter in this city, he summoned Titus to himself, partly so that he might educate him still better, as Chrysostom wants, partly so that when Paul leaves, he [Titus] might train up that church in the true faith. The

---

where "oil" refers to lamp oil, i.e., time.

328 Letter 74 in modern numeration (74.5).

329 The *Synopsis* was a combination of three anonymous ancient treatises published in 1557 and attributed to Dorotheus of Tyre, a 3rd–4th century Syrian saint mentioned by Eusebius (*History* 7.32). It consists of *The Lives of the Prophets*, *The Lives of the Twelve Apostles*, and *The List of the Seventy Disciples*. The third one is the part Balduin is referring to. The entire work is printed in PG 92:521–524, 543–545, 1061–1065.

330 It is the same Nicopolis in all three cases, most accurately located in Epirus, but before the formation of the Roman province of Epirus in A.D. 110, it was in Macedonia. Thrace is immediately to the east of Macedonia, and in Homeric usage included it.

fourth command is concerned with certain others whom Paul likewise calls to himself: "Send Zenas the lawyer and Apollos ahead, solicitously, that nothing might be lacking to them" (v. 13). This Zenas was someone we do not read of elsewhere. Paul calls him a νομικὸν, a lawyer. Flacius thinks that he was experienced in jurisprudence, and gathers from this that Paul commends even to Christian youth the study of the laws and of other liberal arts. But he was of slight fortune and in need of food for the road, which is rare among those who are experienced in jurisprudence. Thus it is more correctly judged that he was a νομικὸς of the same kind as the one of whom Luke 10:25 speaks, or an interpreter of the Mosaic Law, because he is joined with Apollos, the learned Apostolic man from the church of Corinth who is commended on account of his eloquence and experience with the Scriptures (Acts 18:24). He summoned them to himself that he might confer with them about church matters and confirm them more and more in the faith. But he sends them ahead, or as the Greek text has it, wants them to be brought or sent σπουδαίως, solicitously and with care, lest anything should be lacking to them—that is, with necessary food for the road. And since Titus perhaps could not bestow this on them from his own means, he adds a fifth command, which pertains to the whole Cretan church, from which they should seek the expenses necessary for that journey. "And let our people learn," he says, "to excel in good works for necessary uses, that they might not be unfruitful" (v. 14). He considers it to be fair that the church should share necessities with those apostolic men for that necessary journey, as he taught elsewhere: "The one who is instructed in speech should share all good things with the one who has instructed him" (Gal. 6:6).

He calls this "to excel in good works," that is, to be careful to make progress in the good, that it might be plain from their beneficence that their faith has not been unfruitful. Finally, by his custom, he ends the epistle with greetings: "All who are with me salute you." It was for Titus very much a mark of his humaneness and piety, that he easily deserved the love of all Paul's friends, who accordingly asked to be added jointly to the salutation given him. And Paul wants, in turn, to salute those who love him in the faith (v. 15), understanding that there are true Christians in Crete, who not only boast faith with the mouth, but also demonstrate it with works of charity. For them he prays, not only for health and prosperity but also the grace of God, by means of that common prayer that he attaches to all his Epistles, "The grace of God be with you all," meaning the gracious favor of God, with which He has embraced us in His Son, from whom he prays they will never fall away. Indeed, nothing can be more excellent than this prayer, for he who has a propitious God has all things.

Questions from this Part of the Chapter

Question 1

In matters of faith, should one abstain from all disputations whatsoever, since St. Paul wants contentions and disputes of the law to be avoided (v. 9)?

Answer: Contentions and disputes are quite different from sacred disputations. The former seek nothing but victory; the latter seek only the truth. The former make schisms without number among sharers of the same faith; the latter do indeed cause dissensions, but with heretics, and to have disagreements with heretics is not a matter of contention but of piety, Chrysostom says. The former are prohibited by Paul; the latter are usefully retained in the church by the example of Christ and of the Apostles, who also disputed with their adversaries, and because scarcely any way is better for investigating the truth than this sort of comparison of opinions. For as Nazianzen has written in book 1 of *On Theology*,[331] "Truth is brought into the light when it has been drawn out by logical disputations, and like fire from the clash and grinding of stones, so what is true is elicited and as it were, expressed." But one must beware lest empty contentions and disputes arise from useful disputations.

---

331 This sounds like a reference to one of Gregory of Nazianzus' "Theological Orations" (nos. 27–31), but the quotation does not appear in any of them. In fact, the first "Theological Oration" is quite critical of disputation.

For as Augustine writes in *On Christian Doctrine*, [book 2], chapter 31, "The discipline of disputation is very useful for penetrating and solving all kinds of questions that are in the holy writings, yet one must beware the lust of quarreling there, and a certain childish vanity of tricking one's adversaries."[332] Now since we should guard against contentions of this kind in our disputing, let these rules be observed. (1) The disputer should know how to discern the precious from the worthless. That is, he should understand the true opinion rightly, on its foundations, and know the false opinions well, lest he should foist anything falsely on his adversary. This is Irenaeus's rule in the preface of book 4. He says, "It is necessary for one who wishes to convert heretics to know their rules or arguments diligently, for it is impossible for anyone to cure certain sick people, if he is ignorant of the malady of those who are ailing."[333] Hilary has similar comments in book 8 of *On the Trinity*. "We have a twofold concern," he says, "in refuting the idle words of the heretics: first that we teach things that are holy and perfect and sound, lest our speech, wandering off from the roads by way of certain sidetracks and sharp turns, and reemerging from wild rabbit trails, should seek the truth rather than demonstrating it; second, that we reveal to the conscience of all that the things that are being adapted to an appearance of enticing truth by those sophistries of empty and fallacious opinions, are ridiculous and foolish."[334] (2) Nothing should be asserted in disputations without the authority of the divine Scriptures, for Scripture alone is the norm for controversies of faith. Whatever does not agree with it is rejected as easily as it is asserted, as Jerome says on chapter 23 of Matthew. Thus Augustine wanted the canonical books to be supreme in disputations, Letter 163.[335] (3) Arguments of

---

332 *On Christian Doctrine* 2.31.48.
333 *Against Heresies* 4.Preface.2.
334 *On the Trinity* 8.2.
335 Balduin may be referring to Letter 82 in modern numeration, in which Augustine writes to Jerome, "I confess to your Charity that I have learned to yield this respect and honor only to the canonical books of Scripture: of these alone do I most firmly believe that the authors were completely free from error....As to all other writings, in reading them, however great the superiority of the authors

reason should not be advanced except sparingly, and after the opinion has already been sufficiently confirmed from the Scriptures; or to one who is really overdoing it, and for the greater confusion of the adversaries, that they might perish by the same weapons with which they have fought. There is great danger otherwise, entrusting matters of faith to human reasoning, since divine Scripture has no need of human wisdom, as Chrysostom warns in Homily 11 on Genesis. (4) In doubtful questions, which have not been expressly defined in the Scriptures, judgment must be suspended rather than something being rashly determined. Thus Augustine, when he touched upon that question, how God, "even if He does not create souls from heredity,[336] would not still be the Author of the same sin," adds, "It is a great question, and wants another disputation; as far as I can tell, though, a temperate disputation, with moderation, that it might be praised as a cautious inquiry rather than blamed as a hasty assertion. For where there is a dispute about a most obscure matter, and the certain and clear documents of the divine Scriptures are of no help, human presumption ought to restrain itself, doing nothing by deviating to either side" (book 2, *On the Merits and Remission of Sins*, chapter 36).[337] (5) In disputing, victory should not be sought, but truth, whence Licentius in Augustine, book 1 of *Against the Academics*, chapter 3:

"I think that there is no small profit in Philosophy," he says, "since victory is considered unimportant in comparison with seeking the right and the true."[338] (6) There should be no wrangling in disputations. Therefore a humble mind should be brought to them, and one desirous

---

to myself in sanctity and learning, I do not accept their teaching as true on the mere ground of the opinion being held by them; but only because they have succeeded in convincing my judgment of its truth either by means of these canonical writings themselves, or by arguments addressed to my reason. I believe, my brother, that this is your own opinion as well as mine."

336 The Latin is *de traduce*, "from the branch." Thus the theory that God creates the souls of new human beings from the substance of their parents, rather than *ex nihilo*, is called "Traducianism."

337 *On the Merits and Remission of Sins and On the Baptism of Infants* 2.36.(59).

338 *Against the Academics* 1.3.8. This is one of Augustine's early Socratic-style dialogues, and Licentius is one of the participants.

of learning, especially in these questions that have no certain definition from the Scriptures. Thus Augustine, dealing in Letter 112,[339] chapter 21 with that question, "How are we going to see God in eternal life?" warns "that one should not be puffed up against the other, lest while we seek by wrangling to investigate how God can be seen, we should lose the very peace and sanctification without which no one can see God."[340] (7) Let those who dispute use a simple kind of speaking, lest when they adorn the truth with too many words, they might lose the truth through the words. For as Augustine writes in *Questions on Genesis* book 1, the preface,[341] "A disputation is not sought by means of truth, but truth by means of disputation."[342] (8) A disputant should not be a flatterer. Therefore, when there must be a dispute against the enemies of the truth, the truth should be defended with severity. Thus Augustine, because he understood that Proculcian the Donatist had disputed with the orthodox man Evodius, and taken issue with the words of orthodox Evodius, and wrongly interpreted the words of Evodius with which he had quite fervently defended the truth, writes to the Donatist in Letter 147,[343] "If by chance he has said something rather fervently while disputing for his faith and love of the church, something that your dignity would not wish to hear, it should be named not contumacy but confidence, for he wanted to be a debater and a disputant, not a flatterer and a sycophant."[344] (9) Although no one can dispute without syllogistic reasoning, still there is no need for the syllogisms always to be explicit, for often a simple dictum from Scripture suffices to convince an adversary. But if explicit syllogisms are demanded in all things, contentions emerge about logical matters instead of useful

---

339 Letter 147 in modern numeration.

340 *Letters* 147.21.(49).

341 The text reads "book 1, letter 1 (*Epist.* 1)," but the treatise does not contain letters, and the quotation is found in the preface to book 1 (the book on Genesis) of Augustine's *Questions on the Heptateuch*.

342 *Questions on the Heptateuch*, book 1, preface.

343 Letter 33 in modern numeration.

344 Augustine, *Letters* 33.3.

disputations about theological matters. Logic ought to serve Theology, not prescribe to it or dominate it. If these rules have been closely observed, disputation can be carried out against the errors of men, even about sacred things, usefully and without strife and contention. This zeal of contending for the truth is so far from the vice of contention[345] that it rather joins dissenting men together by the bond of peace, as Augustine writes in book 4 of *Against Cresconius*, chapter 3.

Question 2

Is it lawful to remove heretics from life (de vita), because Paul writes, "De vita (avoid) a heretical man after one and another admonition" (v. 10).

Answer: Erasmus reports in his notes for this passage that it was produced in a council by a certain senior theologian, important among the leading men, when it had come into question what passage there was in the canonical writings that commanded a heretic to be subjected to capital punishment. "*Devita*," he said, thinking that *devitare* was Latin for "to remove *from life (de vita)*." The Jesuit Benedict Justinian, in his commentary on this passage, mentions this with the greatest displeasure, and so calls it the fabrication of a most wicked man.[346] Cornelius à Lapide on this passage censures the same thing in Erasmus, adding "Who, I pray, of the Latin interpreters or Fathers, has been so senseless, so foolish, as to say that *divita*[347] is the same as 'to remove *de vita*?'" Cornelius is right, none of the Fathers or learned interpreters were ever so foolish; but your Erasmus has reproached the absurdities of your monks. Foreseeing your calumnies, he introduces a witness for his narrative. He says, "Lest anyone should suspect that this story of mine has been fabricated, I got it from John Colet,[348] a man

---

345 Read *contentionis* instead of *conditionis*.

346 Meaning, a fabrication made by Erasmus to make the theologians look bad, not a fabrication made by the unnamed theologian in Erasmus's anecdote.

347 *Divita* is the form in the Vulgate, and which Balduin used in his earlier comments on v. 10. It means the same thing, but the difference makes the unnamed theologian's mistake even greater.

348 John Colet (1467–1519) was an English churchman and Renaissance scholar

of proven integrity, who was presiding when the thing was done." Nor is there a great difference between this and Thomas' interpretation of the Apostolic dictum. He says in the second part of the second part, question 11, article 3, in the conclusion: "By this very dictum he proves that heretics, if they still be found to be obstinate after one and another correction, should not only be separated from the church through excommunication, but should also be expelled from the world through death." And why is it surprising that for an opinion of such a horrible kind, they should also produce horrible arguments? For others also, intending to prove that heretics should rightly be burned in the sight of the people, have adduced Christ's dictum in John 15:6: "If anyone has not remained in me, he will be thrown out, like a branch, and become dry,[349] and they will collect it and throw it into the fire." Bernhardinus Muscarellus sought his fiery argument against heretics from this passage in his *Practical Criminal Law*, the chapter on the crime of divine lèse-majesté, notes 48 and 49. Also Simanca in his *Institutes* chapter 46, notes 45 and 46. Even the more judicious Papists ridicule theses foolish opinions, not at all undeservedly.

Question 3

Is it rightly denied from this Apostolic dictum, "Avoid a heretical man," that heretics should be subjected to capital punishment?

Answer: Calvin and Beza, who were advocates of this horrible opinion concerning the capital punishment of heretics, disdain this reasoning alleged by some to the effect that nothing is here commanded to the magistrate, but has to do with the minister of the church, whose duty it should not be to subject thieves, murderers, blasphemers, *etc.* to punishment, but only by the legitimate judgment of the church to hand those who do not return to their senses over to Satan, for which reason they will still not depart unpunished. But Beza acts no differently than if that horrible punishment, by which heretics are killed at the sentence

---

(significant in his own right) who befriended Erasmus during the latter's extended stay in England.

349 Read *arescet* instead of *arcescet*.

of the magistrate, had already been abolished in other places. We ourselves cannot allow this, because in this text our Paul treats of heretics as if they were in his see, and how they ought to be dealt with by the minister of the Word, and teaches (rightly, we gather) that it should not be the duty of the minister to hand a heretic over to the magistrate to be killed, even if he has been convicted; for the Apostle has not even a word about this. Now here one also has the passage of Tertullian: What Scripture does not say, it denies (book 4, *Against Marcion*).[350] Elsewhere in Scripture there are arguments of no small moment against that bloody opinion of the Papists and the Calvinists, for instance: that it is said of the New Testament church: "They will not hurt, nor kill, in all my holy mountain, because the earth has been filled with the knowledge of the Lord" (Is. 11:9); that neither Christ nor the Apostles ever ordered capital punishment for heretics, something not even Bellarmine denies; that heretics are commanded rather to grow like tares all the way to the harvest, and are prohibited to be pulled out (Matt. [13:24–30]), which Chrysostom understands as a picture of the heretics (Homily 47 on Matthew), and Cyprian also (Letter 3, book 3); that no one can be compelled to faith, because it is in the mind, over which no man has the power of command; and that it has never been pleasing to good men in the church if rage should be vented upon someone to the point of death, even if he is a heretic, as Augustine says in book 3 of *Against Cresconius the Grammarian*, chapter 50. But heretics should be restrained by another method. The ministers of the church should make inquiries diligently, and observe the doctrines, endeavors, and customs of the heretics, in accord with Paul's warning in Romans 16:17. They should warn those they have observed of their error, from the solid foundations of Scripture, and repeat that admonition once and again, which our Paul desires, and publicly rebuke those who despise the admonitions, and point out their errors to the church, and exhort

---

350 Cf. *Against Marcion* 4.19: "But suppose they sent Him the message for the purpose of tempting Him? Well, but the Scripture does not say so; and inasmuch as it is usual for it to indicate what is done in the way of temptation…so, when it makes no mention of temptation, it does not admit the interpretation of temptation." ANF 3:377.

them to flee them, and cut those who are still obstinate off from the body of the church like putrid members by way of legitimate excommunication, lest the healthy part should be drawn away, according to the example of Paul in 1 Timothy 1:20. The magistrates should embrace the orthodox confession by means of public edicts and rescripts; order the administrators of public offices, political as well as ecclesiastical, to subscribe and to confirm their subscription by oath, according to the example of Joshua in chapter 24, verse 25, Joash in 2 Kings 11:17, and Josiah in 2 Kings 23 verse 3; remove ministers of the church who live impiously and teach wrongly, punish the obstinate with prison or banishment, but stop short of the penalty of death unless the crime of sedition should chance to be combined with the heresy—or of treason, of blasphemy, or the like—matters concerning which the civil laws judge. And heretics have almost always been dealt with in this way, although with some difference.

For in the early church, when the Bishops were deprived of the resources and help of the magistrate, they overcame heretics by excommunication alone, as Paul overcame Hymenaeus and Alexander (1 Tim. 1:20). Afterwards, under the Christian Emperors, they were banished by the Prince, as it is in the chapter *Concerning the Highest Trinity*,[351] Law 2, at the end; or deported, as in each law; or punished arbitrarily as in *Concerning the Highest Trinity*, Law 5.[352] Arius was not punished by Constantine the Great in any other way than by banishment, or exile, as Socrates[353] testifies in chapter 8.[354] Nestorius, too, was not punished by Theodosius and Valentinian except by exile, as Socrates testifies in book 7, chapter [34]. Theodosius enacted a major monetary fine for heretics. Deportation was the gravest penalty of them all, and it is called the final and capital punishment in the last law of the Code, *Concern-*

---

351 This is the first heading in the Code of Justinian.

352 Code 1.3 stipulates different penalties for different ranks of offender: loss of position for clergy and military, banishment from the city for freemen, and "the severest penalty" for slaves. The word "arbitrarily" must refer to this.

353 Socrates of Constantinople, that is, who chronicled the history of the church from 305 to 439 in his *Church History*, and died sometime after 439.

354 The 8th chapter of book 1, that is.

ing the Executor and the Requisitions, book 12.³⁵⁵ Other penalties did accompany it, for instance infamy, the loss of goods and the privileges of entering into legal contracts: of testifying, inheriting, petitioning, serving in the military, but up to the times of Theodosius, it had not come to capital punishment. Nor was there ever anything decreed on this matter by the councils until the Council of Constance in the year of our Lord 1415, which decided something harsher for John Huss and Jerome of Prague, although they had not yet been convicted, contrary to the guarantee given by the magistrate,³⁵⁶ and made the decree that they should be burned. See many more things about this matter in my *Disputation on Heretics*, held in the year 1608.

Question 4

In what sense is a heretic said to be αὐτοκατάκριτος (self-condemned) in verse 10?

Answer: There are some who think more leniently about heresy and heretics, so that they judge them worthy of pity rather than punishment. For they consider a heretic not to err maliciously and contrary to conscience, but only by some persuasion, because he firmly believes that he holds his opinion with entire correctness, and because, having been taken captive by the eyes of the mind, and having been imbued with a false judgment, he thinks the church that he contradicts is not the church of God, but the synagogue of Satan. Celsus Minus is of this opinion in his pamphlet *On Heretics not Having to be Killed*, section 1, page 9. But if you cite against them that saying of our Apostle, that a heretic is αὐτοκατάκριτος after one and another admonition, condemned by his own judgment and convicted in his own conscience, they will reply that "to be αὐτοκατάκριτον" should be understood thus: that heretics, by sinning, are authors of their own condemnation, inasmuch as those who assert that they have judged rightly in selecting the

---

355 This is probably a reference to 12.64.2, but modern editions end with 12.64.1, because 2 was apparently a later addition, not actually part of Justinian's Code.

356 Sigismund of Hungary, soon to be Holy Roman Emperor, had given them a promise of safe conduct if they came to Constance.

correct doctrines for themselves, when they have chosen false doctrine, fall—deceived by their own judgment—into this condemnation that they have imprudently prepared for themselves, the wretches, in which they even wish to persist; and that they should accordingly be avoided as a consequence of their disease, which they do not acknowledge, rejecting all medicine. For if "to be αὐτοκατάκριτον" were the same as "to sin against the conscience," and one had to abandon a man for that reason, they say that the Apostle would contradict himself, since he writes elsewhere that one ought to spare a heretic, and that he should be commended to the light of divine grace if he could ever be enlightened by it. They say these things, but all these things are true of the weak and erring who, having been led astray by others, think that the false doctrine is true, and defend it to the best of their ability for a time—indeed with great zeal, but zeal "that is not κατ' ἐπίγνωσιν" (according to knowledge, [Rom. 10:2])—but may eventually be corrected by diligent explanation, since they allow room for admonitions; for they desire to be taught better things, if they can. Augustine has said of them in *On Baptism*, book [5], chapter 19,[357] that they should be called not "heretics" so much as "erring ones." But heretics defend an opinion—whether devised by themselves or drawn from others—obstinately, although they have been convicted of their error in their conscience, for they listen to no one but themselves, and thus prefer to die in error, rather than be seen to have erred. Augustine writes of these people that they engender or follow false and novel opinions for the sake of some temporal convenience, and especially of glory and preeminence, and that "even when they have been corrected, so that they know what is sound and right, they still resist contumaciously, and are not willing to amend their pestilential and deadly doctrines" (the book *On the Profit of Believing*, chapter 1,[358] and book 18, *On the City of God*, chapter 51).[359]

---

357 *On Baptism against the Donatists* 5.19.26.

358 The part about heretics being motivated by temporal convenience goes with this citation. "He, in my opinion, is an heretic who, for the sake of some temporal advantage, and chiefly for the sake of his own glory and pre-eminence, either gives birth to, or follows, false and new opinions." *On the Profit of Believing* 1.

359 The quotation about contumacious resistance comes from *City of God* 18.51.

The Apostle commands that we warn them, or that they be instructed correctly from Scripture, "once and again," that is, "often." And if they have nothing substantive to argue in return, and yet continue not only to defend their error, but also to propagate it, this is a clear indication that they are sinning against conscience, and have thus been convicted of error by their own judgment; for they could be taught better things, but they are not willing. So Paul writes elsewhere that they "have made shipwreck with respect to faith, conscience having been rejected" (1 Tim. 1:19), and that they have a seared conscience (1 Tim. 4:2): not that they feel no pricks of conscience, but that the pricks have no effect on them. Thus he indicates in our text that they are αὐτοκατάκριτον, that they are convicted by their own judgment and in their conscience, not that they have simply been deceived by some opinion or persuasion. And this can be shown by two arguments from the text. First, because they are commanded to avoid such people after a repeated admonition, but if they were indeed erring, having been deceived, they should not be avoided, but rather received as people who err from the weakness of their judgment, and led back from error to the truth, according to the command of the Apostle (Rom. 14:1), "Receive the one who is weak in the faith." Second, because the reason *why* they should be avoided is added: that they are entirely "overthrown," and they are recalcitrant, and resist demonstrated truth, which is not the mark of a weak and corrupted faculty of judgment, but of a refractory and malicious man. So when the Apostle gives the command (2 Tim. 2:[24-]25) that one must patiently bear with certain men, if perchance God might grant them grace unto repentance, it should be understood not of obstinate heretics, but of the erring who are still teachable. But he judges differently concerning recalcitrant and obstinate heretics, for he "hands them over to Satan, that they might learn not to blaspheme" (1 Tim. 1:20). He prays against them, that the church might be "liberated from those profane and foolish men" (2 Thess. 3:2), and in our text he gives the order to avoid them, for they are αὐτοκατάκριτοι, convicted by their own conscience. They are διεφθαρμένοι τὸν νοῦν (depraved in mind, 1 Tim. 6:5, [cf.] 2 Tim. 3:8), men who by the just judgment of God have entirely lost the power of judging and understanding, having been utterly blinded, that they might continue to φιλάττειν (maintain) the same θέσιν (position, thesis) shamelessly, even if they have been refuted a thousand times, "growing worse, erring and seducing others into error" (2 Tim. 3:13), which is why it is not at all undeservedly that men who have been rejected by God and "handed over to a reprobate mind" [Rom. 1:28] should be guarded against, and fled.

Theological Aphorisms from this Part of the Chapter

1. Foolish questions and absurd disputes about things of no import are alien to the ecclesiastical chair (v. 9), for "the one who speaks, let him speak the declarations of God" (1 Pet. 4:11). Therefore those who are eager to entertain themselves and others at a council with fables and little stories, or who desire to seem subtle by tossing around pros and cons, should not be tolerated at all. The speech of the Lord is simple, intended not for arrogance, but for understanding; not for the petty glory of the teacher, but for the benefit of the hearers. This is why St. Paul repeats this admonition about avoiding foolish questions and useless disputes so many times (1 Tim. 4:7, 2 Tim. 2:23). For he knows the custom of some younger men who, when they are going to speak to the people, put forth only grand and sublime words, depart from a simple manner of speaking that consists principally of morals, and try to captivate the popular ear with the quarreling of scholastic terms and disputations. You could say they are like that Elihu in the history of Job who says, "Listen to me, and I will show you my wisdom, for I am full of words, and the breath of my belly compels me, and my stomach is like new wine without a vent, which bursts new bottles" (Job 32:10, 18–19).

2. Those who err in the faith, whether deceived by their own opinion or led astray by the persuasion of others, should receive admonitions willingly, or else their error degenerates into heresy, and they are overthrown and hardened (v. [11]). For every heresy has been conjoined with hardening, first in the heresiarchs, who not only err themselves, but also overthrow the faith of others (2 Tim. 2:18) whom

they lead astray (2 Tim. 3:13), and "introduce destructive sects" (2 Pet. 2:1). Indications of these hardenings are not obscure: (1) πώρωσις τῆς καρδίας (callousing of the heart), which is attributed to other hardened men (John 12:40, Eph. 4:18) when they are moved by no sensation of divine threats. (2) ἀπαλγησία (insensitivity to pain), when they no longer feel the pain of a wounded conscience, for they are said to have a seared conscience, or one cut off, as it were, with a branding iron (1 Tim. 4:2). (3) πνεῦμα [κατανύξεως] (a spirit of stupefaction, or a spirit of deep sleep (Is. 29[:10]), when they are in part inflamed by hatred for those who are giving good warnings, and in part suffering the conflicts of thoughts that are accusing and defending each other [Rom. 2:15], yet which do not concern them. (4) They are corrupted in the mind (1 Tim. 6:5, 2 Tim. 3:8), or blinded in such a way that they do not want to acknowledge their errors, even though they have been demonstrated to the eye—nor indeed are they able to, by the just judgment of God, whose oft-repeated admonitions they have spurned. (5) Finally, they even become blasphemers of the celestial truth that they contradict. We have an example of men of this kind in Acts 19:9 and 13:45–46. Teachability can guard against all these things. For man is prone to errors, which are removed from many through faithful instruction, while others who are wise only in themselves, perish by themselves.

3. We should avoid heretics (v. 10) in the same way we should beware false prophets (Matt. 7:15), and beware of pseudo-apostles as of dogs (Phil. 3:2). Nor should we believe every spirit (1 John 4:1), and we should "observe those who cause dissensions and offenses against sound doctrine" (Rom. 16:17). Let this be done (1) when we abstain from association with them, as far as this can be done. For although it is permitted to live with them politically, we would have to exit the world otherwise (1 Cor. 5:10). Still, that association with those who have not been rightly instructed is perilous, for "their speech spreads like a cancer" (2 Tim. 2:17). "Their throat is an open grave, they deal deceitfully with their tongues" (Ps. 5:11). They make a pretense of Christianity, and go to battle against Christ, as Athanasius says in his Oration 2 Against

the Arians.³⁶⁰ Thus Chrysostom has judged in Homily 47 on Acts that the threats of heretics should not be feared as much as their flatteries, and St. John wants not even a greeting to be spoken to heretics (2 John 10). And he himself would not even enter the bath house in which Cerinthus was washing.³⁶¹ (2) When their rites are avoided and their orations are not heeded, for all the words of heretics are suspect, Athanasius says in Oration 4 Against the Arians, and experience teaches how easily those who have been among foreigners, and have not been able to attend rites other than those of heretics, have imbibed their poison with great danger—theirs, and that of many others. (3) When we do not read the books of heretics, for nothing is more pernicious than an evil book. For fine words are discovered there, specious sophistries constructed to deceive, fallacious arguments arranged with great zeal, by which the inexperienced are easily deceived. Leo expressed a fine judgment on this matter in Letter 93,³⁶² chapter 15. "Although there are in the writings of heretics certain things that seem to have the appearance of erudition and piety, they are yet not free of poison." For as Gregory writes in book 5 of *Morals*, chapter 11, "Heretics mix things that are right with things that are perverse, that by displaying the good things, they might draw the hearers to themselves, and by producing the evil things, they might corrupt them with a hidden pestilence."³⁶³

4. Although the life of all men is a pilgrimage, since "we have no lasting city here, but seek the city that will be" (Heb. 13:14), still the ministers of the church are especially pilgrims, just as Paul rarely

---

360 Cf. the second discourse (Oration): "The Arians are not fighting with us about their heresy; but *while they pretend us, their real fight is against the Godhead Itself*" (2.18.32, NPNF² 4:365). Another similar statement is found in the first discourse: "Why then, if they think as Jews, are they not circumcised with them too, instead of *pretending Christianity, while they are its foes*?" (1.11.38, NPNF² 4:328).

361 St. Irenaeus writes in *Against Heresies* 3.3.4, "There are also those who heard from [St. Polycarp] that John, the disciple of the Lord, going to bathe at Ephesus and perceiving Cerinthus within, rushed out of the bath-house without bathing, exclaiming, 'Let us fly, lest even the bath-house fall down, because Cerinthus, the enemy of the truth, is within.'" Cerinthus was an early gnostic teacher.

362 Gregory the Great, *Letter 103* in modern editions.

363 Gregory the Great, Morals in Job 5.11.28 (*PL* 75.694B).

stayed in one place. In our text, he writes that he is going to winter at Nicopolis (v. 12). In the case of the Apostle, indeed, this was not surprising, because the care of all the churches was resting on him (2 Cor. 11:28), but it does not seem that this can be said for the other ministers of the Word, since they have surely been placed over some assembly. Yet a fourfold migration of these men occurred from time to time. One is by violence, when having been ejected from their post by enemies of the truth, they are compelled to go away into exile, the way Paul left Damascus in a basket, having been sent away by the disciples (Acts 9:25). Another is by choice, when they betake themselves elsewhere because of private business matters, or sometimes even to friends for the sake of enjoyment, which is often part of being human, and has not been forbidden to the ministers of the church, as long as it is moderate. The third is dutiful, when they move by reason of their office, for the sake of looking after other churches, a kind of pilgrimage that was familiar to Paul. The fourth is the necessary kind, when having been ejected by famine or pestilence or war, or even persecution of one's person, they are compelled to betake themselves to flight. It pertains to this kind when they are lawfully called to another church, which they are able to lead more fruitfully.[364] In all these migrations of theirs, they must be mindful of the way of all flesh, and arrange their road accordingly, in such a way that they might not be excluded from the heavenly fatherland.

5) Those who are sent elsewhere in the church's name should be sent solicitously, as our Paul warns in verse 13; that is, with decent provisions, for no one "performs military service at his own expense," nor does anyone "plant a vineyard who may not eat of its fruit" (1 Cor. 9:7). For this purpose, among others, there must be an accounting of the church's money, that it might not be exhausted one of these times, but the collections might suffice for the things that are needed.

---

364 This fourth kind would seem to be simply a broader version of the first kind ("by violence"), at least until this "more fruitful" consideration is added, which is confusing in itself, as it doesn't seem to involve necessity or compulsion at all. It seems Balduin must mean that a minister who is offered a chance for a "more fruitful" ministry is actually *obligated* to take it.

6) It behooves the pious to be generous in good works (v. 14), not only because it has to do with piety and integrity of life, but also because it has to do with munificence to the poor and the ministers of the church, so that if the public collection (*sumtu publico*) should chance to fall short, their own abundance might supply the need of those people. This is that splendid fruit of faith without which we boast of the Gospel in vain. For "those who serve the Gospel also make a living from the Gospel, as the Lord ordained" (1 Cor. 9:14). "Therefore he who is catechized in the Word should share in all good things with he who catechizes him" (Gal. 6:6).

7) "Salvation and blessing"[365] is a pious prayer that obtains from God whatever things are best for us—namely, if it should arise from those who love us in the faith (v. 15); that is, from the partners who share our faith, whose hearts the Holy Spirit has kindled with sincere love for us. A blessing of this kind, which comes down from heaven, is a sign of His love, for angels also have saluted men out of love for them (Judg. 6:12, Luke 1:28), and God Himself salutes us out of His boundless love for us, as often as He announces the promises of grace to us, and publishes the blessing bestowed on those who observe His Law. Let us therefore learn to bless each other too, out of a sincere love for one another, not doubting but that pious prayers may be the vehicles of the divine blessing of which all are made partakers who show themselves worthy of it. May God, the font of all blessing, fill us with a blessing of this kind, of salvation and grace, and may His grace be and remain with us all, through Christ. Amen.

The End Of the Commentary on St. Paul the Apostle's Epistle to Titus

---

365 These are not the words of the Vulgate for Titus 3:15, or Balduin's own translation above. Perhaps it is a paraphrase.

The Epistle of St. Paul to Philemon
(Παύλου τοῦ Ἀποστόλου πρὸς τὸν Φιλήμονα ἐπιστολή)

Introduction
Of the Occasion, Argument, and Division of this Epistle

Even though there was formerly no lack of those who doubted whether this was a letter of St. Paul and whether we could be built up from it, they nevertheless had no other proof for their doubt than that it was only written to recommend, not to teach, as Jerome remarks in the preface to Paul's letters.[366] But there was never a doubt in the orthodox Church about this matter; besides, the customary blessing is added close to the end, by which he seals with his own hand as a special sign that it is his authentic letter, and so distinguishes it from a forged letter circulated under his name. He writes about this: "The greeting of Paul with my own hand, which is the token in every letter I write. The grace of our Lord Jesus Christ be with you all" (2 Thessalonians 3:17).

Specifically, however, this letter is the shortest of all, very intimate, written to a private person about private business. Philemon was a citizen of Colossae, since his slave Onesimus is said to have been from Colossae (Colossians 4:9). Since Philemon was well-known among them and rich, his large household employed many slaves. Among them was Onesimus, who, after he had stolen something from his owner, as can be gathered from Philemon 18, fled from Colossae to Rome. The

---

366 Jerome, Preface to the Pauline Epistles (Romans–Philemon) in the Vulgate.

apostle Paul, who was then in his first imprisonment, converted him to faith in Christ after he repented of what he had done. For this reason, Paul calls him "his son whom he begat while he was in chains," as is stated in Philemon 10. Since for some time he had been very useful to the imprisoned apostle, when he wrote his letter to the church in Colossae, he also sent him back to his owner with this commendation, and asked him as a friend to receive the runaway slave back favorably. Paul applied very powerful persuasion and used wonderful skill to make this serious offense pleasing to Philemon's heart, and restored Onesimus to him with the highest commendation.

Therefore, even though no article of faith is openly treated in this letter, yet an example of the apostle's seriousness and gentleness does shine forth here. He deals with the subject in great humility, while he shows by this example that access to grace is closed off to no man, not even to a runaway slave and thief, nor must anyone definitely despair of salvation. The apostle has to be concerned even about slaves, and must deal gently with repentant sinners, because they have the same Redeemer we do. Slaves must not be taken away from their masters (for Paul does not try to keep this Onesimus even though he was useful to him in his chains, but sends him back to his owner), because finally all Christians ought to be fair rather than overly attached to someone. With these names this letter does not apply only to Philemon, but it is the κειμήλιον [treasure] of the whole Church, because the letter supplies many things useful for all of us. For the purpose of teaching, we divide it into two parts. The first part concerns kindness, and makes known Philemon's godliness, faith, and love, and this is easily found in what he would write up to verse eight.

The second part embraces the commendation of Onesimus, which is defended with many clear proofs, from verse eight to the end. May the Most Holy Trinity be with us, as we treat this part of His most holy Word in the manner and way we ought, and beneficially apply it to our profit. Amen.

The First Part of the Text [Philemon 1–7]

Παῦλος δέσμιος Χριστοῦ Ἰησοῦ, καὶ Τιμόθεος ὁ ἀδελφὸς Φιλήμονι τῷ ἀγαπητῷ καὶ συνεργῷ ἡμῶν

1. Paul, a prisoner of Christ Jesus, and brother Timothy to Philemon, our beloved colleague.

Καὶ Ἀπφίᾳ τῇ ἀγαπητῇ, καὶ Ἀρχίππῳ τῷ συστρατιώτῃ ἡμῶν, καὶ τῇ κατ' οἶκόν σου ἐκκλησίᾳ

2. And to beloved Apphia, and to Archippus, our fellow-soldier, and to the congregation at your house

Χάρις ὑμῖν καὶ εἰρήνη ἀπὸ θεοῦ πατρὸς ἡμῶν, καὶ κυρίου Ἰησοῦ Χριστοῦ

3. Grace to you and peace from God our Father and the Lord Jesus Christ

Εὐχαριστῶ τῷ θεῷ μου, πάντοτε μνείαν σου ποιούμενος ἐπὶ τῶν προσευχῶν μου

4. I thank my God every time I mention you in my prayers

Ἀκούων σου τὴν ἀγάπην καὶ τὴν πίστιν, ἣν ἔχεις πρὸς τὸν κύριον Ἰησοῦν, καὶ εἰς πάντας τοὺς ἁγίους

5. When I hear about the love and faith you have toward the Lord Jesus and toward all the saints

Ὅπως ἡ κοινωνία τῆς πίστεώς σου ἐνεργὴς γένηται ἐν ἐπιγνώσει παντὸς ἔργου ἀγαθοῦ τοῦ ἐν ὑμῖν εἰς Χριστὸν Ἰησοῦν

6. So that the sharing of your faith becomes effective in the knowledge of every good which is in you toward Christ Jesus

Χάριν γὰρ ἔσχον πολλὴν καὶ παράκλησιν ἐπὶ τῇ ἀγάπῃ σου, ὅτι τὰ σπλάγχνα τῶν ἁγίων ἀναπέπαυται διὰ σοῦ ἀδελφέ

7. For we have great joy and encouragement in your love, because the inward parts of the saints have been refreshed through you, brother

Notes in text.[367]

---

[367] Verse 7 (Greek): Σπλάγχνα and *viscera* (KJV: "bowels") are consistently translated "inward parts." Balduin discusses this in the last paragraph of his com-

Analysis and Explanation of Part One

The introduction in the first three verses conforms to the usual parts of a letter. He lists the author, those addressed, and the greeting, in all of which he has scattered some seeds of the contents, which is for the benefit of Philemon, whom he wants to try to persuade. Timothy is associated with Paul as author: "Paul, a prisoner of Christ Jesus, and brother Timothy" (v. 1).

He does not call himself an apostle, as he does in other letters, because he did not want to be entangled here by anything which belongs to the office of an apostle. Rather, he calls himself a captive, because he wrote about his chains: "and indeed a captive of Christ" [v. 9], because he was in chains on account of the Gospel. With this epithet, moreover, he wants to move Philemon's heart, for "the chains of Christ" are equivalent to being a captive. Those who have this name can boast that they were counted worthy to suffer shame for the name of Christ [Acts 5:41]. With their favor the godly can do even more than to receive back a runaway slave. "For who will not feel awe," says Chrysostom, "who will not tremble when he hears about the chains of Christ? Who will not discard his pride in awe of this name, to say nothing of one young slave?"[368]

He associates to himself Timothy as author, just as he did in the letter to the Colossians [1:1], which he had written at the same time. In this way he shows compassion for Onesimus, because he has in Timothy a witness of his chains and of his paternal feelings for Onesimus, and thus a partner in his request. He also does this to influence Philemon's heart, for when these two holy men agree on one matter, he will not be able easily to refuse them anything [cf. Matt. 18:19]. He calls this Timothy a "brother," namely, his brother and Philemon's brother, that is, a partner in faith, or a Christian. He was obliged in the same way to remind Philemon of this, for we are obliged to "do good to all, but

---

ments on this section below, just before the questions.

368 Chrysostom, *Philemon*, NPNF[1] 13:547.

especially to those who are of the household of faith" (Galatians 6:10).

Those addressed in the letter are Philemon, our beloved helper, and Apphia, the very dear sister, and Archippus, our fellow-soldier, and the Church in his house (vv. 1–2). Philemon, as was said, was a citizen of Colossae who had been converted by Paul to the faith of Christ, and for that reason owed himself to Paul, as he says in verse 19. He calls Philemon "beloved." Jerome comments that Paul did not say ἀγαπημένῳ, "beloved," but ἀγαπητῷ, that is, "estimable." The difference between "beloved" and "estimable," he says, is that someone who does not deserve the love can be called "beloved," but the one who deserves to be loved is called "estimable."[369]

He also calls him his συνεργός, because he also takes part in the work of Christ, as Jerome explains it,[370] that is, because he confesses this same faith in Christ and reveals this by what he does, just as do Paul and other godly people. Theophylact thinks that he was a minister of the Church, and takes note here of the repeated emotion (τὸ πάθος). For if Philemon is beloved, he says, he will forgive Onesimus; if he is a fellow-worker, he will not keep a slave, but send him back for the ministry of the Word, whose worker and minister he is. Calvin also thinks that Philemon belonged to the class of pastors, because he is called Paul's συνεργός. But, since all believers are commanded to be συνεργοὶ τῇ ἀληθείᾳ (3 John 8), we judge that the best interpretation of all is that of Ambrose, who thinks he was given this title because he faithfully promoted the affairs of the Church, and greatly aided the course of the Gospel to the best of his ability. Although he was not clergy, he says, nevertheless the Church's needs were important to him because of his zeal; for this reason, he calls his participation a work.

And how eager he was in this effort to promote the teaching of the Gospel becomes clear from the fact that he had a house church, to which Paul also wrote a letter. In his introduction, Theodoret wrote that in this letter Paul arranged a gathering of believers, for which reason that house continued for many generations to be a church dedicated to

---

369 Jerome, *Philemon*, PL 26:607.
370 Jerome, *Philemon*, PL 26:607.

God.³⁷¹ Those who assembled in this house were abundantly assisted by Philemon, for he was generous. He "refreshed the inward parts of the saints," as Paul wrote about him (v. 7). Therefore, even if at this time he was not yet clergy, afterwards he was made bishop of Gaza.³⁷²

Further, Theophylact thinks that Apphia was probably Philemon's wife, whom Paul also calls ἀγαπητῇ, "beloved," because she was worthy of love on account of her confession of faith and devotion to godliness. The Latin version adds "sister," which word is not in the Greek text.³⁷³

Archippus presided over the Church at Colossae; Paul wrote about him: "Say to Archippus: Take heed to the ministry you have received in the Lord, so that you fulfill it" (Colossians 4:17). This is why he calls him συστρατιώτην, "fellow soldier," as he also considered Epaphroditus worthy of this title (Philippians 2:25). He connects the Church of Philemon with these people, that is, his whole family and those who gather in his house for worship, just as he commands them to greet "Nymphas and the church which is in his house" (Colossians 4:15).

Therefore, the apostle invites all these people to intercede for the welfare of one runaway slave, so that he would be received favorably by his owner as a model of extraordinary kindness.

He uses the greeting which is common also in other letters: "Grace to you and peace from God our Father and the Lord Jesus Christ" (v. 3). Grace is the first principle of our salvation, and is equivalent to the mercy of God, through which we are saved, as written above (Titus 3:5).³⁷⁴ Peace follows from grace. We have peace in our consciences, as Paul writes: "Being reconciled, we have peace with God" (Romans 5:1).

Paul prays for both [grace and peace] from God and from Christ, because their essence and power is the same. The Son does the same thing the Father does, but with this distinction of order, that the Father is considered to be the efficient cause and the Son the meritorious

---

371 Theodoret of Cyrus, *Commentary on the Letters of St. Paul*, 2:261.

372 Dorotheus, *Synopsis*.

373 USB fifth edition shows a variant reading here, placing τῇ ἀδελφῇ, "sister," in the text, and listing τῇ ἀγαπητῇ as the variant reading.

374 That is, in Balduin's commentary on Titus which precedes this.

cause of our salvation. The Father is called God and the Son is called Lord, not because the Son is not God or the Father is not Lord, but because by means of His obedience the Son acquired for Himself a special lordship over people, since victors in war have lordship over those whom they snatched out of the hands of enemies and set free.

Up to this point, the beginning of this letter has been the standard one; now he seeks the good will and binds the heart of Philemon to himself in many ways, as he looks for an opportunity to intercede for the runaway slave.

First, he points out the love he demonstrates by praying persistently for him. "I thank my God every time I mention you in my prayers" (v. 4). Every time I remember you (but I remember you every time I pray), I thank God for your goodness. He wrote similarly to Timothy: "I thank God that without ceasing I remember you in my prayers" (2 Timothy 1:3). For it is Paul's custom to make mention in his prayers of the saints whose faith and works were known, partly by giving thanks that God had given them such a heart, and partly by praying that He would strengthen them in good.

Then he points out what virtue of Philemon it is for which he gives thanks, and at the same time praises his godliness: "When I hear," he says, "about the love and faith you have toward the Lord Jesus and toward all the saints" (v. 5). Two special things are necessary in a Christian man: faith and love. Faith is directed toward Christ; love is directed toward the saints. Faith, just like man's heart, is godly, for faith in Christ makes us children of God (John 1:12). But love is the result of faith; faith is recognized from love, because faith works through love (Galatians 5:6). This is why St. James writes: "Just as the body without the spirit is dead, so faith without works is dead" (James 2:26).

Therefore, he now commends these two things in Philemon, and puts him forward as an example of a truly godly man. Because he recognizes that all good comes from God, he thanks God for this man. Since news of Philemon's virtues had traveled from Phrygia to Rome, they must have been all the greater. Theophylact, however, regarded these words as exerting great force on Philemon to embrace his runaway slave. Because he embraces all the saints or believers in love, he ought also to embrace Onesimus with the same love (for he is a believer) as he is seen to love the Lord. To be fair, he pointed out above that Philemon revealed his faith in kindness and mercy toward others.

For this reason, when Paul heard about his faith, he prayed for him without any limit: "So that the sharing of your faith becomes visible in the knowledge of every good which is in you in Christ Jesus" (v. 6). By "the sharing of faith" he means the faith shared with the other saints, as Chrysostom and Theophylact think,[375] or more correctly according to Jerome,[376] being generous to the saints, as his faith goes beyond them and he shares himself with still others. He wants this sharing of faith to become visible, as the Latin Vulgate says; the Greek, however, does not have ἐναργής, "visible," but ἐνεργής, "effective, industrious." Therefore, the apostle wants Philemon's faith to share itself so that it works toward others the works of love, with the goal that they would know that it is all good, that is, that Philemon and his whole house would overflow in showing love, and that they have truly been made rich in Christ Jesus in whom they believe. The overflowing of their goodness never becomes known more than when others receive the benefit of it. But he adds "in Christ Jesus," by which he means that all this kindness goes toward those in Christ who are in need; he includes in his accounts whatever is given to those in need in his name.

He says that Philemon's kindness toward the poor is very great: "For I have great joy and encouragement in your love, because the inward parts of the saints have been refreshed through you, brother" (v. 7). His words are very tender, suitable for greatly influencing Philemon. He calls him "brother" to remind him of the faith he shares with all believers, and thus also with Onesimus; he speaks of the love, that is, his kindness with which he has previously served those in need and generously cared for their good. He adds a double fruit of this kindness: first in the apostle himself who had joy and encouragement from it. In Greek it is χάρις instead of χαρά, just as Erasmus notes in 2 Corinthians

---

375 Chrysostom, *Philemon*, NPNF[1] 13:550.
376 Jerome, *Philemon*, PL 26:610.

1:15,[377] although there are several examples of this. In Syriac χαράν is *chanata*. "May He grant you joy in place of this sorrow" (δώησει χαράν ἀντὶ τῆς λυπῆς τάυτης, Tobit 7:17). A line of Theodotion's version of Leviticus 1:16 has φύσις in place of φύσᾳ.

Therefore, the apostle was filled with joy when he heard about Philemon's kindness, and with encouragement because the apostle's efforts on this man had also not been useless, but had achieved such a beautiful fruit of faith. There was a second fruit on the part of the poor whose inward parts were refreshed by his kindness, that is, they were very much cheered because of his protection in their need. He says that the inward parts of the saints were refreshed; some properly take this as meaning that Philemon satisfied their inward parts by feeding the hungry. For an empty stomach rumbles and boils, but stops that when it is filled with food. But without doubt he wants to show how much they were cheered, since they had been furnished not just with one but with many kindnesses in their need, to such an extent that this joy had even penetrated the inner chambers of their hearts. For in Scripture "inward parts" are not infrequently put in place of the heart itself or of the seat of compassion and mercy, and so there is "the inward parts of mercy" [Luke 1:78; Col. 3:12]. Jerome says that this is the apostle's idiom, so that when he wants to point to the full measure of love, he always calls it "inward parts."[378]

Questions on this Part of the Chapter

Question 1

In verse 2 the apostle writes about the church in the house of Philemon, but elsewhere he writes about the church in the house of Nymphas

---

[377] In 2 Cor. 1:15 UBS has χάριν in the text; Bruce Metzger (*A Textual Commentary on the Greek New Testament*, p. 576) calls χαράν "a scribal modification."

[378] Jerome, *Philemon*, PL 26:611.

(Colossians 4:15). Do these individual churches detract anything from the unity of the Church?

Answer: We believe in one Church, according to the words, "My dove, my undefiled is but one; she is the only one of her mother, she is the choice one of her that bore her" (Song of Solomon 6:9). However, the unity of the Church does not depend on the place, since the assemblage of the believers does not have only one location in the world, but is scattered here and there. For this reason the Church is said to be divided by reason of the accident [of its location], but to be one by reason of its essence. Therefore, the unity of the Church is spiritual, that is, all its members are united under the one head, Christ. St. Paul writes about this unity: "There is one body, and one Spirit, even as you are called in one hope of your calling, one Lord, one faith, one baptism, one God and Father of all" (Ephesians 4:4–6).

Therefore, even if there are many individual churches at some place in the separate towns, villages, and houses of the believers, nevertheless all of them come together in this unity, because they all have one founder, called God, and they all have one final goal, which is eternal salvation. They all have the same means, the same faith, the same sacraments, the same Word, the same laws and statutes; they all have the same Spirit by whom they are guided, they all have the same head, Christ, by whom they are stirred up, and in whom as members they grow together into one people, into one body, into one fellowship.

Just as one sun is visible in all the places of the world, but its rays are scattered everywhere, so there is one Church in the world, but its members are spread far and wide in the world. Irenaeus[379] writes about this unity of the Church in many places that, although it is scattered throughout the whole world, nevertheless it carefully preserves the apostolic faith; it has one mind and one and the same heart; it proclaims, teaches, and hands this down unanimously; and it is furnished with one mouth.

---

379 Irenaeus, *Against Heresies,* book 1, chapter 3 (ANF 1:319–20).

Question 2

When in verse 5 Paul praises Philemon's love and faith in God and all the saints, is it correct to conclude that he also believed in the saints?

Answer: Jerome asks at this place how he could have the same faith in Christ Jesus and in His saints,[380] and answers that Paul was saying the same thing as is said in Exodus 19:9 [14:31]: "The people believed God and Moses, His servant." He adds that one and the same faith is placed in Moses and in God, and whoever believes God cannot otherwise retain his faith unless he also believes in His saints. For love and faith in God is not complete if it holds onto hatred and disloyalty toward His ministers. From this Bellarmine gathers that he also ought to have faith in saints.[381] Cornelius à Lapide writes in his commentary on this letter that it follows from this text that whoever honors and calls on the saints does not take anything away from Christ; on the contrary, in this way he honors and calls on Christ.[382] Jerome says that this is taught here; but Jerome explains that what he calls believing in the saints is undoubtedly really believing what is written about the saints. For he directly adds to the words cited above:

"But what I say is this: Anyone who has believed in God the Creator cannot believe unless he has first believed that what was written about His saints is true. For example, that Adam was formed by God, that Eve was made from his rib and side, that Enoch was transported [directly to heaven], that Noah [and his family] alone in the world were saved from shipwreck, etc."[383]

Therefore, Jerome distinctly does not assign the same faith to God and the saints, but he assigns confidence to God, but only the historical narrative to the saints. This confidence is only found in believers, but trust in the historical narrative can also be found in the ungodly, and for that matter even in devils. Therefore, believing God is not the same

---

380 Jerome, *Philemon*, PL 26:609.
381 Bellarmine, *Eternal Happiness of the Saints*, book 1, chapter 20.
382 Cornelius à Lapide, *Comentaria in scripturam sacram*.
383 Jerome, *Philemon*, PL 26:609.

thing as believing in God; Augustine carefully distinguishes between these.[384] He says that believing God is believing that what He says is true; to believe in Him is to love Him. He describes this confidence as being the result of love, without which the confidence would be hypocritical. Elsewhere he calls it clinging to God by cooperating well with the working of God.[385] Thus at the exodus the people believed God and they also believed in Him, that is, they placed their confidence in Him. But they believed Moses as His helper, that is, they believed that all the commandments of God he related to them were undoubtedly true; but they did not believe on Moses, as if they placed their confidence in him.

Augustine writes: "We believe Paul, but we do not believe on Paul. We believe Peter, but we do not believe on Peter."[386] He writes: "Not unless we must believe in Him who is God."[387] Therefore, what Jerome writes about this passage is very true; no one can have confidence in God who has not believed what was written about the saints.[388] But Bellarmine takes from this that whoever calls on the saints as the saints and friends of God ought to believe and hope in them in the same way he does in the patriarchs.[389] For believing in the saints is not the same as believing what was written about the saints; Jerome demands the former from believers, but not the latter.

If we look at the words of Paul correctly, then what Jerome wants (although otherwise very true) was not what Paul intended; Benedict also says this.[390] Justinian observed in his commentary on this passage: Paul says nothing about their faith in what was written about the saints. Bellarmine, however, says that what Paul intended was that faith and love would be directed to God and our neighbor, but in different ways. For love is indeed properly directed toward God and our neighbor;

---

384 Augustine, sermon 18, de temp. and *John*, tractate 29, NPNF¹ 7:185.
385 Augustine, *Psalms*, Psalm 77, NPNF¹ 8:369.
386 Augustine, *John*, tractate 29, NPNF¹ 7:185.
387 Augustine, *John*, tractate 67, NPNF¹ 7:321.
388 Jerome, *Philemon*, PL 26:609.
389 Bellarmine, *Eternal Happiness of the Saints*, book 1, chapter. 20.
390 Benedict, *Interpretation*.

faith is also properly directed toward God, but not without works of godliness and kindness through which it is at work in our neighbors. This is stated in scholastic terms in this way: Love toward God and our neighbor is an action produced in us, but faith is an action produced toward God alone, and only toward our neighbor when it is commanded. Next after his friends they fault Paul for saying here that whoever speaks against the heretics regarding the reverent veneration of the saints is dancing completely outside the circle. This is not only said for that one reason, but he adds another reason, because Paul was obviously not speaking about dead saints, but about believers who were still alive, whose inward parts Philemon could refresh with his kindness. We willingly support Justinian in all of this, and often take note that the example they praise agrees with the Jesuits.

But lest we think this expresses Paul's intention, they are most correct of all who judge that Paul commends two virtues in Philemon, faith and love, and that these are to be distinguished by who they are directed toward. Faith is directed toward God, but love is directed toward the saints. This is why in the Greek text different prepositions are used; he ascribes faith to Philemon πρὸς τὸν κύριον Ἰησοῦν, since we come to Christ with faith; but he ascribes love to Philemon εἰς ἁγίους, since love is active toward the saints and reveals the faith. This explanation removes all difficulties.

Theological Maxims from this Part

1. All believers, even if they are not in the ministry, nevertheless can be helpers of the ministers of the Word, just as Paul called Philemon, a citizen of Colossae, his συνεργός (v. 1), since he clearly advanced the course of the Gospel by his kindness and godliness and compliance [with Paul's request to free Onesimus]. For unless the ministry is supported with the necessary expenses and gets compliance from those who listen, the whole structure of the Church will fall down. Therefore, the teachers and the listeners produce works on each side for the Church, and consider whatever they can do to provide the teaching

of the Gospel to be an honor. This is why God gave His teachers to the Church, "so that the saints are perfected for the work of the ministry, for the edifying of the body of Christ, until we all come into the unity of the faith and of the knowledge of God," etc. (Ephesians 4:12–13).

2. The private house of every Christian ought to be a church, as was Philemon's house (v. 2). That is, this ought to be completely clear to every Christian man who believes in God, loves Word and sacraments, serves God and his neighbor with prayers and godly compliance, and diligently abstains from everything which is against the Law of God. There truly is the house of God, which He fills with His blessing and chooses as His dwelling, as the Savior promised: "If anyone keeps My words, we will come to him and make our abode with him" (John 14:23). This was also true of the house of Zechariah, the priest (Luke 1 [:57–64]), of Zacchaeus (Luke 19:9), of Lazarus of Bethany (Luke 10:38), of the widow of Zarephath (1 Kings 17 [:10–16]), etc.

3. The ministers of the Church are "fellow-soldiers" (v. 2) among themselves, because the ministry is warfare in which they must fight against heretics, against the reprobate, against manifold vices, against the world, and against the devil. This is why Paul exhorts Timothy: "Fight the good fight, keeping faith and a good conscience" (1 Timothy 1:18 [–19]). Accordingly, just as soldiers must endure many things, such as hunger, cold, heat, and the like, so also many misfortunes work against the ministry, all of which are overcome by the hope of victory. So Paul writes to Timothy a second time: "Work as a good soldier of Jesus Christ. No one who is serving as a soldier of God gets entangled in the affairs of this life, so that he may please him who chose him to be a soldier" (2 Timothy 2:3[–4]).

4. The very best wish which anyone can desire for his neighbor is grace and peace from God the Father and the Lord Jesus Christ (v. 3). For grace includes the favor and mercy of God toward sinners, and peace includes reconciliation with God. No man is more blessed than he who has a gracious God. He has a peaceful conscience, unlimited access to God, and is certain that his prayers are heard, while otherwise those who are not yet reconciled to God cannot pray, as Isaiah 1:15 states.

5. We make mention in our prayers of godly people, as the example

of Paul shows (v. 4), not only to bring their needs to God, but also to give thanks for the gifts God has granted them. For this means to realize that God is the fountain which liberally gives all good works, and consequently to honor Him with heart, mouth, and works. Nothing better can be conceived in the mind or expressed by the mouth or explained with the pen; nothing can be said more briefly or heard more joyfully or understood more agreeably or done more fruitfully, as Augustine says somewhere.

6. There are two special virtues of a Christian: faith and love. Faith is directed toward God, and love toward our neighbor. Faith embraces the grace of the Father and the merit of the Son; love embraces others with works of mercy. Faith justifies, while love is the result in those who have been justified. Faith works through love [Gal. 5:6], but both are indivisibly connected with each other, so that faith which does not carry on works of love is in vain, for "faith without works is dead" (James 2:26). And in this text faith is said to be "effective in the knowledge of every good" (v. 6). Therefore, if we are truly believers, we will not neglect works of love nor forsake our neighbor in his distress; in all things we will show that we are rich in faith, and these riches will overflow in works of love. For this reason St. Paul exhorts: "As we have opportunity, let us do good to all people, especially to those who are of the household of faith" (Galatians 6:10).

7. They are bound in Christ Jesus to do good works (v. 6). For just as good works have their source in Christ, they in turn are directed to Him, or are done to His honor and glory. This is the difference between good works in the reborn and virtues in unbelievers. Good works arise from faith and are done on account of the glory of God, and for that reason are pleasing to God; but the virtues of unbelievers do not arise from faith and are done on account of their own glory. Consequently, they are not acceptable to God, no matter how splendid, imposing, and extraordinary they are. For, as Jerome says, every virtue apart from Christ is a vice, and those who do not promote the glory of Christ with all their efforts and actions are not Christians.[391]

---

391 Jerome, *Philemon*, PL 26:610.

8. Helping others ought to give us joy, just as Paul writes that he had "great joy and encouragement in the love with which Philemon refreshed the inward parts of the saints" (v. 1 [7]). It is evidence of true love that it does not begrudge another's happiness but rejoices in it (1 Corinthians 13:4 [13:6]). But those who prefer to see others perish in their distress grow feeble when they hear that others are living happily. Therefore, let us be filled with love so that this jealousy is far from us; but let us not refrain from helping them in their distress; rather our joy should be to hear that others are rejoicing; this is what it means to "rejoice with those who rejoice" (Romans 12:15).

9. Doing good to the poor is refreshing their inward parts (v. 7). For those who groan under the burden of poverty experience a wonderful cooling from the help of the godly and generous brothers. This "mercy is as welcome," says Sirach, "in time of affliction, as clouds of rain in the time of drought" (Ecclesiasticus 35:26). From this we learn that we also should refresh the inward parts of others. We should not shut up the fountains of liberality, but "disperse them abroad" (Proverbs 5:16). We should practice mercy toward others, so that we also obtain mercy on the day of tribulation. But "whoever stops up his ears at the cry of the poor will himself cry out and not be heard" (Proverbs 21:13).

The Second Part of the Text [Philemon 8–26]

Διὸ πολλὴν ἐν Χριστῷ παρρησίαν ἔχων ἐπιτάσσειν σοι τὸ ἀνῆκον	8. Because of this, although I could be very bold in Christ in inflicting on you what is your duty
Διὰ τὴν ἀγάπην μᾶλλον παρακαλῶ, τοιοῦτος ὤν, ὡς Παῦλος πρεσβύτης, νυνὶ δὲ καὶ δέσμιος Ἰησοῦ Χριστοῦ	9. Nevertheless, because of love I ask you, such as I am, to be sure old Paul, now also a prisoner of Jesus Christ

Παρακαλῶ σε περὶ τοῦ ἐμοῦ τέκνου ὃν ἐγέννησα ἐν τοῖς δεσμοῖς μου, Ὀνήσιμον

Τόν ποτέ σοι ἄχρηστον, νυνὶ δὲ σοὶ καὶ ἐμοὶ εὔχρηστον

Ὃν ἀνέπεμψα· σὺ δὲ αὐτόν, τοῦτ' ἔστιν τὰ ἐμὰ σπλάγχνα· προσλαβοῦ

Ὃν ἐγὼ ἐβουλόμην πρὸς ἐμαυτὸν κατέχειν, ἵνα ὑπὲρ σοῦ διακονῇ μοι ἐν τοῖς δεσμοῖς τοῦ εὐαγγελίου

Χωρὶς δὲ τῆς σῆς γνώμης οὐδὲν ἠθέλησα ποιῆσαι, ἵνα μὴ ὡς κατὰ ἀνάγκην τὸ ἀγαθόν σου ᾖ ἀλλὰ κατὰ ἑκούσιον

Τάχα γὰρ διὰ τοῦτο ἐχωρίσθη πρὸς ὥραν, ἵνα αἰώνιον αὐτὸν ἀπέχῃς

Οὐκέτι ὡς δοῦλον, ἀλλ' ὑπὲρ δοῦλον, ἀδελφὸν ἀγαπητὸν μάλιστα ἐμοί, πόσῳ δὲ μᾶλλον σοὶ καὶ ἐν σαρκὶ καὶ ἐν κυρίῳ

Εἰ οὖν με ἔχεις κοινωνόν, προσλαβοῦ αὐτὸν ὡς ἐμέ

Εἰ δέ τι ἠδίκησέν σε, ἢ ὀφείλει, τοῦτο ἐμοὶ ἐλλόγα

10. But I ask you for my son whom I have begotten in my chains, Onesimus

11. Formerly useless to you, but now very useful to you and to me

12. I have sent him back; but you receive him who is my own inward parts

13. I desired to keep him with me, so that on your behalf he could serve me in the chains of the Gospel

14. But I did not want to do anything without your opinion, lest the good you do would be done out of necessity rather than voluntarily

15. For perhaps, then, he went away for a time so that you would receive him back forever

16. Not now as a slave, but more than a slave, to be sure a brother greatly loved by me, and how much more by you, both in flesh and in the Lord

17. If, therefore, you regard me as a partner, then receive him just as me

18. If he has injured you in any way or owes you anything, put it on my account

Ἐγὼ Παῦλος ἔγραψα τῇ ἐμῇ χειρί, ἐγὼ ἀποτίσω: ἵνα μὴ λέγω σοι ὅτι καὶ σεαυτόν μοι προσοφείλεις	19. I, Paul, have written with my own hand that I will pay it, lest I should say to you that you owe me yourself and even more
Ναί, ἀδελφέ, ἐγώ σου ὀναίμην ἐν κυρίῳ: ἀνάπαυσόν μου τὰ σπλάγχνα ἐν κυρίῳ	20. Also, brother, let me have the benefit of you in the Lord: refresh my inward parts in the Lord
Πεποιθὼς τῇ ὑπακοῇ σου ἔγραψά σοι, εἰδὼς ὅτι καὶ ὑπὲρ ἃ λέγω, ποιήσεις	21. I have written to you, confident that you will obey, and knowing that you will do even more than I say.
Ἅμα δὲ καὶ ἑτοίμαζέ μοι ξενίαν: ἐλπίζω γὰρ ὅτι διὰ τῶν προσευχῶν ὑμῶν χαρισθήσομαι ὑμῖν	22. But at the same time also prepare a room for me, for I hope that by the aid of your prayers I will be given to you
Ἀσπάζεταί σε Ἐπαφρᾶς ὁ συναιχμάλωτός μου ἐν Χριστῷ Ἰησοῦ	23. Epaphras, my fellow captive in Christ Jesus, greets you
Μᾶρκος, Ἀρίσταρχος, Δημᾶς, Λουκᾶς, οἱ συνεργοί μου	24. [As do] Mark, Aristarchus, Demas, Luke, my helpers
Ἡ χάρις τοῦ κυρίου ἡμῶν Ἰησοῦ Χριστοῦ μετὰ σοῦ πνεύματος ὑμῶν, ἀμήν	25. The grace of our Lord Jesus Christ be with your spirit. Amen.
Πρὸς Φιλήμονα ἐγράφη ἀπὸ Ῥώμης διὰ Ὀνησίμου οἰκέτου. Ἐν στίχοις λζ	26. This was sent from Rome to Philemon by the slave Onesimus.

Analysis and Explanation of Part Two

[St. Paul] introduces the commendation of Onesimus in this part of the chapter very skillfully, and firmly introduces many proofs. The purpose of his letter appears in verses 10 and 11: I implore you for my son, Onesimus: receive him favorably, etc. The first point for persuasion is derived from the person of Philemon, who was the most zealous of the saints. From this the apostle drew great hope that Philemon would grant his request.

"Because of this, although I could be very bold in Christ Jesus by commanding you to do what is proper, I rather implore because of love" (vv. 8–9). As an apostle Paul could have admonished this ordinary man, but he did not want to make use of his right and preferred to implore and to obtain what he wanted by asking for it. He writes that he had great boldness, that is, the privilege (παρρησίαν) to command in Christ Jesus, whose apostle he is, that he do this, τὸ ἀνῆκον, or what Philemon was capable of doing, or what was his duty. What he is to do is what [Paul] has already described, namely, being generous toward those who are miserable and distressed. He could command him to do this also for Onesimus, but he prefers to give up his right and obtain it by asking.

The second point is derived from Paul's nature: "Because of love I rather implore this," he says, "since I am Paul the old man, and now also a prisoner of Jesus Christ" (v. 9). These words are very emotional, for Paul who could command asks. He asks the owner to act out of pity toward the miserable Onesimus and out of love toward the one he was angry with. He asks as an old man of advanced age. He is a prisoner of Jesus Christ, whose chains he carries around as if in a triumphal procession and considers it an honor to do so. Since he is this, Paul does not think that Philemon can deny him anything.

The third point is derived from the person of Onesimus, who had so far been Philemon's slave, but now had become Paul's son; because he had been converted to faith in Christ, he was worthy of that name, of love, and of kindness. "I implore you," Paul says, "for the son I begot in chains, Onesimus" (v. 10). Onesimus was by birth a Phrygian, by circumstances a slave, who fled from his owner because of theft, and met Paul who was in chains, and now had the hope of freedom and of reconciliation with his owner. In his chains Paul instructed Onesimus in the true faith, converted him to Christ, and in this way made him his spiritual son whom he begot through the Word. He used this same way of speaking about the conversion of the Corinthians (1 Corinthians 4:15), and called the Galatians his children for whom he travailed in birth until Christ was formed in them (Galatians 4:19). He did not lose his nationality by becoming Paul's son, but continued firmly in faith, returned to Paul, and became Paul's servant, as Jerome writes. But at last he was an excellent teacher in the Ephesian church and made the successor of Timothy in the episcopate, which Ignatius forcefully advocates; he is said to have obtained the crown of martyrdom under Trajan.[392] Therefore, this point has great authority, because Paul is not interceding only for a thief or for a fugitive, but for his son, whose evil deeds could be covered over by the subsequent improvement of his life and the sanctity of his faith.

The fourth point is derived from his usefulness. "Once he was useless to you, but now he is useful both to me and to you" (v. 11). He is making a play on the name Onesimus, for Ὀνήσιμος in Greek means useful. He means to say: If once his life did not correspond to his name, he has now corrected that, and the deceiver will be truly Onesimus, who can usefully serve both of us. I sent him back to you by that name, but the crime of Onesimus does not come along because of his humble repentance (ταπείνωσις). He writes that when he was a thief he was only useless; now, however, since he has become reconciled, it is not the time to stir up his crime; rather, it is useful kindly to receive him who has improved his conduct and can be of use to others.

The fifth point is derived from fairness; because Paul prescribes the kindness for himself in advance, it is explained that this favor would be fair. "But you, receive him, that is, my inward parts" (v. 11). He is emotional (πάθος), because he calls Onesimus his inward parts. Because he was his son begotten in Christ, he now loves him very tenderly as his inward parts, and he takes into account everything which can happen to him. Therefore, he could not overlook the one who loves Paul, who is even his inward parts.

He loves Onesimus as his inward parts because (1) he begot him in

---

392 Ignatius of Antioch, *Letters*, 12-14. Trajan was the Roman emperor from 98–117.

his old age, for such children are generally more dear to their parents, just as it is written about Joseph: "Israel loved Joseph more than all his children, because he begot him in his old age" (Genesis 37:3). [Paul loves Onesimus] (2) because he begot this son in chains, for those who are born to us in dangerous times are loved by us more intensely, just as the patriarch Jacob loved[393] his son Benjamin, not only because he was born last, but also because his mother died bringing him to the light of life; for this reason he was called Benoni, "the son of sorrow" [Gen. 35:18].

The sixth point is derived from the sign. I wanted to keep him with me, he says (v. 13). This is a definite indication that Onesimus was a useful man, since Paul was reluctant to send him away, and he only kept with him people who were useful and worthy because of their love for the good.

The seventh point is derived from fairness, "so that he would serve me in my chains in place of you" he says (v. 13).[394] Philemon ought to serve Paul in his chains as his apostle who converted him to faith in Christ, and Onesimus did this for him. Therefore, it was fair that he should overlook that he was loved before because of his slavery, but now Philemon should receive the returning Onesimus as a human being. But he calls them "the chains of the Gospel," because he did not sustain them on account of some crime, but on account of his confession of the teaching about Christ.

The eighth point is derived from his many duties: "But I did not want to do anything without consulting you, lest the good you do would be done out of necessity rather than voluntarily" (v. 14). Paul could by rights make use of and keep with him the one he had begotten through the Gospel. But he wanted rather to submit this to the will of Philemon and to restore his slave to him. If Philemon wanted to send Onesimus back to Paul who was in chains, then it would be established that he was not forced to do this, but did it willingly, since he would

---

393 Read *dilectiis* instead of *delitiis*.

394 Read *ut pro te mihi ministraret in vinculis, ait v. 13* instead of *ut pro me tibi ministraret in vinculis, ait v. 31*.

first receive him back favorably. Therefore, just as Paul adapted himself to Philemon by sending back the slave he could have kept with him, so Philemon also ought to adapt himself to the apostle by receiving the fugitive he sent back favorably.

The ninth point is derived from the providence of God. For Philemon ought to reflect that his slave did not flee away from him by chance or accidentally, but God wanted to make use of his flight as the means for his conversion. For He had put Paul into chains at this time, by whom Onesimus would be supplied with eternal salvation. "For perhaps he went away from you for a time so that you could receive him back eternally" (v. 15). By means of a humble choice of words (ταπείνωσις) he softens Onesimus' flight, for he does not say that he "fled away," but that he "went away," ἐχωρίσθη, separated from him only by space, not by heart, because now he has been made your comrade in faith. He did not go away for a long time, but only for an hour, or only for a short time, as the words are used in Galatians 2:5.

But he went away so that you could receive him back eternally. Some explain αἰώνιον as the time of your life, or as long as you lived, as Horace says, "may you serve eternally," that is, may you live a long time. Others judge that Paul was looking back at a Hebrew custom according to which if slaves do not want to make use of the law of liberty because they love their owner, his wife, or his children, it can nevertheless be permitted to them by law that they are said to serve לעולם, eternally, that is, until the Year of Jubilee (Exodus 21:6; Deuteronomy 15:16).

This is why the apostle indicates that Philemon should not so greatly press the point of Onesimus' fleeing, as though for that reason he was unworthy to be received back. Rather, this flight provided a great advantage, because now he was truly restored to him as a comrade in faith, whom he could keep with him as long as he pleased, even for the time of his life. In this way the brief flight would be sufficiently compensated. But when he adds that his fleeing away happened τάχα, "perhaps," some judge that he is not doubting, but affirming; for that reason they translate "truly, clearly." But Jerome applies this to the extraordinary providence of God, by which a Christian was made out of a fugitive slave and thief; he writes that Paul expressed doubt because God's judgments are hidden, and it is rash to speak about what is doubtful as if it were certain.[395]

The tenth point is derived from the status of Onesimus, who now returns to Philemon not as a slave but as a brother or a comrade in faith, who deserves to be embraced. For as John writes: "We ought to receive such people so that we are co-workers with the truth" (3 John 8). "Now not as a slave," Paul says, namely, "you should receive him, but instead of as a slave as a brother very dear to me, but how much more to you, both in flesh and in the Lord" (v. 16). The Latin version has "slave," but the Greek original has ὑπὲρ δοῦλον, which Jerome translates "more than a slave" or "better than a slave,"[396] for he had now by conversion been made a brother of both Paul and Philemon, both of whom confessed the same faith.

For all who have been reborn in Christ are brothers among themselves because of the faith they share. Christ does not blush to call them His brothers (Psalm 22:22; John 20:17; Hebrews 2:11–12). Paul, however, calls Onesimus his brother in the highest degree, "very dear to me," because of the love he had shown him in his chains.

From this, then, comes the point about the greater: "but how much more to you both in flesh and in the Lord," which is the eleventh point in order. It has this meaning: If someone otherwise unknown to me is nevertheless such a beloved brother because he received faith and because of the service he rendered me for a short time, how much more ought he to be received by you, since he was once part of your family and has now also been made a partaker of your faith? This is why he calls Onesimus Philemon's twofold brother, (1) in flesh and (2) in the Lord. Some take "in flesh" to mean that they were mutually joined to each other by blood, for they were also called brothers related by blood. But Theophylact correctly explains that Onesimus served Philemon as a slave in carnal and ordinary things as his household slave, so that he deserved to be loved on that account. Now, however, he is a brother in the Lord because of the faith they shared in the Lord Jesus. Because of

---

395 Jerome, *Philemon*, PL 26:613.
396 Jerome, *Philemon*, PL 26:614.

this he is worthy of much greater love because he is a slave not only to you but also to the Lord who is over him, to you with virtuous service, but to the Lord with faith and godliness.

The twelfth point is derived from the comparison: "If you regard me as a comrade, receive him just as me" (v. 17), that is, if you love me, love also him whom I love. If you spit him out, then also spit me out and despise me in court. For I acknowledge Onesimus as my partner, without whom you cannot do anything for me. For he is my other self; I reckon that whoever hates him also hates me.

The thirteenth point is the repayment of the damages. Since Philemon could bring up Onesimus' theft, Paul offers to repay it himself. "If he has injured you in any way or owes you anything, put it on my account. I, Paul, have written with my own hand that I will pay it, lest I should say to you that you owe me yourself" (vv. 18–19). These quite restrained words report Onesimus' crime who was disloyal to his owner and made off with something. The apostle does not use the word "theft," but calls it an "injury" or "damage," either because he wanted to diminish the guilt of the theft, or because it was estranged or demolished, which Onesimus could not undo by repaying it.

However, so that the damage would be repaired, and to make it easier for Philemon to receive back the now converted thief, Paul interposes himself as the one who gives security and who by his own autograph promises to repay the debt. Philemon ought to have confidence in this all the more willingly because he owed his whole self to the apostle as his teacher, by whom he had been converted to faith in Christ. The apostle silently points to this, and leaves the sting in the mind of Philemon with the aim of commending him. He wants [Philemon] to decide for himself how much he owes the apostle, and whether it would be right to accept this guarantee of repaying the debt and to take Onesimus back into favor, overlooking his previous crime.

St. Paul uses these points to defend his commendation [of Onesimus], to which he finally adds this very emotional conclusion: "Also, brother, let me have the benefit of you in the Lord: refresh my inward parts in the Lord" (v. 20). There is twofold emotion (πάθος) in this verse: first, because he is certain of getting what he has asked for from his brother. In Greek there is a particle of assertion, ναὶ ἀδελφέ, "Certainly brother, let me have the benefit of you," that is, "I am certain that you will not refuse me your kindness, but you will do this because of the Lord in whom we are brothers, so that I will know that my commendation carries great weight with you."

Others say that the particle ναί in this place has this meaning: "Do these things for me, brothers, so that I may have the benefit of your friendliness." Elsewhere, it means that something is true, as in 2 Corinthians 1:17. Elsewhere, it means entreaty, as in Revelation 22:20.

Because in Greek he says ὀναίμην, he is without a doubt making a play on the name Onesimus, as if he wanted to say, "If you are not going to take advantage of him who has been your slave for a long time because of his disloyalty, I am nevertheless convinced that I will have the benefit of your kindness."

The second [emotional element here] is that he asks him to "refresh his inward parts," which Jerome thinks is said ambiguously.[397] This word "inward parts" could be understood either of Onesimus whom he called his inward parts above in verse 12, or of Paul himself who will be wonderfully revived if some kindness is shown to this miserable man because of his becoming surety for him. Both could be understood, for Philemon's kindness would refresh both Onesimus, who had returned to his owner who had previously hated him, and Paul, who would rejoice that his effort in restoring this fugitive man was not in vain.

A third emotional element (πάθος) is added in the following verse. "I have written to you, confident that you will obey, and knowing that you will do even more than I say" (v. 21). The apostle praises Philemon's compliance which he had learned to know from other things. For this reason he trusted that he would also now give abundant reason for him to be assured that he would do what he asked and even more than he asked. With rhetorical skill he brings to an end his commendation of Onesimus with these very penetrating feelings.

Now he sprinkles in a few other things, and first asks that a room be prepared for him in Colossae, because he hopes to be released [from

---

397 Jerome, *Philemon*, PL 26:615.

prison]. "But at the same time also prepare a room for me, for I hope that by the aid of your prayers I will be given to you" (v. 22). These words do have some reference to the matter of Onesimus. For when Philemon heard that the apostle will be there very soon, it became easier for him to receive Onesimus, lest it seem that this apostle's hope was mistaken.

But even if Paul did not need a large room, but could be satisfied with one small room, he nevertheless asks that a room be prepared for him, in part to give evidence of his love for Philemon. For when we love someone a lot, and know that we are also loved by them, we do not need to coax them to do their duty with much flattery of words, but can boldly state what we want, since firm friendship easily overcomes all trouble. In part, he was also looking for a suitable home for himself, from which he could teach people that he was by no means without duties. Jerome wrote about this: "The room was to be prepared more for the apostle than for Paul."[398]

He is coming to a new city to preach the Crucified One, and he is bringing teachings they have not heard before; he knows that many will flock to him, and it was necessary that the house be located in a frequented part of the city which they could easily come to. Then, the place needed to be free from anything inappropriate; it needed to be large enough to hold many listeners, not close to the theater, and not in a detestable or shameful neighborhood. Last, it needs to be located on ground level, rather than in an attic, etc.

The apostle, however, adds the source of his hope that he will be released, namely, the prayers of the saints that God would give them this teacher, so that he could complete what he had begun to build among them. From this we can conclude that the Church committed its apostle to God in prayer even when he was stuck in chains.

He then includes greetings to Philemon from several friends by name. "Epaphras, my fellow captive in Christ Jesus, greets you, [as do] Mark, Aristarchus, Demas, Luke, my helpers" (vv. 23–24). We find similar greetings in the letter to the Colossians (4:10–14), since that

---

398 Jerome, *Philemon*, PL 26:616.

letter was written at the same time and was brought by Onesimus.

Epaphras was a faithful teacher of the Colossians, whom he calls his "fellow servant" (Colossians 1:7); some think that he was one of the seventy disciples [Luke 10:1]. Here he calls him his "fellow captive." Jerome writes about this epithet that Paul with his parents was from the Gyscali region of Judea; when that whole province was devastated by the Romans and the Jews scattered over the earth, Paul moved to the city of Tarsus in Cilicia.[399] Epaphras was a captive for a time in the same place; after he learned about Christ, he and his parents settled in Colossae, a city in Asia [Minor]. But Jerome does not place much value on this narrative.

Epaphras is called Paul's "fellow captive," as is also Aristarchus (Colossians 4:10), because they were thrown into chains together with Paul in Rome. That persecution affected not only the apostle, but also his companions.

Jerome thinks that Mark was the writer of the Gospel [according to Mark], but opposed to that is the fact that Mark the evangelist was not Paul's comrade, but Peter's helper, whom he therefore calls his son (1 Peter 5:13). Irenaeus calls him Peter's disciple, comrade, and interpreter.[400] Jerome calls him his describer.[401] Other ecclesiastical writers prove that Paul did not know Mark the evangelist, because at the time Paul preached the Gospel at Rome, Mark was the bishop of the Church of Alexandria, as they teach from Basil.[402] We judge, then, that this Mark was the son of Mary, to whose house Peter returned after being led out of prison by an angel (Acts 12:12). He was the cousin of Barnabas; Paul strove with Barnabas about this Mark (Acts 15:39), about whom he said some things in his letter to the Colossians (4 [:10]).

---

399 Jerome, *Philemon*, PL 26:617.

400 Irenaeus, *Against Heresies*, book 3, chapter 1, ANF 1:414; Eusebius of Caesarea, *Ecclesiastical History*, book 2, chapter 15, NPNF[2] 1:116; Epiphanius, *Panarion*, 51; Chrysostom, *Matthew*, Homily 59, NPNF[1] 10:364–71.

401 Jerome, *Philemon*, PL 26:618.

402 Basil of Caesarea, *Adversus Eunomium*, book 5.

I have said[403] that Aristarchus was a Thessalonian from Macedonia, whom Paul calls his "fellow prisoner" (Colossians 4:10), because it is stated that he was led away from Jerusalem to Rome together with Paul (Acts 27:2).

Demas was the one about whom Paul wrote during his final imprisonment that he had forsaken him because he loved the world (2 Timothy 4:10).

Luke the evangelist came from Antioch, "whose praise is written in the Gospel throughout all the churches" (2 Corinthians 8:18). He was Paul's comrade on his journeys, as it is said at the same place, to whom he is thought to be indebted for his Gospel.[404] Tertullian writes: "They used to attribute the arrangement of Luke's Gospel to Paul. He began to be seen among the masters, which his disciples published."[405]

Paul calls all of these συνεργοί, his helpers, because they confessed the teaching of the Gospel together with Paul with the same faith and firmness.

At the end, the apostle adds the usual wish: "The grace of our Lord Jesus Christ be with your spirit. Amen" (v. 25). This wish has in mind everything he mentioned at the beginning of the letter, although at first it was said only about Philemon. He requests the grace of our Lord Jesus Christ for their spirit; this is a synecdoche, that is, for the whole man, for when it is well with the spirit, the whole man prospers.

Questions on this Part of the Chapter

Question 1

If the believers are the apostles' children, as stated in verse 10, then it follows that the apostles are their fathers. Why, then, did Christ say to His

---

403 That is, in Balduin's comments on Colossians 4:10.
404 Eusebius of Caesarea, *Ecclesiastical History*, book 3, chapter 4, NPNF² 1:137.
405 Tertullian, *Against Marcion*, book 4, ANF 3:347.

disciples, *"Call no man your father on earth, for one is your Father, who is in heaven" (Matthew 23:9)*?

Answer: The spiritual begetting of people which happens through the Word for life is chiefly attributed to God from whom we are said to be born (John 1:13). But when He makes use of the works of His servants in the work of salvation, His servants also for this reason share in this title of honor; in fact, they are even called "saviors" (Obadiah 21). For all that, there is only one Savior, our God.

So Paul calls himself the father of the Corinthians when he writes: "Although you have ten thousand instructors in Christ, you do not have many fathers: for through Christ Jesus I have begotten you in the Gospel" (1 Corinthians 4:15). Thus the prophets were sometimes called "fathers" (2 Kings 2:12), and their disciples are called the "sons of the prophets" (2 Kings 4:38); the usage today is that the teachers of the Church are considered worthy of the name "fathers."

But when Christ forbids calling anyone "father," he is not simply withdrawing this title of honor from people; otherwise, He would be abolishing the Fourth Commandment, in which we are commanded to honor father and mother; rather, He forbids it in a certain respect.

The Jesuit Barradius thinks Christ is giving counsel to those who aspire to perfection; these counsels [Matt. 23:5–10] refer first to those who seek wealth, then to those who seek honor, then to those who seek to be parents.[406] This is why He says: "Call no one your father or mother on earth," once you have said your last good-bye to them, for "you have a Father in heaven, God."

But this is false. Christ was not speaking there with those who were aspiring to perfection, which the papists think are the monks, but with the crowd and His disciples. He was not prescribing a counsel, but reproving the pride[407] of the Pharisees who aspired to titles of honor. He makes no mention of mother, but the Jesuit adds that on his own. Finally, nowhere does He forbid saying good-bye, but rather wants us

---

[406] Barradius, *Commentaria in concordiam et historiam evangelicam.* volume 3, book 8, chapter 24.

[407] Read *fastum*.

to support them in their old age (Ecclesiasticus 3:12), and honor them all the days of our lives (Tobit 4:3).

Therefore, these words of Christ are not speaking about disowning parents, but about propriety, lest we put some man in front of or equal to God. The Pharisees did this by claiming for themselves alone out of the pride of their hearts the right to be teachers and fathers over others; this is why they long to hear the words "rabbi" and "fathers."

Therefore, Christ does not want everyone to be called our father by nature, but for reasons of concession and honor. For God alone is our Father by nature, from whom we have both natural and spiritual life, even though we have both of them through men, who for that reason share secondarily in this name of honor for reasons of concession [cf. Eph. 3:14–15]. We have natural life through our natural parents, whom God Himself calls father and mother (Exodus 20:12; Ephesians 6:2). But we have spiritual life through the teachers of the Church, who beget us through the Gospel in Jesus Christ.

The Fathers explain it this way. Jerome writes on Matthew 23: "It is one thing to be a father or teacher by nature, something else to be one by tender feeling. If we call a man 'father,' we are conferring honor to his age; we are not pointing out the Creator of our life."[408]

Chrysostom writes: "'Do not call him father,' not as if they should not call anyone father, but lest they neglect Him whom they ought chiefly to call Father. Chiefly in this way no one is a teacher or a father before Him, for He is the cause of all teachers and fathers."[409]

Theophylact writes: "In saying, 'Call no man your father,' he is not prohibiting the honor given to parents, since He desires that we should honor parents and especially our spiritual fathers; rather He is inducing us to acknowledge the true Father, namely, God."[410]

Augustine writes on Psalm 77: "On account of honor and because of concern for godliness, Paul calls his disciples his dear children, although he elsewhere does not neglect what was said by the Lord: 'Do

---

408 Jerome, *Matthew*, p. 261.
409 Chrysostom, *Matthew*, Homily 72, NPNF[1] 10:438.
410 Theophylact, *The Explanation of the Gospels*, p. 197.

not call anyone father on earth, for you have one Father, God.' He did not say this, to take away from this word the customary way of speaking about human honor, but lest the grace of God by which we are reborn to eternal life would be ascribed to the nature, power, or even the holiness of some man. For this reason, when Paul says, 'I begot you,' he means in Jesus Christ and through the Gospel, lest anyone suppose that he is God."[411]

There are similar statements.[412]

Question 2

Is it permitted sometimes to doubt the plans of God, as Paul seems to doubt when he writes about Onesimus, "Perhaps, then, he went away for a time so that you would receive him back forever, not as a slave, but instead of a slave as a greatly loved brother" (vv. 15–16)?

Answer: In the explanation of the text we said that the apostle refers these words to God's foreknowledge and plans for the conversion of Onesimus. God directed his flight so that he came to Paul and was converted to faith in Christ through Paul's teaching. Therefore, there is no doubt at all about God's plan. Some think that the Greek particle τάχα does not denote doubt but affirmation, since Paul was quite certain about it.

But since it is not certain where Paul got this conviction from, we stick with the Vulgate's usage of perforsitan, "perhaps," just as the Greek word is employed in Romans 5:7, and there translated by Luther as *vielleicht*, "peradventure." The meaning is that perhaps it happens according to the extraordinary plan and providence of God that he fled away from you so that on this occasion he would be entrusted to my instruction, and be restored to you afterwards as a comrade in faith. This is Paul's conclusion from what happened, but it appears to be only a conjecture, because Paul was not sure.

This is why we ask whether it is permitted to doubt God's plans. For all that, it is written: "My counsel will stand, and I will do all I want"

---

411 Augustine, *Psalms*, NPNF[1] 8:371.
412 Augustine, *Summary Meeting*, diei 3, c. 7.

(Isaiah 46:10); "I am God, and I do not change" (Malachi 3:6).

Therefore, since Onesimus' flight took place according to the extraordinary plan of God, as what happened teaches, so that he would become the slave of Christ through Paul's Gospel, why does Paul doubt that plan of God, since he knows that God's plan is nothing else than what God has stated, namely, that they would do what He wants and has wisely arranged, according to which He governs everything, whether by what He does or by what He permits to happen?

God actively carries out His plan in good things, according to which "God does whatever He wants in heaven and on earth" (Psalm 135:6), and "works all things according to the counsel of His good pleasure" (Ephesians 1:11). God acts permissively in evil things, since God's will is connected with that permission with respect to the good goal toward which God leads the evil action.

For as Augustine says, it does not happen apart from His will, since it will not happen unless He permits it to happen, nor does He permit it unwillingly, but willingly. He does not permit good to happen in an evil way, unless He can omnipotently make good out of the evil.[413]

In this way Christ was handed over into the hands of His enemies by the plan of God the Father, who permitted this handing over to happen, and decided to permit it, with this saving and very glorious goal of restoring salvation to human beings. In the same way, He permitted Onesimus' flight to happen according to His plan and with the goal that he would be converted to Christ by talking with the prisoner Paul. In this way God's plan is always certain and unchangeable, just as God Himself is unchangeable; He would not be God if His decrees could change. For this reason there is no doubt that He will do everything He has decided from eternity, although what He has decided is hidden from us before it happens.

On our part, God's plans can be doubtful in two ways. First, when nothing definite is stated in Scripture about what kind of things will happen, for we are not permitted to think about divine things apart from Scripture. "All the counsel of God is declared" to us (Acts 20:27),

---

413 Augustine, *Handbook*, chapter 100, NPNF¹ 3:269.

but not about details or about all that will happen. In general I can be certain that God will not allow anything evil to happen unless He can make something good out of it. Nevertheless, Paul could not be certain about whether God permitted Onesimus' flight so that he would be converted; for that reason he preferred to doubt what he could not describe as certain.

Then, Scripture itself seems to make us doubtful about God's will, as generally happens in temporal things. For example, Benhadad, king of Syria, asked Elisha whether he would recover from his disease, and the prophet answered him, "You will recover," "although the Lord showed me that he would surely die" (2 Kings 8:10). Again, Isaiah told Hezekiah, "Set your house in order, for you will die" from your sickness "and not live" (Isaiah 38:1). But this did not happen; rather, the king prayed and his life was prolonged for fifteen years. Again, through Jonah the Lord said to the Ninevites: "Yet forty days and Nineveh will be overthrown" (Jonah 3:4). Nevertheless, this did not happen, because the Ninevites repented. Nothing can really be established as certain about God's plan from these examples.

But this rule of Gregory the Great must be observed: God knows how to change His mind sometimes, but He never changes His plan.[414] By "plan" he understands God's decree and eternal will about something, which He never changes, and for that reason it is most certain. By "mind," however, he understands the explanation of His will either about some good thing or about a penalty, which was made known not, of course, according to His immutable decree, but because of either our merits or secondary causes. So when Elisha said to Benhadad of Syria, "You will recover," he was declaring God's mind made known according to secondary causes, for all his strength had not yet become sick, and the means of restoration were still present. But when he adds, "The Lord showed me that he would surely die," God's plan was divinely unveiled to him and revealed that he would certainly be dying because of his evil merits.

So the Lord's mind, assisted by secondary causes, was announced

---

[414] Gregory the Great, *Reflections on Job*, book 12, pp. 56–57.

to Hezekiah, "You will die and not live," because all your strength is becoming weak; without this strength he could not naturally live, not even by the king's merits, because he was sufficiently ripe for death; but in the counsel of God it was decided that he would live fifteen more years, which God graciously gave to him when he prayed.

Thus the mind of the Lord, proceeding from their merits, was spoken to the Ninevites that they would perish in forty days, but in the counsel of God it was decided and extended to them, because their repentance was known to God.

Gregory writes about Hezekiah: Through the prophet God spoke about the time he deserved to die; but through His bountiful mercy He postponed his time for dying, which He knew before time [began].[415] The prophet was not deceitful, because he learned the time of death at which that man deserved to die. Nor are the Lord's decisions destroyed when out of God's bounty the years of his life were increased, for also this was foreseen before time [began], etc. Therefore, since the mind of God can be changed for these reasons, it often happens that people decide from the mind of God that they cannot establish anything as certain concerning God's plans, even though they are unchangeable. This is why the prophets often speak hesitantly about the relaxation of temporal punishments, such as Joel 2:14 and Jonah 3:9, even though there is no doubt that God has from all eternity established these things as certain.

The practical application of this question is that we are not to decide by our own judgment about God's plans. Our judgment can be wrong for many reasons in matters which are not stated clearly in Holy Scripture. Even though God's plan is unknown to us, it is still firm forever. It does not depend on fleeting human judgment, but on God's unchanging decree.[416]

---

[415] Gregory the Great, *Reflections on Job*, book 12, p. 57.
[416] See Augustine, *Genesis*, book 6, chapter 17, pp. 198–99.

Question 3

Paul took Onesimus' debt onto himself, and bound himself to pay it by means of his autograph (vv. 18–19). It is asked, then, whether it is godly and proper for a Christian man to become surety for another?

Answer: We should understand becoming surety or security to mean binding his faithfulness to pay another's debt, so that if the first debtor does not pay, then he will make amends to the creditor.

The canonists debate at length on this matter. Who can become surety? Can someone who has become surety be allowed to demand a price from the debtor for becoming surety for him? In these cases, the one who becomes surety is obligated to make amends to the creditor in place of the first debtor. Can the first creditor be obligated to restore losses to the one who became surety? Other questions are similar to these. In all these cases it is always taken for granted that becoming surety is permitted.[417]

But whether an agreement to become surety is permitted can still be debated. To be security for another has a very great appearance of Christian love, since many are in need of money; nothing is ever loaned to them unless another becomes surety for them. The one who becomes surety is security to the creditor that he will pay what was borrowed (Jen. Germ. Tom. X, fol. 468 seqq.).

But blessed Luther, in the booklet he published in 1524 on trade, generally opposes this practice.[418] For he judges that a godly man should not become surety for anyone, not only because of the danger that he will give occasion for the proverb, "Give security, and harm is present,"[419] but also for other reasons which he treats there at length.

First, he stresses the sayings of Solomon in Proverbs which deal

---

417 See Juan Azor, *Istitutionum moralium, in quibus universae quaestiones ad conscientiam recte, aut prave factorum pertinentes breviter tractantur tomus* . . . (Lugduni: Cardon & Cavellat, 1616–25), book 11, chapter 21; Jodocus Lorichius [1613], *Thesaurus novus utriusque theologiae theoricae et practicae* (Friburgi Brisgoiae: Böckler, 1609), s.v. "fidejussor."

418 Luther, *Trade and Usury* (1524), AE 45:231–310.

419 Erasmus, *Adages*, 597.

Philemon 8-26

not only with the danger of surety (6:1–2; 20:16; 27:13), but also seem entirely to prohibit such guarantees ("Do not be one who strikes hands, or who becomes surety for debts," 22:26), to which are related other sayings in Proverbs (11:15; 17:18).

Then, he says that those who become surety should not trust people so much. While they certainly believe that the first debtor is acting in good faith and will pay the debts, yet the human heart is deceptive; God alone knows this best of all, and He does not want us to put our trust in man.

Third, the one who becomes surety trusts himself too much, as if he can always pay, when his life and all his abilities are in the hands of God. We can establish nothing certain about this for the future. For this reason, they always quickly get themselves in trouble with their rashness, just as the patriarch Judah promised that he would bring his brother Benjamin back from Egypt, but he would have had to be left behind as a slave in the house of Pharaoh in place of his brother for whom he became surety, if God had not arranged things differently (Genesis 43:9; 44:32).

Fourth, the merchants are strengthened in their covetousness by those who become surety. If there was no such security, many ordinary people would be very content; however, since they have those who pledge for them, they always grasp for more, and also seek to get riches in illegal ways.

For these reasons Luther disapproved of giving security, and rather recommended that we give generously according to our ability to our neighbor gratuitously and mutually, to lift him out of his poverty. He did not make the kind of loan which must be allowed in buying and selling, but recommended setting up what could be completed with ready money, etc.[420]

But it really cannot be denied that Holy Scripture does not entirely disapprove of becoming surety, but rather commends it as a duty of love. "A good man will be surety for his neighbor" (Ecclesiasticus 29:14); our Paul became surety for Onesimus; and Christ Himself is

---

[420] Luther, *Trade and Usury* (1524), AE 45:252–55.

called our "surety" [Heb. 7:22], who freed us with His precious blood. Christ also wants us to make a loan (Luke 6:35).

When, however, Luther speaks somewhat harshly about becoming surety, we must know that he is describing the perfect Christian who also lives among perfect Christians, as we all ought to be, where whoever receives a loan pays it back willingly. If this happens, there is scarcely any need for becoming surety. But since people are actually filled with deceit, he recommends that we either become surety for no one, lest we deceive them and assist in the deception of others, or that we become surety in such a way that we are also ready to lose our money and willingly to pay it for the debtor. This is why he writes that "it is decreed according to Scripture that no one shall become surety for another, unless he is able and entirely willing to assume the debt and pay it himself."[421] This decree is stated: "Do not give surety beyond your means, and if you give surety, be concerned as one who must pay" (Ecclesiasticus 8:13).

Thus he writes that whoever wants to give a loan should give it to Christians (that is, to honest and honorable people who do not want to deceive anyone).[422] But if he has given money for a loan, but not [to Christians], and must abandon the income, then let him not loan any more, unless he wants to make good his own loss. This also agrees with the command: "Assist your neighbor according to your ability, but take heed to yourself lest you fall" (Ecclesiasticus 29:20).

From this we can conclude that there are two kinds of security, one of which is not only ruinous, but is simply forbidden to Christians; the other is permitted but not commanded as a duty of love.

Rashly becoming security or surety is prohibited, when he becomes surety for all without distinction, without considering the circumstances of who he is becoming surety for, whether he is worthy of this, whether he has contracted a debt for proper reasons (for gluttons, gamblers, and prodigal people also contract debts, for whom it is ungodly to be security; rather, he is asking us out of love for another man's

---

421 Luther, *Trade and Usury* (1524), AE 45:257.
422 Luther, *Trade and Usury* (1524), AE 45:256.

property, not to help someone out of ruin), whether he will pay, and whether the one becoming surety has enough in his own goods that without loss to his own needs he can pay the debt of another. Those who do not ponder these things, but become security for others perhaps for a tiny profit, harm themselves. They trust themselves and others very much; they offer to the others for whom they are security an opportunity for sinning, who with this confidence in the foreign money of the guarantor either worry about their own skin, or seek excessive profit. Solomon writes about these guarantors: "A man void of understanding strikes hands and becomes surety for his friend" (Proverbs 17:18). This kind of rash and improvident becoming surety Luther opposes with his arguments. Solomon acts against these especially in the passages cited. They sin against God, against themselves, against their neighbor, and against their own family, as Luther's arguments teach.

Then there is the security which is permitted when he knows that his neighbor is in need of our works, in things which are necessary, and even intends to give it back. He also knows that he has enough in his goods that, especially if the primary debtor cannot pay, he nevertheless wants to and can pay. In providing security, everything must be done without conceit; on this see Ecclesiasticus 29:8–10. This kind of becoming surety is not sinful, but a beautiful duty of love. Solomon advises whoever becomes security for his neighbor in this way either to urge the debtor to pay or to pay it himself (Proverbs 6:3).

Theological Maxims from this Part

1. Out of respect for human feelings we ought sometimes to give up some of our rights; consider the example of Paul who entreated Philemon when he could have ordered him to have compassion on his fugitive slave (vv. 8–9). God Himself, who rules the whole world, asks and entreats those whom He knows beforehand are bound by His commands. Paul writes that he entreats in Christ's stead, exhorting God through himself, that we would be reconciled to God (2 Corinthians 5:20). This is the way parents act with children, magistrates with sub-

jects, owners with slaves, who often accomplish more with gentleness than with commands. For this reason Paul wants parents to beware of stirring up their children to wrath (Ephesians 6:4). What a magistrate can accomplish with harshness is shown by the example of Rehoboam (1 Kings 12:16).

2. The elderly are to be honored, and consequently listened to, submitted to, obliged when that is permitted, served with what they require. Paul, an elderly captive, hoped to accomplish something by becoming surety (v. 9). "Rise up before the gray head, says the Lord, and honor the face of the old man" (Leviticus 19:32). The poet Juvenal writes about the way the aged are treated;

> They believed that this great crime must be honored with death
> If youth will not rise in the presence of an old man, and if
> Some boy does not rise in the presence of a bearded one,
> although he is still looking after
> The corn at home, and large heaps of acorns
> He was so venerable that he had been walking for four years
> And was so equal to sacred old age that he had the first down
> [on his cheeks].[423]

But they are to rise in the presence of old men, even if something is given to their honorable requests; they are to yield to their admonitions; they are to pay attention to their counsels, according to Sirach's admonition: "Do not slight the discourse of the sages, but busy yourself with their maxims, because from them you will gain instruction and learn how to serve great ones" (Ecclesiasticus 8:8).

3. Prisoners of Christ are martyrs (v. 9), and their chains are the chains of the Gospel (v. 13). Therefore, their martyrdom is not a dishonor, but part of their glory, for it has been given to them by God not only to believe in Christ, but also to suffer for Him (Philippians 1:29). For that reason, the apostles, like green twigs which had been cut off, "departed from the presence of the council, rejoicing that they were counted worthy to suffer for the name of Jesus Christ" (Acts 5:41). "But let none suffer as a thief or a murderer or an evildoer or as a busybody

---

423 Juvenal, *Satires*, 13:54–59. Loeb Classical Library, vol. 91.

in other men's matters. Yet if anyone suffers as a Christian, let him not be ashamed, but let him glorify God in that name" (1 Peter 4:15–16).

4. The ministers of the Church become fathers to their hearers, as often as they turn them from their sins to God. So Paul called Onesimus "his son" begotten through the Gospel (v. 10). For the Word of God is that incorruptible seed through which we are reborn (1 Peter 1:23). Therefore the ministers should love their hearers as their children and their inward parts, as the example of Paul shows (v. 12). They should feel respect for them as their fathers, and they in turn are among them as brothers and sisters reborn from the same seed. This harmony is fitting for Christians and pleasing to God, who wants us "carefully to keep the unity of the Spirit in the bond of peace" (Ephesians 4:3), and "to esteem each other with brotherly love" (Romans 12:10).

5. No danger or trouble should relieve us of the duties of godliness and kindness, for even in chains Paul instructed Onesimus in the true faith, converted him, and made him his spiritual son; from his chains he sent him back to his owner, and anxiously worked so that he would be received favorably. Many make an excuse for neglecting their opportunities to do good and being stingy because of the poverty of their blessings, the feebleness of their health, and the like. But the opportunity to serve other godly people can never be lacking, even if it cannot be done with our resources. In chains Paul could only do this by teaching, encouraging, commending, and advising others. Just these are the duties of love, by which we are able to give evidence of our faith to our neighbor. "Therefore, let us not become slow in doing good, for in due season we will reap a harvest if we do not give up" (Galatians 6:9).

6. Our kindnesses are not to be forced, but voluntary (v. 14), just as God looks for voluntary worship from us (Psalm 110:3). "God loves a cheerful giver" (2 Corinthians 9:7; Ecclesiasticus 35:11). For this reason, when Paul asks the Corinthians for alms for the foreign brothers [in Palestine], he writes: "If your mind is willing, it is acceptable according to what you have, not according to what you do not have" (2 Corinthians 8:12), and: "Let each one give as he has determined in his heart, not grudgingly or out of necessity" (2 Corinthians 9:7). So when

contributions for building the tabernacle were undertaken, Moses said to the people: "Let everyone bring it to the Lord voluntarily and from a willing heart" (Exodus 35:5). He writes: "The people rejoiced, because they gave their offering willingly" (1 Chronicles 29:9).

7. Slaves must not be alienated from their lords, even if this could happen with some appearance of godliness, just as Paul could now have made use of his work of converting Onesimus to faith while in chains and applied this occasion to his freedom, but he did not want to do this against Philemon's will. For that reason he sent him back to his owner (vv. 13-14). He himself teaches elsewhere: "Let everyone remain in the same calling in which he was called. Were you called as a servant? Do not be concerned, but if you can get free, do so" (1 Corinthians 7:20-21). The Lord's commandment is that we do not covet another's manservant or maidservant (Exodus 20:17). It also happens that whoever by force or deceit estranges household servants from their owner, no matter what pretext he uses, disapproves of Paul's example who, even though Onesimus was useful to him, sent him back to his owner.

8. Some evils can occasionally happen because of the good goal which he who did the evil did not intend, just as Onesimus fled from his owner so that when he was restored to him he had now been converted to eternal faith in Christ (v. 15). This is arranged by the Lord, who directs His providence so that even evils in the world serve someone's good. Augustine says that the omnipotent God who has the highest power and is the highest good does not in any way permit any evil to be in His works, unless being always omnipotent and good He also works good through the evil.[424] Again he says that He most perfectly arranges the evil wills so that, when things which are good are used in an evil way, He even uses the evil wills in a good way.[425] So Joseph was sold by his brothers into Egypt, indeed by the ill will and hatred of his brothers, but nevertheless not without the extraordinary arrangement of God who in this way took care of His people. Joseph himself said: "God sent me into Egypt ahead of you to preserve your

---

[424] Augustine, *Handbook*, chapter 11, NPNF¹ 3:240.
[425] Augustine, *City of God*, book 11, chapter 17, NPNF¹ 2:214.

life" (Genesis 45:5), and again: "You thought evil against me, but God meant it for good, in order to raise me up and preserve many people" (Genesis 50:20). He also allowed Hezekiah to be tested by the sin of pride when he displayed his treasures to the king of Babylon, with the goal of knowing what was in his heart (2 Chronicles 32:31). Therefore, let us have a quiet mind in misfortune; let us not despair of a true conscience in sins, entrusting our affairs to the Lord, who makes "all things work together for good for those who love Him" (Romans 8 [:28]). "Cast all your care on Him," Peter says, "because He cares for you" (1 Peter 5:7). Gregory says that sometimes God hurls down the pride hidden in the mind by clearly employing the flesh.[426]

9. The Christian faith has great strength, since it can even make our slaves into our brothers. After his conversion, Paul no longer wants to call Onesimus Philemon's slave, but his brother in the Lord (v. 16). For in Christ Jesus "there is neither slave nor free, neither male nor female, for all are one in Jesus Christ" (Galatians 3:28). This unity is made up of the unity of faith, of Baptism, of God, and of all spiritual privileges, which God distributes among the believers without distinguishing between gender and standing in life. He can change the circumstances of slaves and others of little value into that of people who can support others.

10. Because they share faith and spiritual goods, believers ought to carry out the duties of human kindness to each other. Because of this κοινωνία Paul asked that Onesimus be received (v. 17). The true sharing of goods does not mean that we have resources and riches in common, but that our neighbor is assisted with what he requires, just as members of one body, as Paul encourages us to love and harmony with each other (1 Corinthians 12:20[-26]). Therefore, just as we are benefited by the kindness of God our Father, so it is right that we also carry out kindnesses to our brothers, especially when we are not unaware that Christ Himself is present in this sharing, who receives these acts of love as done to Him (Matthew 25 [:40]).

11. The sharing of faith also includes the sharing of the trials of the

---

[426] Gregory the Great, *Reflections on Job*, book 26, chapter 13.

saints, just as Paul took Onesimus' blame onto himself (v. 18). Let us also take some of the trials from our neighbor onto ourselves. This is "bearing one another's burdens" (Galatians 6:2), and imitating Christ who allowed our sins to be charged against Him in order to free us from those sins, while He "who did not know sin was made sin by God, so that we would be made the righteousness of God in Him" (2 Corinthians 5:21). So let us also prevent the trials of others even at our own loss, if it is necessary, according to St. John's admonition: "We perceive the love of God in that He laid down His life for us, and we ought to lay down our life for our brothers" (1 John 3:16).

12. It is permitted to become security for others, as Paul's example shows (v. 19). With his autograph he pledged for Onesimus. But this is to happen with a godly intention, not to get some gain, so that we are prepared to pay if the first debtor does not pay. This will truly be a work of love, which Sirach commends in a good man (Ecclesiasticus 29:14). There is much about this in Question 3 above.

13. Believers owe everything to their teachers by whom they were instructed in true faith and educated in the ways of the Lord; they know that they watch over their souls. In that way Paul said to Philemon, whom he had converted, "you owe me yourself" (v. 19). No greater kindness can be transferred from one man to another than the sharing of heavenly teaching, because of which we ought to be all the more ready to do other works for them. Paul writes, "If we have sown for you spiritual things, is it a great thing if we reap your carnal things?" (1 Corinthians 9:11).

14. The highest praise is when the hearers do more than the teachers hoped from them, as Paul is confident Philemon will do (v. 21). This is evidence of an obedient soul by which the inward parts of teachers are refreshed, so that they can patiently bear the troubles of their office, since they see that "their labor is not in vain in the Lord" [1 Cor. 15:58], but bears fruit superabundantly. For this reason the apostle admonishes, "Obey those who have the rule over you, and submit yourselves; for they watch over your souls as those who will give an account" (Hebrews 13:17).

15. Prayers and intercessions for others bear great fruit before God.

Paul hopes to be freed from his chains by the prayers of the saints (v. 25), as happened to St. Peter (Acts 12:5–11). Therefore, let us pray devotedly for those who are in distress, who are sick, who are suffering injustice, and the like, according to the admonition of the apostle James (5:14, 16–18). Especially, however, let us entrust the distressed condition of the Church to God in our prayers, that He would put an end to the raving of our enemies, preserve truth and peace among us, and keep us in true faith until the end. To Him be honor and glory forever. Amen.

End of the Comments on St. Paul the Apostle's Letter to Philemon

Works Cited

Augustine of Hippo

    City of God • **De civitate Dei** (CCSL 47–48) • *The City of God (FC 8, 14, 24) (NPNF¹ 2)*

    Genesis • **De Genesi ad litteram** (CSEL 28.1) • *The Literal Meaning of Genesis (ACW 41)*

    Handbook • **Enchiridion ad Laurentium, de fide, spe et caritate** (CCSL 46) • *A Handbook on Faith, Hope, and Love (ACW 3) (NPNF¹ 3)*

    John • **In Johannis evangelium tractatus** (CCSL 36) • *Tractates on the Gospel of John (NPNF¹ 7)*

    Psalms • **Enarrationes in Psalmos** (CCSL 38–40) • *Explanations of the Psalms (ACW 29–30) (NPNF¹ 8)*

    Sermo 18 • *Sermon 18*

    Summary meeting • **Breviculus conlationis cum Donatistis** (CSEL 53) • *A Summary of the Meeting with the Donatists (WSA I.22)*

Azor, Juan

    ***Institutionum moralium, in quibus universae quaestiones ad conscientiam recte, aut prave factorum pertinentes breviter tractantur tomus . . .* Lugduni: Cardon & Cavellat, 1616–25**

Basil of Caesarea

    Adversus Eunomium libri v *(PG 29)*

Barradius

    ***Commentaria in concordiam et historiam evangelicam.* Moguntiae: Mylius, 1618**

Bellarmine, Robert

    Eternal Happiness of the Saints • ***De aeterna felicitate sanctorum libri quinque.* Cologne: Bernhard Wolter, 1618** • *The Eternal Happiness of the Saints,* **translated by John Dalton, London: Thomas Richardson and Son**

Works Cited

Benedictus, Johannes
> *Interpretation* • **Biblia Sacra iuxta vulgatam quam dicvnt editionem: a mendis qvibus innumeris / scatebat, summa cura paríque fide repurgata, atque ad priscorum probatissimorúmque exemplariorum normam, adhibita interdum fontium autoritate, Ioannis Benedicti Parisiensis theologi industria restituta . . . Adiecta est in fine Hebraicarum, Graecarum, caeterarúmque peregrinarum vocum . . . interpretatio.* **Parisiis: Prostant apud Carolam Guillard & Gulielmum Desboys, 1552**

Chrysostom
> *Matthew* • **In Matthaeum homiliae** *(PG 57–58)* • *Homilies on the Gospel of St. Matthew (NPNF¹ 10)*
> *Philemon* • *Homilies on Philemon (NPNF¹ 13)*

Cyprian
> *De bono patientiae* • *On the Advantage of Patience (ANF 5:484–91)*

Dorotheus of Tyre
> *Synopsis* • **Sulpitii Seueri Sacrae Historiae à Mundi exordio ad sua usque tempora deductae, libri II: Item Dorothei Episcopi Tyri . . . De vita Prophetarum et Apostolorum Synopsis.** **Coloniae Agrippinae: apud Jo. Gymnicum, 1573**

Epiphanius of Salamis
> *Panarion* • **Contra Octoaginta Haereses Opus, Panarium, Sive Arcula, Aut Capsula Medica appellatum.** **Basel: Robert Winter, 1543** *(PG 41–42)* • *The Panarion of Epiphanius of Salamis,* trans. by Frank Williams. Leiden: Brill, 1987, 1994

Erasmus, Desiderius
> *Adages* • **Adagiorum chiliades Des. Erasmi Roterodami qvatvor cvm sesqvicentvria, ex postrema autoris recognitione.** **Basileae: Froben, 1559** • *Adages (CWE 30–36)*

Eusebius of Caesarea
: *Ecclesiastical History* • **Eusebii Pamphili, Ruffini, Socratis, Theodoriti, Sozomeni, Theodori, Evagrii, et Dorothei ecclesiastica historia, sex propè seculorum res gestas complectens . . . chronographia insuper & lectionis sacrae historiae luculenta methodo exornata. Basel: Eusebius Episcopius & Nikolaus Episcopius, 1570**; *Eusebii Pamphili Episcopi Caesariae Palaestinae, Ecclesiasticae historiae lib. X, Wolfgango Musculo interprete.* **Basel: Froben et Episcopius, 1557**; *Historiae Ecclesiasticae libri decem, partim Ruffino in nouem prioribus libris, partim Ioanne Christophorsono, libri ultimi, interpret.* **Basileae: Petrinus, 1579** *(GCS 9)* • *The Ecclesiastical History (FC 19) (NPNF² 1)*

Gregory the Great
: *Reflections on Job* • **Expositio in Librum Job, sive Moralium libri XXV** *(PL 75)* • *Morals on the Book of Job (LFC 18, 21, 23, 31)* • *Moral Reflections on the Book of Job (CS 258)*

Ignatius of Antioch
: *Letters* • *The Apostolic Fathers: Greek Texts and English Translations*, trans. Holmes. Grand Rapids: Baker Acad., 2008

Irenaeus
: *Against Heresies* • **Libri quinque Aduersus portentosas haereses Valentini & aliorum, accuratius quàm antehac emendati, additis Graecis quae reperiri potuerunt. Geneva: Jean LePreux and Jean Petit, 1570**; *Adversus haereses (PG 7)* • *Against Heresies (ANF 1)*

Jerome
: **Biblia sacra iuxta vulgatam versionem, ed. Robert Weber. Stuttgart: Deutsche Bibelgesellschaft, 1994** • *Preface to the Pauline Epistles (Romans–Philemon) in the Vulgate*
  Epistolae *(CSEL 54–56)* • *The Letters of St. Jerome (NPNF² 6)*

Works Cited

Matthew • ***Commentarii in Euangelium Matthaei*** *(PL 26)* • *Commentary on Matthew (FC 117)*

Philemon • ***Commentarii in IV epistulas Paulinas (ad Galatas, ad Ephesios, ad Titum, ad Philemonem)*** *(PL 26; CCSL 77C)*

Juvenal
: *Satires (Loeb Classical Library 91)*

Lapide, Cornelius à
: ***Commentaria in omnes d. Pauli epistolas.*** **Antwerp: Martinus Nutius, 1621**

Lorichius, Jodocus
: ***Thesaurus Novus Utriusque Theologiae Theoricae Et Practicae.*** **Friburgi Brisgoiae: Böckler, 1609**

Luther, Martin
: *Trade and Usury* • ***Von Kauffshandlung und wucher*** • *Trade and Usury (1524) (AE 45:231–310)*

Metzger, Bruce
: *A Textual Commentary on the Greek New Testament United Bible Societies 1971*

Tertullian
: ***Adversus Marcionem*** *(CCSL 1)* • *Against Marcion (ANF 3)*

Theodoret of Cyrus
: ***Interpretatio in quatuordecim epistolas S. Pauli*** *(PG 82)* • *Commentary on the Letters of St. Paul, translated by Robert Charles Hill, Brookline, Massachusetts: Holy Cross Orthodox Press, 2001*

Theophylact
: ***In quatuor Evangelia enarrationes.*** **Basel: Andreas Cratander, 1525** • *The Explanation of the Gospels. House Springs, Mo.: Chrysostom Press, 2007*

Index of Persons

Adelphius (or Adolphus) 121

Alexander of Alexander (Alessandro Alessandri) 44, 88, 90, 105

Ambrose of Milan 52, 75, 85, 87, 96, 101, 117, 121, 136, 212

Ambrosiaster 121n

Andreae, Jakob 15n, 172n

Andronicus, Emperor (Andronikos I Komnenos) 137

Anglicus, Joan ("Pope Joan") 87

Anselm of Canterbury 23, 93, 118

Anselm of Laon 93n–94n

Antiochus the Sophist 99

Aquila of Sinope (or Aquila Ponticus) 113

Aquinas, Thomas 21, 161, 185n, 197

Aratus 72

Aristotle 37–38, 45, 58n, 143, 188

Arius 120, 199

Athanasius 76, 85, 97, 121, 161, 204–205

Augustine of Hippo 9, 18n, 20, 21, 22, 34, 43n, 52, 71, 74, 92, 103, 109, 118, 147, 157, 161, 167, 181, 185, 188, 193–196, 198, 201, 219, 222, 237–238, 239, 241n, 248

Azor, Juan 242n

Baronius 3, 111

Barradius 236

Basil of Caesarea 102, 234

Basilides 3

Bede 161

Index of Persons

Bellarmine, Robert 50, 53, 54, 60-61, 67, 166, 174-176, 185n, 198, 218-220

Berenice (or Pherenice) 86-87

Bernard of Clairvaux 135-136, 140, 151-152

Beza, Theodore 15, 92, 115, 116, 172, 197-198

Bucanus, William (Gulielmus) 116

Caligula, Emperor 88

Callimachus of Cyrene 41, 43

Calvin, John 115, 197, 212

Camaterus, Basil (Basil II Kamateros) 137

Camerarius, Philippe 86, 137

Candaules 85n

Canterus, Guilelmus (or Willem Cantor) 45

Casaubon, Isaac 111

Cato 89

Cerinthus 205

Chemnitz, Martin 64

Chrysostom, John 2, 8, 33, 59, 65, 68, 74-75, 80, 94, 98-99, 118, 120, 121, 133, 167, 188, 190, 192, 194, 198, 205, 211, 215, 234n, 237

Cicero (Marcus Tullius Cicero) 42, 45

Claudius, Emperor (Tiberius Claudius Caesar Augustus Germanicus) 91

Clement of Alexandria 56, 147

Clement of Rome 93

Cleopatra 90

Clodius (Publius Clodius Pulcher) 86n

Cloppenburch, Johann 122n

Coelius Rhodiginus *See* Rhodiginus, Caelius

Colet, John 196-197

Constantine, Emperor 92n, 97, 136, 199

Constantius II, Emperor 97n, 136n

Conti, Natali (Noël le Comte or Natalis Comes) 43

Cornelius à Lapide 22, 53-54, 60, 63-64, 93-94, 167, 196, 218

Coster, Francis 67

Cresconius the Grammarian 181n, 196, 198

Creta 32

Creticus 88n-89n

Ctesias 86

Cucretum 32

Cyprian 25, 55, 190, 198

Cyrenius (Quirinius) 147

Cyril of Alexandria 20

Demophilus 101

Diodorus Siculus 86n, 110

Diogenes Laërtius 42

Dionysius (Pseudo-Dionysius the Areopagite) 109

Dorotheus of Tyre 190, 213n

Eleazar (ben Simon) 147-148n

Enjedinus, Georgius 122-123n

Epicurus 188

Epimenides of Knossos 41-43, 45, 58-59

Epiphanius of Salamis 92, 93, 110, 168, 186, 234n

Erasmus, Desiderius 32-33, 44, 92, 121, 167, 196-197, 215-216, 242n

Eugene III, Pope 135

Index of Persons

Eunomius 120

Eusebius of Caesarea 2, 31, 56, 85, 92, 110, 111, 186n, 190n, 234n, 235n

Evodius 195

Faustus the Manichee 157

Favorinus 45

Flacius Illyricus, Matthias 191

Franzius, Wolfgang 170

Fulgentius (St. Fulgentius of Ruspe) 18, 118

Gaius Oppius 90n

Gelasius I, Pope 167

Gennadius of Marseille 93n

Gratian 93n

Gregory of Nazianzus 167, 192

Gregory the Great 74, 139, 144, 161, 166, 205, 240-241, 249

Gyges 85

Gyraldus (Giglio Gregorio Giraldi) 41-42

Hermogenes 185

Herodotus 85

Hesiod 41

Hesperus 32

Hilary of Poitiers 193

Hofmann, Daniel 17

Homer 1, 185, 190n

Horace 48, 229

Hosius of Cordoba 96-97, 136

Huber, Samuel 17, 27

Huss, John 200

Hyperius, Andreas 23

Hypsicratea 87

Ignatius of Antioch 56, 85, 227

Innocent III 22

Irenaeus 47, 87, 143, 193, 205n, 217, 234

Isidore of Pelusium 161

Isidore of Seville 111

Jerome 7, 8, 10, 14, 19, 20, 21-23, 31-32, 38, 40, 41, 44, 48, 52-54, 57, 59-60, 66, 68-69, 72, 73, 79, 80, 81, 82, 85, 90, 92, 103, 108-109, 114, 115, 120-121, 143, 148, 149, 152, 156, 162, 163, 166-167, 177-178, 182, 185-187, 189, 190, 193, 208, 212, 215, 216, 218-219, 222, 227, 229-230, 232, 233, 234, 237

Jerome of Prague 200

John of Jerusalem 31

Johann of Drusius (Johann Clemens van der Driesche) 32

Josephus 47, 147

Jovinian 143

Judas of Galilee 147

Justin 86

Justin Martyr 86n

Justina, Empress 96n

Justinian, Benedict 31, 49-50, 54, 56, 66, 167, 168, 196, 219-220

Justinian, Emperor 88n, 199n, 200n

Juvenal 88-91, 246

Koskenniemi, Erkki 42n

Lerius, Joao 85

Licentius 194

Index of Persons

Licinius 92
Livia 88
Livy 90
Lombard, Peter 22, 185n
Lorichius, Jodocus 242n
Lucan 89
Lucilius, Gaius 45
Lucretia 91
Luther, Martin 60-62, 66, 73-74, 76, 143, 154n, 164, 169n, 238, 242-245
Lycurgus 85
Lyra (Nicholas of Lyra) 166
Macarius of Egypt 101
Marcion 3, 143, 198, 235n
Melanchthon, Philip 97n
Menander 72
Messalina, Valeria 91
Metzger, Bruce 216n
Minus, Celsus 200
Mithridates (VI) 87
Muscarellus, Bernhardinus 197
Nazianzen *See* Gregory of Nazianzus
Nero 90-91
Nestorius 71n, 199
Nicephorus (Nikephoros Kallistos Xanthopoulos) 101
Nicetas (Niketas Choniates) 167
Nonius Marcellus 90

Origen 21-22, 42, 160

Ostorodus (Christoph Ostorodt)..129n

Ovid... 41, 44, 89, 91

Pareus (or Paraeus), David..17, 116

Pausanias 86-87

Pererius, Benedictus (Benedict Pereira)... 176

Pererius (Isaac de la Peyrère) 17

Phavorinus *See* Favorinus

Philostratus..99

Photinus of Sirmium 124n

Pindar..101

Piscator, Johann 15, 21, 23, 115

Platina, Bartolomeo.. 87

Plato.. 41, 45, 85

Plautus.. 189n

Pliny the Elder 32, 48

Plutarch.. 79n, 100

Polybius.. 43, 44

Polycarp 143, 205n

Proculcian the Donatist... 195

Prosper of Aquitaine 117n

Quintilla..92

Rhodiginus, Caelius (Lodovico Ricchieri) 36, 43, 45, 105

Sardanapalus..86

Scaligeri, Joseph Justus 32

Semiramis..86

Seneca the Younger 99, 105, 152

Index of Persons

Sigbert of Gembloux 87

Sigismund of Hungary 200n

Simanca 197

Smalcius, Valentinus 170

Socinus *See* Sozzini, Fausto

Socrates of Constantinople 199

Sophronius of Jerusalem 2

Sozzini, Fausto 121n, 124, 126-131, 170

Spiridion of Tremithus 64

Statius 44

Sternacki, Sebastian 129n

Strabo 35-36, 43, 45

Suetonius 88, 91

Suidas 110

Symmachus 113

Tacitus 47n

Terence 45

Tertullian 38, 55, 92-93, 141-142, 167-168, 177, 185, 198, 235

Thecla 167-168

Theodore of Mopsuestia 71n, 121n

Theodoret of Cyrus 14, 59, 71, 167, 186, 212-213

Theodosius I, Emperor 136

Theodosius II, Emperor 199-200

Theodotion 216

Theophylact 8, 9, 14, 35, 81, 120-121, 143, 167, 212, 213, 214-215, 230-231, 237

Theopompus 161

Theudas 147

Tibullus, Albius 89

Trajan, Emperor 227

Ulpian 88

Ulysses 88

Valentinian II, Emperor 96, 136

Valentinian III, Emperor 199

Zanchius, Jerome (Girolamo Zanchi) 115-116

Zeno 188